Feminism

OPPOSING VIEWPOINTS®

Other Books of Related Interest in the Opposing Viewpoints Series:

Abortion
AIDS
American Values
America's Children
Biomedical Ethics
Censorship
Child Abuse
Civil Liberties
Culture Wars
The Family in America
Homosexuality
Male/Female Roles
Mass Media
Sexual Values
Social Justice
Teenage Sexuality
Violence in America

Feminism

OPPOSING VIEWPOINTS®

David Bender & Bruno Leone, *Series Editors*

Carol Wekesser, *Book Editor*

OPPOSING VIEWPOINTS SERIES®

Greenhaven Press, Inc., San Diego, CA

Greenhaven Press, Inc.
PO Box 289009
San Diego, CA 92198-9009

Cover photo: Alan Watson

Library of Congress Cataloging-in-Publication Data

Feminism : opposing viewpoints / Carol Wekesser, book editor.
     p.   cm. — (Opposing viewpoints series)
  Includes bibliographical references (p.   ) and index.
  ISBN 1-56510-178-2 (lib. : acid-free paper) — ISBN 1-56510-179-0 (pbk. : acid-free paper)
  1. Feminism. 2. Feminism—United States. [1. Feminism. 2. Women's rights.] I. Wekesser, Carol, 1963–   . II. Series: Opposing viewpoints series (Unnumbered)
HQ1154.F444 1995
305.42'0973—dc20   94-4974
                                            CIP
                                            AC

Every effort has been made to trace the owners of copyrighted material.

"Congress shall make no law . . .
abridging the freedom of speech,
or of the press."

First Amendment to the U.S. Constitution

The basic foundation of our democracy is the first amendment
guarantee of freedom of expression. The Opposing Viewpoints
Series is dedicated to the concept of this basic freedom and the
idea that it is more important to practice it than to enshrine it.

Contents

Why Consider Opposing Viewpoints?

"The only way in which a human being can make some approach to knowing the whole of a subject is by hearing what can be said about it by persons of every variety of opinion and studying all modes in which it can be looked at by every character of mind. No wise man ever acquired his wisdom in any mode but this."

John Stuart Mill

In our media-intensive culture it is not difficult to find differing opinions. Thousands of newspapers and magazines and dozens of radio and television talk shows resound with differing points of view. The difficulty lies in deciding which opinion to agree with and which "experts" seem the most credible. The more inundated we become with differing opinions and claims, the more essential it is to hone critical reading and thinking skills to evaluate these ideas. Opposing Viewpoints books address this problem directly by presenting stimulating debates that can be used to enhance and teach these skills. The varied opinions contained in each book examine many different aspects of a single issue. While examining these conveniently edited opposing views, readers can develop critical thinking skills such as the ability to compare and contrast authors' credibility, facts, argumentation styles, use of persuasive techniques, and other stylistic tools. In short, the Opposing Viewpoints Series is an ideal way to attain the higher-level thinking and reading skills so essential in a culture of diverse and contradictory opinions.

In addition to providing a tool for critical thinking, Opposing Viewpoints books challenge readers to question their own strongly held opinions and assumptions. Most people form their opinions on the basis of upbringing, peer pressure, and personal, cultural, or professional bias. By reading carefully balanced opposing views, readers must directly confront new ideas as well as the opinions of those with whom they disagree. This is not to simplistically argue that everyone who reads opposing views will—or should—change his or her opinion. Instead, the series enhances readers' depth of understanding of their own views by encouraging confrontation with opposing ideas. Careful examination of others' views can lead to the readers' understanding of the logical inconsistencies in their own opinions, perspective on why they hold an opinion, and the consideration of the possibility that their opinion requires further evaluation.

Evaluating Other Opinions

To ensure that this type of examination occurs, Opposing Viewpoints books present all types of opinions. Prominent spokespeople on different sides of each issue as well as well-known professionals from many disciplines challenge the reader. An additional goal of the series is to provide a forum for other, less known, or even unpopular viewpoints. The opinion of an ordinary person who has had to make the decision to cut off life support from a terminally ill relative, for example, may be just as valuable and provide just as much insight as a medical ethicist's professional opinion. The editors have two additional purposes in including these less known views. One, the editors encourage readers to respect others' opinions—even when not enhanced by professional credibility. It is only by reading or listening to and objectively evaluating others' ideas that one can determine whether they are worthy of consideration. Two, the inclusion of such viewpoints encourages the important critical thinking skill of objectively evaluating an author's credentials and bias. This evaluation will illuminate an author's reasons for taking a particular stance on an issue and will aid in readers' evaluation of the author's ideas.

As series editors of the Opposing Viewpoints Series, it is our hope that these books will give readers a deeper understanding of the issues debated and an appreciation of the complexity of even seemingly simple issues when good and honest people disagree. This awareness is particularly important in a democratic society such as ours in which people enter into public debate to determine the common good. Those with whom one disagrees should not be regarded as enemies but rather as people whose views deserve careful examination and may shed light on one's own.

Thomas Jefferson once said that "difference of opinion leads to inquiry, and inquiry to truth." Jefferson, a broadly educated man, argued that "if a nation expects to be ignorant and free . . . it expects what never was and never will be." As individuals and as a nation, it is imperative that we consider the opinions of others and examine them with skill and discernment. The Opposing Viewpoints Series is intended to help readers achieve this goal.

David L. Bender & Bruno Leone,
Series Editors

Introduction

"Few social movements can claim to have so radically, and rapidly, transformed a culture as feminism has America."

Nina J. Easton, Los Angeles Times Magazine, *February 2, 1992*

Feminism has helped women achieve many advances in the twentieth century. They have gained the vote, achieved increased economic freedom, expanded their educational opportunities, entered traditionally male careers, and helped make discrimination illegal. According to a 1991 Gallup poll for *Newsweek*, 74 percent of female respondents said that women were better off than ten years before with regard to economic and social status, and 81 percent said that women's legal rights had improved.

Today, a majority of Americans continue to support the goals of mainstream feminism. As Betty Friedan, considered by many the founder of modern feminism, states:

> The women's movement is an absolute part of society now. It is in the consciousness, part of the way women look at themselves and are looked at. . . . The great majority, polls say 65 to 75 percent of women of America, of all ages, absolutely identify with the complete agenda of the women's movement: equal opportunity for jobs, education, professional training, the right to control your own body—your own reproductive process, freedom of choice, child care—the whole agenda.

But while a majority of Americans espouse many feminist ideals, a majority also reject the label "feminist." According to a 1992 *Time*/CNN poll, 63 percent of American women do not consider themselves feminists. The figures are even lower among young women: A recent poll conducted by R.H. Bruskin found that only 16 percent of college women "definitely" consider themselves feminists. As writer Nina J. Easton explains:

> Ask women if they consider themselves feminists, and most will say no. For despite a raising of our collective consciousness that made *Ms.* a courtesy title and put child care on the national agenda, most Americans still view organized feminism with distrust. Substitute the term "feminism" for "women's movement" in public-opinion polls and support plummets. To many, the term *feminist* still evokes images of hairy-legged, humorless extremists who view men as the enemy.

Is it important that so many people have a negative perception of feminism? Perhaps not. Some might argue that the label is meaningless and that what is important is that most people support the movement's basic tenets. But many feminists are concerned with the public's negative perception of their movement and seek to understand the causes of this perception and to find ways to combat it.

The reasons for people's avoidance of the feminist label are many. As Easton states, one negative perception of feminists is that they are man-haters, who blame men for all of the world's ills. While the "man-hating" image of feminists may be an unfair generalization, that stereotype is an obstacle the movement must overcome if it is to attract new members. As Marie C. Wilson, executive director of the Ms. Foundation for Women, urges, "I hope we can find a way to address the question, 'How can you be for women and not against men?' "

Another reason many women may avoid the feminist label is the movement's association with lesbianism. Prior to the advent of the gay rights movement, many lesbians joined the women's movement as a way to work for equality. This tie between feminism and lesbianism disturbs some heterosexual women who do not wish to be identified with a "lesbian agenda."

This attitude, argues attorney Urvashi Vaid, former director of the National Gay and Lesbian Task Force, is simply a reflection of homophobia. Feminist and author Naomi Wolf, however, disagrees: "A lot of the women I speak to actually aren't homophobic. But they are resistant to feminism because the word is synonymous with lesbianism. . . . We are asking them not to be afraid of the stigma attached to feminism by homophobia, to identify themselves in a way that even gay people . . . have trouble doing."

The tie between lesbianism and feminism is related to another reason many women avoid calling themselves feminists: the belief that the movement represents only the interests of extremists in society and does not address the needs of average women. For example, when radical feminists speak of fighting "patriarchy" in religion and society or label all heterosexual intercourse as rape, they are expressing views most women do not share. Radical feminist theory may hold little interest for many American women who are struggling with the day-to-day hassles of modern life: balancing career and family and striving to be excellent workers, partners, and parents. "Women's stressed and stretched lives force them to balance jobs, household management, child and elder care without adequate support systems," says Harriett Woods, president of the National Women's Political Caucus. Women do not want to contemplate the theories of extremist feminists, Woods concludes, but seek "a practical way to get some space and control in their lives."

As Woods implies, many average women shun the feminist label because they believe the movement has not done enough to help them. Others, however, do not embrace the label because they believe the feminist movement has outlived its usefulness. As *Time* magazine states, women's fight for equality has "largely been won." This view is especially common among young women, who in general face far fewer obstacles to achieving their educational and career goals than did their mothers.

Another theory about why the feminist label is unattractive to many women blames the negative perceptions concerning feminism on a media-driven "backlash" against the movement. This backlash, proponents of the theory believe, took hold in the 1980s after the immense strides women made in the 1970s.

Susan Faludi, author of *Backlash: The Undeclared War Against American Women*, is the foremost advocate of the backlash theory. Faludi and others argue that while people at first appreciated what feminism had accomplished for women, some men began to be threatened by women's real accomplishments. These people then defensively began blaming feminists for "nearly every woe besetting women, from depression to meager savings accounts, from teenage suicides to eating disorders to bad complexions," Faludi argues. She concludes that this backlash, perpetuated and popularized in the media, poses a great threat to feminism and must be recognized and fought if women are to successfully counter the negative perceptions many Americans now have of feminism.

Other feminists, however, believe the movement itself is responsible for some of the negative perceptions. As Rene Denfield, a 26-year-old feminist author, states: "I don't believe males in the media conspired to undermine feminism. The term's negative connotations stem directly from the movement itself. We're told we'll be raped, sexually harassed, and treated unequally at work—which, if we listened, would leave us feeling hopeless." Denfield and others maintain that feminism must change if it is to attract young converts and rid itself of its negative connotations.

How feminism can meet the needs of today's women and continue to be a vital movement is one of the issues debated in *Feminism: Opposing Viewpoints*. The book explores feminist issues of the past, present, and future in the following chapters: Historical Debates on Women's Rights; How Does Feminism Affect Women? How Does Feminism Affect Society? Is Feminism Obsolete? What Should the Goals of Feminism Be? Feminism is an important, controversial movement that elicits heated arguments concerning personal, political, and public issues. The authors in this book present opinions ranging from the reactionary to the radical that will shed light on how feminism is perceived and how it continues to affect society.

Historical Debates on Women's Rights

Feminism

Chapter Preface

In 1848, the first U.S. women's rights convention was held in Seneca Falls, New York. This marked the beginning of the women's movement in the United States, which ultimately led to women's gaining the right to vote in 1920, seventy-two years later. None of the organizers of the Seneca Falls convention— Elizabeth Cady Stanton, Susan B. Anthony, and Lucretia Mott—lived to see women vote.

It may be difficult for most people to understand why it took so long for Americans to decide that women deserved the right to vote. After all, today the vote is considered a basic right of all citizens. But until the beginning of the twentieth century, voting and all political issues were considered the domain of men. Women ran the home; men ran the world outside the home. To allow women to vote meant acknowledging that women had the intelligence to make political decisions. Perhaps more importantly, it meant allowing women into a traditionally male domain.

This one issue—whether women should share power and control in areas traditionally governed by men—was a central debate in the early twentieth century. The following chapter presents a variety of early twentieth-century views concerning women's right to vote, to use birth control, and to compete with men. The authors, both men and women, provide a fascinating glimpse into how women were perceived a century ago.

"We demand that . . . woman shall have a voice and a vote."

Women Should Have the Right to Vote

National American Woman Suffrage Association

In 1890, the National Woman Suffrage Association and the American Woman Suffrage Association joined to form the National American Woman Suffrage Association. This organization became the primary force in attempting to gain women the right to vote. The following viewpoint is the association's 1904 Declaration of Principles. In the viewpoint, the authors state that women comprise half of the population, yet have no voice in governing. A democratic nation such as the United States cannot permit the continued oppression of one segment of its population. Therefore, the authors conclude, women must be given the right to vote.

As you read, consider the following questions:

1. Why does the fact that women own property make the inability to vote even more oppressive, in the authors' opinion?
2. How have changes in industry made it vital that women be able to vote, according to the authors?
3. How will women acquiring the vote benefit the nation as a whole, in the authors' opinion?

National American Woman Suffrage Association, "Declaration of Principles," 1904, reprinted in *The History of Woman Suffrage*. Vol. 5, Appendix to Ch. 4, Ida Husted Harper, ed. New York: American Woman Suffrage Association, 1992.

When our forefathers gained the victory in a seven years' war to establish the principle that representation should go hand in hand with taxation, they marked a new epoch in the history of man; but though our foremothers bore an equal part in that long conflict its triumph brought to them no added rights and through all the following century and a quarter, taxation without representation has been continuously imposed on women by as great tyranny as King George exercised over the American colonists.

So long as no married woman was permitted to own property and all women were barred from the money-making occupations this discrimination did not seem so invidious; but to-day the situation is without a parallel. The women of the United States now pay taxes on real and personal estate valued at billions of dollars. In a number of individual States their holdings amount to many millions. Everywhere they are accumulating property. In hundreds of places they form one-third of the taxpayers, with the number constantly increasing, and yet they are absolutely without representation in the affairs of the nation, of the State, even of the community in which they live and pay taxes. We enter our protest against this injustice and we demand that the immortal principles established by the War of the Revolution shall be applied equally to women and men citizens.

Half the Citizenry Has No Voice

As our new republic passed into a higher stage of development the gross inequality became apparent of giving representation to capital and denying it to labor; therefore the right of suffrage was extended to the workingman. Now we demand for the 4,000,000 wage-earning women of our country the same protection of the ballot as is possessed by the wage-earning men.

The founders took an even broader view of human rights when they declared that government could justly derive its powers only from the consent of the governed, and for 125 years this grand assertion was regarded as a corner-stone of the republic, with scarcely a recognition of the fact that one-half of the citizens were as completely governed without their consent as were the people of any absolute monarchy in existence. It was only when our government was extended over alien races in foreign countries that our people awoke to the meaning of the principles of the Declaration of Independence. In response to its provisions, the Congress of the United States hastened to invest with the power of consent the men of this new territory, but committed the flagrant injustice of withholding it from the women. We demand that the ballot shall be extended to the women of our foreign possessions on the same terms as to the men. Furthermore, we demand that the women of the United

States shall no longer suffer the degradation of being held not so competent to exercise the suffrage as a Filipino, a Hawaiian or a Porto Rican man.

The remaining Territories within the United States are insisting upon admission into the Union on the ground that their citizens desire "the right to select their own governing officials, choose their own judges, name those who are to make their laws and levy, collect, and disburse their taxes." These are just and commendable desires but we demand that their women shall have full recognition as citizens when these Territories are admitted and that their constitutions shall secure to women precisely the same rights as to men.

Gen. Rosalie Jones crossing the Delaware.

James H. Donahey/Cleveland *Plain Dealer*, February 15, 1913.

When our government was founded the rudiments of education were thought sufficient for women, since their entire time was absorbed in the multitude of household duties. Now the number of girls graduated by the high schools greatly exceeds the number of boys in every State and the percentage of women students in the colleges is vastly larger than that of men. Meantime most of the domestic industries have been taken from the home to the factory and hundreds of thousands of women have followed them there, while the more highly trained have entered the professions and other avenues of skilled labor. We demand that under this new régime, and in view of these changed conditions in which she is so important a factor woman shall have a voice and a vote in the solution of their innumerable problems.

Other Injustices

The laws of practically every State provide that the husband shall select the place of residence for the family, and if the wife refuse to abide by his choice she forfeits her right to support and her refusal shall be regarded as desertion. We protest against the recent decision of the courts which has added to this injustice by requiring the wife also to accept for herself the citizenship preferred by her husband, thus compelling a woman born in the United States to lose her nationality if her husband choose to declare his allegiance to a foreign country.

As women form two-thirds of the church membership of the entire nation; as they constitute but one-eleventh of the convicted criminals; as they are rapidly becoming the educated class and as the salvation of our government depends upon a moral, law-abiding, educated electorate, we demand for the sake of its integrity and permanence that women be made a part of its voting body.

In brief, we demand that all constitutional and legal barriers shall be removed which deny to women any individual right or personal freedom which is granted to man. This we ask in the name of a democratic and a republican government, which, its constitution declares, was formed "to establish justice and secure the blessings of liberty."

"Of all the forms of Feminism, the movement known as 'votes for women' is the most innocuous."

Women Should Not Have the Right to Vote

Prestonia Mann Martin

Many Americans opposed women's gaining the right to vote. Some believed it would burden women, others feared it would harm the nation. In the following viewpoint, Prestonia Mann Martin expresses her belief that voting is a man's job. Voting, she states, would distract women from their domestic duties and would harm the nation by having those ignorant about government making decisions. Martin was a leading opponent of women's suffrage. She and her husband, John Martin, co-authored the book *Feminism: Its Fallacies and Follies*, from which the viewpoint is excerpted.

As you read, consider the following questions:

1. What comparison does Martin make between shoveling coal and voting?
2. In what specific ways does the author believe women's voting would harm society?
3. Suffragists believed that society would be better if women voted. How does the author refute this idea?

Excerpted from Mr. and Mrs. John Martin, *Feminism: Its Fallacies and Follies*. Book 2 (pp. 312-14, 320-26). New York: Dodd, Mead & Co., 1916.

Of all the forms of Feminism, the movement known as "votes for women" is the most innocuous; indeed its relative unimportance in the scheme of the universe has never been adequately described. That women take it so seriously might be regarded as one of the drollest manifestations of lack of humour were it not obvious that their importunities rest upon a childish delusion, quite solemnly held, regarding the value of the ballot. Their absurd indignation at being excluded from it is only comprehensible when we realise the degree of exaggerated envy and veneration which they attach to the privilege from which they are being excluded.

"But the question of suffrage is so simple," protested a suffragist to me. "It is only justice; simple justice. It is *unfair* to exclude women from the privilege of the ballot."

Equality and Coal

Why is it unfair? Is it unfair to deprive them of the privilege of wearing trousers, or serving on juries, or bearing arms, or dying in the trenches?

Is it unfair to deprive a person of something they don't want? Is it unfair or unjust to exclude a woman from a privilege which is a privilege only in some one else's judgment, not in hers?

In most families the custom obtains that while the woman orders most things, the man of the house orders the coal. Coal seems to belong to the outside world, along with lumber and bricks and earth and the like. Moreover, the man often tends the furnace; stoking is his job. Somebody has to order the coal; coal is in his province; he is the suitable person; therefore he does it. The custom has arisen spontaneously, no laws to that effect having been enacted, and seems, as far as one can observe, to work satisfactorily to all concerned. One never hears that it is a matter of "simple justice" that the woman should order the coal, or at least HALF of the coal! One does not hear her imploring to be allowed to share this privilege with her man. If he dies then she must take his place and order the coal; but she does not seem to feel that her privileges have been thereby extended, or her status in society raised—neither she nor does any one else. Indeed, she is rather commiserated than congratulated, as one having to assume an extra burden.

Voting at political elections is a part of the ordinary, humdrum routine of life. It is to carrying on government, what ordering coal is to a household. Somebody has got to vote because, unfortunately, we have to have a government, just as, in our climate, we have to burn fires, and therefore have to order fuel. But there is nothing joyous, nothing exhilarating, nothing elevating about either act, nothing that confers an atom of weight or a spark of glory upon those who perform it. . . .

THE ONLY WAY

Speaker— "The only way we can gain woman's suffrage is by making our appeal through our charm, our grace, and our beauty."

John Held Jr., *Judge*, November 9, 1912.

Some half a century behind the times the woman suffrage movement to-day is full of certain quaint anachronisms. With the single exception of the supposed use that working women could make of the vote to raise their wages (quite illusory, since men have not voted themselves into higher wages), the movement is naïvely irrelevant to the real needs of the day. At a time, for example, when the electorate is becoming already so enormous that the mechanical counting of votes is difficult and the expense of elections quite beyond their value to the country, it proposes to double the number of votes. Common sense calls for simplification of governmental machinery; but women suffragists call for more confusion and complexity. At a time when all indications point to the decay of the family they would transfer still more human energy from it to the State. At a time when the home needs renovating from garret to cellar, they call upon women to undertake "municipal housekeeping." At a time when woman's personal influence, as guardian and teacher and nurse to her children, as guide, philosopher and friend to her husband, as benefactor to her friends, to strangers and to the poor at her gates, is urgently called for, woman suffrage demands that she be given the vote in order to have "something to do." At a time when society is already too masculine in its ideals and pursuits it would have woman add her presence to masculine ideals and pursuits and thus upset still more the normal balance. When she needs above all things to assert HERSELF and to count for all she is worth, it would cheapen her by throwing her into the welter of public affairs. At a time when, by long efforts, a generous legal provision has been made for her, favouring her above man before the law—it demands for her a political equality which is likely to annul these special privileges and, indeed, in suffrage States, has already done so. At a time when men are allowing their sense of political responsibility to slacken and take every excuse to avoid political and jury obligations, it is paving the way to further laxness by making it possible for them to "leave it to the women." At a time when compulsory voting laws are being called for to force men to vote at all, women are being told that the vote is a precious possession, which they should make every sacrifice to obtain. At a time when the immigration problem and the assimilation of foreign influences are becoming increasingly difficult, it would add the immigrant woman to the immigrant man, as a voter, and double the size of the ignorant and venal vote. At a time when the family has received a damaging blow by the wholesale exodus of women into industry, it proposes to add one more attraction and occupation to engage them still further in outside matters. At a time when the ranks of fallen girls is augmented by the many who have lost the protection of home, it proposes to throw them still more into association with men in politics and expose them to further temptation. At a time when social justice demands, through collectivism, a wider distribution of wealth, it proposes to inject into public affairs the individualistic anti-collectivist influence of women (wholly valuable in the family). At a time when it is difficult for any man to clear himself of the suspicion of self-seeking in politics, and when therefore it is peculiarly desirable that there shall be a body of citizens who shall be, like Caesar's wife, "above suspicion," and thus able to push reforms in a whole-hearted and disinterested manner, it proposes to rob society of this invaluable asset and reduce both sexes to the same level of always suspected self-interest.

The Force of a Gun

At a time when half the world is at war and the truth is made plain that the government of all nations rests upon force, and that no law is worth a scrap of paper more than the force of the gun behind it, woman suffragists propose that women shall encumber government with special laws, which they themselves could not enforce, and which men must, therefore, be prepared to die for if necessary. The male voter is committed to the task of backing up his vote with his fist or his gun in case it can be enforced in no other way. A woman's vote has no guaranty behind it and therefore she can never be a citizen in the same sense that a man is a citizen. (At most she can only become a sort of left-handed or morganatic citizen—never quite legitimately wedded to the State.) She can vote only by courtesy as a sort of honourary citizen, a citizen emeritus, not an active, sustaining member of the body politic. As boys playing "soldier," with sticks for guns, the woman voter carries a gun that won't go off. She casts her ballot when and where men suffer her to do so. She can neither secure the ballot nor hold it without his consent. She may rail at this as much as she likes; but such is the case, and nobody is to blame for it except Nature, which made her the weaker.

It is true that not every man could enforce his vote; the cripple could not. But, after all, disabled men are a handful; while disabled women (physically) are the whole sex. Moreover, the man's disability may be temporary and he may one day recover his strength. But womanhood is an infirmity from which women rarely, if ever, wholly recover.

Many women think that they want to vote because they do not quite know what voting is about. They don't realise that its object is to make laws. And laws, as every woman knows, are a nuisance. Who wants to be always making laws, always trying to rule and repress and regulate other people's affairs? What pleasure can there be in perpetually worrying your fellow-beings with more laws; have they not troubles enough already! Women have no affinity with laws; they lack the aptitude either to make laws or to obey them. In a world of women there would be few laws made, and fewer still enforced. It is woman's way to get along somehow, from hour to hour, compromising with each difficulty as it arises. And there is much to be said for this method.

Voting for Williams

The good woman who has been wheedled into joining the suffrage sisterhood is fascinated by the notion that with a vote she could reform society. She would clean the streets with her vote—as though it were a broom! (The streets of Paris and of Berlin are clean and not a woman's vote has made them so.) She would abolish saloons. (They have been abolished in numerous States where she does not vote.) She would banish vice. (Denver continues a hotbed of vice, uneffected by twenty years of women's voting.) She would prohibit child-labour. (Which no woman's State has done.) She would protect women in factories. (Which is best done in the older States, where she does not vote.)

Nevertheless she persists in thinking that with a vote she could go forth and slay every dragon, like Don Quixote with his lance. I have talked with women who seemed to be under the

25

impression that a polling booth is a place with a row of little boxes, like nests in a hen house, and you drop a ballot in this box if you want clean streets, and in that if you want pure milk and fresh vegetables, and in this box if you want the price of butter to go down, and in that if you don't want your husband to stay out so late nights, and in this if you want more subway trains—anything you want! Voting is just like writing a letter to Santa Claus.

One woman, whom I interrogated before an election a few years ago, as to her precise objects in wishing to vote, said that with a vote she meant to bring in economy, justice and efficiency in government. She intended, she said, to vote for the Good, the Beautiful and the True. "Now, see here," I protested, "you *can't* vote for the Good, the Beautiful and the True. They're not printed on the ballot papers. What you *have* to vote for is just William H. Taft, or William R. Hearst, or William J. Bryan or some other William—it's *Williams* you have to vote for—not the Good, the Beautiful and the True!"

Suffragists assure us that their very presence in man's savage and barbarous world would soften and civilise it. Yet women have entered business by the thousands; have they altered business by their influence? They have entered journalism in shoals; have they effected any change in newspaper methods? Is the press any the less vulgar, less sensational, less prying, less unscrupulous, for her presence in the editorial office? The press is susceptible to pressure, but it must come from the box office, from the advertiser, from the reader. Woman in the home, as reader, as buyer, as wife of an advertiser can affect journalism; as employé of the press she has no influence. Neither business, nor journalism, nor politics becomes more moral, more refined, more honest, more humane because of her participation in them. She is the subordinate when she enters man's world, and takes on more colour than she imparts. Her presence in man's world does not turn it womanward. She is out of her element there. She has no purchase on the situation. She cannot lift man's world a hair's-breadth above HIS level because it is *his* world. He made it; he controls it; he understands it—at least better than she does. She can influence his world best by staying out of it and creating a world of her own, very different from his, the influence of which he will nevertheless not escape.

"Birth control is the means by which woman attains basic freedom."

Women Should Have Access to Birth Control

Margaret Sanger

Margaret Sanger (1883-1966) was a feminist who believed women were oppressed by their inability to control their own reproduction. Sanger, a nurse in New York City, saw the plight of poor women with too many children and was motivated to promote women's right to birth control. In the following viewpoint, Sanger argues that women not only have a right, but also a responsibility, to control their reproduction. The viewpoint is excerpted from Sanger's book *Woman and the New Race*.

As you read, consider the following questions:

1. How does women's inability to control reproduction affect society, in Sanger's opinion?
2. Why were women unable to control reproduction, according to the author?
3. How will birth control benefit society, in the author's opinion?

Excerpted from Margaret Sanger, *Woman and the New Race*. New York: Brentano's, 1920.

The most far-reaching social development of modern times is the revolt of woman against sex servitude. The most important force in the remaking of the world is a free motherhood. Beside this force, the elaborate international programmes of modern statesmen are weak and superficial. Diplomats may formulate leagues of nations and nations may pledge their utmost strength to maintain them, statesmen may dream of reconstructing the world out of alliances, hegemonies and spheres of influence, but woman, continuing to produce explosive populations, will convert these pledges into the proverbial scraps of paper; or she may, by controlling birth, lift motherhood to the plane of a voluntary, intelligent function, and remake the world. When the world is thus remade, it will exceed the dream of statesman, reformer and revolutionist. . . .

The Harms of Submissive Maternity

Woman has, through her reproductive ability, founded and perpetuated the tyrannies of the Earth. Whether it was the tyranny of a monarchy, an oligarchy or a republic, the one indispensable factor of its existence was, as it is now, hordes of human beings—human beings so plentiful as to be cheap, and so cheap that ignorance was their natural lot. Upon the rock of an unenlightened, submissive maternity have these been founded; upon the product of such a maternity have they flourished.

No despot ever flung forth his legions to die in foreign conquest, no privilege-ruled nation ever erupted across its borders, to lock in death embrace with another, but behind them loomed the driving power of a population too large for its boundaries and its natural resources.

No period of low wages or of idleness with their want among the workers, no peonage or sweatshop, no child-labor factory, ever came into being, save from the same source. Nor have famine and plague been as much "acts of God" as acts of too prolific mothers. They, also, as all students know, have their basic causes in over-population.

The creators of over-population are the women, who, while wringing their hands over each fresh horror, submit anew to their task of producing the multitudes who will bring about the *next* tragedy of civilization.

Women's Ignorance About Reproduction

While unknowingly laying the foundations of tyrannies and providing the human tinder for racial conflagrations, woman was also unknowingly creating slums, filling asylums with insane, and institutions with other defectives. She was replenishing the ranks of the prostitutes, furnishing grist for the criminal courts and inmates for prisons. Had she planned deliberately to

28

achieve this tragic total of human waste and misery, she could hardly have done it more effectively.

Woman's passivity under the burden of her disastrous task was almost altogether that of ignorant resignation. She knew virtually nothing about her reproductive nature and less about the consequences of her excessive child-bearing. It is true that, obeying the inner urge of their natures, *some* women revolted. They went even to the extreme of infanticide and abortion. Usually their revolts were not general enough. They fought as individuals, not as a mass. In the mass they sank back into blind and hopeless subjection. They went on breeding with staggering rapidity those numberless, undesired children who become the clogs and the destroyers of civilizations.

The Sorrow of Unplanned Pregnancies

Alas! Alas! Who can measure the mountains of sorrow and suffering endured in unwelcome motherhood in the abodes of ignorance, poverty, and vice, where terror-stricken women and children are the victims of strong men frenzied with passion and intoxicating drink?

Elizabeth Cady Stanton, *Eighty Years and More*, 1898.

Today, however, woman is rising in fundamental revolt. Even her efforts at mere reform are . . . steps in that direction. Underneath each of them is the feminine urge to complete freedom. Millions of women are asserting their right to voluntary motherhood. They are determined to decide for themselves whether they shall become mothers, under what conditions and when. This is the fundamental revolt referred to. It is for woman the key to the temple of liberty.

Even as birth control is the means by which woman attains basic freedom, so it is the means by which she must and will uproot the evil she has wrought through her submission. As she has unconsciously and ignorantly brought about social disaster, so must and will she consciously and intelligently *undo* that disaster and create a new and a better order.

Women's Responsibility

The task is hers. It cannot be avoided by excuses, nor can it be delegated. It is not enough for woman to point to the self-evident domination of man. Nor does it avail to plead the guilt of rulers and the exploiters of labor. It makes no difference that she does not formulate industrial systems nor that she is an in-

29

stinctive believer in social justice. In her submission lies her error and her guilt. By her failure to withhold the multitudes of children who have made inevitable the most flagrant of our social evils, she incurred a debt to society. Regardless of her own wrongs, regardless of her lack of opportunity and regardless of all other considerations, *she* must pay that debt.

She must not think to pay this debt in any superficial way. She cannot pay it with palliatives—with child-labor laws, prohibition, regulation of prostitution and agitation against war. Political nostrums and social panaceas are but incidentally and superficially useful. They do not touch the source of the social disease.

War, famine, poverty and oppression of the workers will continue while woman makes life cheap. They will cease only when she limits her reproductivity and human life is no longer a thing to be wasted.

Two chief obstacles hinder the discharge of this tremendous obligation. The first and the lesser is the legal barrier. Dark-Age laws would still deny to her the knowledge of her reproductive nature. Such knowledge is indispensable to intelligent motherhood and she must achieve it, despite absurd statutes and equally absurd moral canons.

The second and more serious barrier is her own ignorance of the extent and effect of her submission. Until she knows the evil her subjection has wrought to herself, to her progeny and to the world at large, she cannot wipe out that evil.

The First Step: Birth Control

To get rid of these obstacles is to invite attack from the forces of reaction which are so strongly entrenched in our present-day society. It means warfare in every phase of her life. Nevertheless, at whatever cost, she must emerge from her ignorance and assume her responsibility.

She can do this only when she has awakened to a knowledge of herself and of the consequences of her ignorance. The first step is birth control. Through birth control she will attain to voluntary motherhood. Having attained this, the basic freedom of her sex, she will cease to enslave herself and the mass of humanity. Then, through the understanding of the intuitive forward urge within her, she will not stop at patching up the world; she will remake it.

"It is a bad thing to blaspheme against life; and that pseudo-scientific theory of birth-prevention was the foulest blasphemy of all."

Birth Control Harms Society

Vance Thompson

Childbirth is a miracle, and no one should attempt to prevent it through birth control, Vance Thompson asserts in the following viewpoint. Thompson believes that society should revere women for their ability to bear children, should protect babies, and should not try to control the number of babies born. Thompson, an antisuffragist during the early 1900s, wrote the book *Woman*, from which this viewpoint is excerpted.

As you read, consider the following questions:

1. What criticisms does Thompson have of the views of George Bernard Shaw?
2. Why does the author believe that it is futile to attempt to control reproduction?
3. What is society's duty, in Thompson's opinion?

Excerpted from Vance Thompson, *Woman*, (pp. 213-22). New York: Dutton, 1917.

Passion-pulled lovers go swaggering into marriage as though it were a tavern.

Then children—

Perhaps many children—

The endless stream of babies—

What do you fancy man, looking about his man-made society, and seeing everywhere about him milk-fed evidence that the cosmic process is going on—what do you fancy man finds to say?

How Man Has Mismanaged Society

I might quote physicians; I might quote judges on the bench; I might quote a few weary women; but just to show the thing at its worst, I shall quote that noisy ventriloquist, Bernard Shaw:

"The artificial sterilization of matrimony is the most beneficial of modern discoveries for the well-being of the community."

You understand?

Man has mismanaged his social organization so absurdly that in a world of ample wealth and space, there are underfeeding and slum-crowding in one section, while, a few miles up the river, some old man dyspeptic squats in the isolation of a wide park behind a palisade of millions. And because man has muddled things—because he has made life unjust and cruel—he goes sniffing round the slums, exclaiming: "The trouble is there are too many children." He sees the heart-break, hunger, misery, dirt, scandal he has made in the world; he is horribly perturbed, for he is a sentimentalist—even Shaw is a kind of perverted sentimentalist; and he says: "Something must be done about it"; and he calls a congress together and summons all the doctors and sociologists and eugenists and in comes Shaw—a foot-length of grouse-colored hair on his chin; and Shaw takes a little child and sets it in their midst, saying: "Behold, the pale criminal! This monster is responsible for all the social misery, hunger, scandal, crime and degeneration of the community"; whereupon the old doctors and the old sociologists and the old eugenists and the old judges (in gowns) and the passionate young professors howl their hatred of the criminal and his crime; then Shaw picks up his mighty ink-bottle and bashes the baby's brains out; for—

"It is the most beneficial of modern discoveries for the well-being of the community."

An Infamy Worse than Murder

Most beneficial of modern discoveries—reverently, here, I should like to call upon the name of my Creator; irreverently I should like to go out into my garden and swear vilely among the palm-trees—they, too, are busy about the reprehensible business of the life-process. But I shall not take refuge in anger. I shall not even tell George Bernard Shaw that his infamy is a worse infamy than murder, for it is the infamy of soul-killing. He would not know what I meant. He is still squatting in the childish materialism of the last century, when the soul-lessness of man seemed a plausible explanation of the way matter has. One grave, measured word, however, I shall say: Homicide is less loathesome than animicide. The common murderer may have acted on an impulse of drunkenness or wrath; he may repent—anyway he may pay loyally with his own criminal life; he may, in that last moment of repentance, cease to be a murderer; but the cold-blooded Malthusian soul-murderer is always a murderer, day and night, indoors and out, for his vileness pervades every conscious and unconscious moment of his life. And having made this statement, without anger and without emphasis, I ask you to glance once again at the statistical fool who stands, trying to stop the cosmic process by poisoning the well of babyhood or by closing to the curious, down-swarming monads the gates of life.

The Cosmic Balance

Cheer up; I too will give you some statistics.

Living humanity is composed of about one billion, two hundred thousand millions of human beings, the number of men and women being approximately equal at any given time.

Of these there die annually 35,879,520 of both sexes.

Daily there die 98,848 male and female.

In an hour 4,020 die.

In a minute 67 die.

In every second just a fraction more than one human being dies. Now as these stream out of life there streams in at the other pole precisely the same number of human entities—no more, no less; the cosmic balance is absolute. Life, like a pendulum, swings in and out of matter, steady, unfailing in regularity, ceaseless in activity. When, in an hour four thousand and twenty human entities pass through the gate of ebony and death, there enter, in that same hour, exactly four thousand and twenty human entities by the ivory gate of birth. It is the out-breathing and in-breathing of the cosmic life. It is balanced and it is eternal.

Do you think the mountebanks can stop its endless flow? That they can check it? That they can vary the rate of influx and efflux by closing sterilely the gates or poisoning the human wells of life? Not even by that one life and a fraction that comes and goes with the second can they alter the eternal balance of life. In and out the mighty force swings, according to a law as immutable as that which sways the cosmic suns.

It is certainly possible "artificially to sterilize matrimony" in certain people—the paupers science keeps, like rabbits, for experiment; it is quite possible; but only blind ignorance could fancy it

33

would stop the ebb and flow of the cosmic tide of life. All this ignorant clamor about sex-control belongs to the maudlin and senti-
mental science, which reached its climax in the last century and
is, fortunately, dying down with decent rapidity. It has done its
worst. You and I, whether man or Woman Emergent, may safely
assume it will soon be buried in the grave of filthy and aban-
doned heresies against life. It is a bad thing to blaspheme against
life; and that pseudo-scientific theory of birth-prevention was the
foulest blasphemy of all—begotten by the dark and sterile powers
of life-denial.

You can't stop the stream of babies—the endless tidal stream
of babies that swings in and out of life.

The Threat of Feminism

The woman's movement is a movement towards progressive
national degeneration and ultimate national suicide. Already the
evidence is conclusive that the effects of Feminism upon the
inalienable function and immemorial duty of woman—the bearing of children—are so appalling as to threaten the perpetuation
of the best part of the nation. The one duty to society which
women alone can discharge is the bearing of children.

John Martin, *Feminism: Its Fallacies and Follies*, 1916.

Are they pathetic or absurd—these heady young professors,
who have attained the dizzy intellectual heights of Shaw; these
earnest little doctors, who are still blasting away in the aban-
doned quarries of *ante-bellum* science; these idle and compassionate women, who are picturesquely interested in the "lower
classes"—pathetic or absurd in their hysterical efforts to stop the
rhythmic pulse of the life-force?

Too much water going over Niagara Falls?

Well, you cannot stop it by dipping out a cupful *above the
falls*—not even if you use a sterilized cup. . . .

Woman as a Temple

Now it is mysteriously true that Woman—even without a wed-
ding-ring—is still the gate of the body and the gate of the soul.
Wherever she is, whatever she is, whoever she is in the social
organism, still is she, awesomely, the Gate.

Where she is, what she is, who she is—all these are matters
society is perfectly justified in busying itself about; it may go
just as far as its power permits in drilling her or restraining her.
It may even make laws about the way she shall fulfill her duty
to the conservation of race. In fact, since we are socially orga-

nized animals, our society may do what it pleases with us, so long as it does not interfere with the cosmic law. Now society may decree that all race-mothers shall dress in yellow petticoats or wear rings in their ears; there is only one thing it cannot do—stop that condition of earth-life which is a result of the positive and negative currents of life. In other words, it cannot, in spite of pseudo-science, alter the equilibrium of life and death. Babies will keep on coming. This law is cosmic. They come by a mandate higher than that of man-made law.

They come through the Gate.

When once man has got it into his wanton head that the body of Woman is a temple and not a tavern, there will be no more trouble about the babies.

As it is the children, adventuring into life, come through the Gates, whether they are sacred or profane. They come through the gates of the tavern, even as they come through the gates of the temple.

And you and I, their contemporaries in life, have only one imperative duty: To stand with drawn swords round the cradle.

That is all; "what, ho, here is a new human being—on guard!"

Practically I don't care a hang what you do to the woman—runaway wife, tainted divorcée, lawless prowler and thief of love; you may boil her in oil or put her in the pillory, if that is the kind of thing your society enjoys; but what you cannot do is lay your mucky hand on the child. It is not guilty of breaking any of your good and proper laws. And society's implacable duty is to stand round the bedside where a child is born with swords drawn for its protection and with trumpets singing a welcome. . . .

There are moments that hold all the future, because they contain all the past; and such a moment is the birth of a child—any child, every child.

What? The coming into life of a little noetic monad? Yes; for in his baby hand he holds all the future of the race. He is the messenger of Phanes, the Manifestor. And I hail Woman's entrance, as a peer, into the rule and government of earth-life, because I know that she will indeed guard—with drawn sword—the sacredness and honor of that life.

She will have none of man's silly and criminal way of muddling the babies out of life; she will, instead, make a fair, large room for them in it. Already she has taught man a little of the spiritual significance of marriage; she must teach him also the sacred significance of the birth of a little child—the monad, holding in its tiny hand the seed of immortality.

"Those fundamental physiological habits of body which handicap women cannot be denied."

Women Are Weaker Than Men

John Martin

John Martin (1865-1956), an educator, lecturer, and author, was on the New York City Board of Education and a professor at Rollins College in Winter Park, Florida. He and his wife, Prestonia Mann Martin, staunch opponents of woman's suffrage, wrote the book *Feminism: Its Fallacies and Follies*, from which the following viewpoint is excerpted. In the viewpoint, Martin maintains that women are physically and mentally weaker than men. Consequently, women should not attempt to compete in business and other male domains.

As you read, consider the following questions:

1. How does college life affect young women, in the author's opinion?
2. What examples from the animal kingdom do feminists cite to bolster their views, and how does the author refute these views?
3. Why is it important that women not try to be like men, according to Martin?

Excerpted from Mr. and Mrs. John Martin, *Feminism: Its Fallacies and Follies*. Book 1 (pp. 12-20). New York: Dodd, Mead & Co., 1916.

Feminism seeks to approximate woman's life and work to man's life and work. Women, it teaches, should be educated like men; they should do the same work as men in politics—voting, legislating, administering; they should follow industrial careers like men; they should reduce to a minimum the demands of motherhood and, like men, subordinate the home to their "life's work." "Feminism can be defined philosophically," says Mr. W. L. George," as the levelling of the sexes."

Now, if it be admitted that women are in body and mind different from men, there is a preliminary obstacle, hard to evade, to the working out of this programme, and therefore Feminism is concerned to show that there is little ·difference in nature between men and women. Most of the characteristics that distinguish women from men are acquired, it contends, through the conventional training and environment to which they are subjected in a man-made world.

Feminists Deny Differences Between Men and Women

It is difficult to discover any characteristics that Feminists allow are feminine. Though the existence of those fundamental physiological habits of body which handicap women cannot be denied, even they are pooh-poohed, minimised and ignored. "I find that an average of sixty per cent. of girls enter college," says Miss M. Carey Thomas, president of the Bryn Mawr College, "absolutely and in every respect well, and that less than thirty per cent. make, or need to make, any periodic difference whatever in exercise or study from year's end to year's end."

In the same spirit, a president of a woman's college in England tells a feminist group that she finds young women can study hard, take examinations, and keep up with all their work by exercising a little strength of will when they have headaches and pain. It is good for them, she thinks, not to allow trifling bodily ailments to check their pursuit of knowledge.

Scientific and medical opinion is emphatically in opposition to the statements of feminist heads of colleges at this point. It recommends, not that exercise and study be pursued without regard to periodic variations of bodily condition; but that closer attention be paid to the effect of college life on the girl's bodily functions. A medical study made in 1912, of three hundred and fourteen girls in the University of Chicago, "showed that 32 per cent. changed their type of menstruation during the year under the stress of university life. The physical director was able to improve the type of only fourteen of these girls."

Similar testimony is given about women in business. Respecting a set of observations made by Engelmann, it is stated [by Havelock Ellis], "As is to be expected, great suffering during menstruation is found in the business woman, averaging in those here considered, 83 per cent.; but this varies, even in the same class of business, with the character of the work. The girl behind the counter, who is on her feet most of the day, with but little space for change of position, shows 91 per cent.; those who sit, bookkeepers and stenographers, show 82 per cent., and those who have a certain freedom of motion—floorwalkers—cash girls—packers—are noted with only 78 per cent."

So impressed is Dr. G. Stanley Hall, after a wide and thorough examination of medical and historical evidence, concerning the importance of the lunar period to the physical, mental and emotional life of adolescents that he surmises "the time may come when we must even change the divisions of the year for women, leaving to man his Sunday holiday each week and giving to her the same number of Sabbaths per year, but in groups of four successive days per month."

Woman Not Destined for Intellectual Efforts

To demand for women civil rights equal to those exercised by men is equivalent to demanding the end of your power. The exterior aspect alone of women reveals that she is not destined for hard physical labor, nor prolonged intellectual efforts. Her sphere is another, but not less beautiful. She puts poetry into life. By the power of her grace, the glance of her eye, the charm of her smile she dominates man, who dominates the world. Man has strength which you cannot take from him; but you have seduction which captivates his strength. Of what do you complain? Since the world began you have been queens and rulers. Nothing is done without you. It is for you that all fine work is accomplished.

But the day in which you become our equals, civilly and politically, you will become our rivals. Take care, then, that the charm that constitutes your whole strength shall not be broken. For then, as we are incontestably the more vigorous and better equipped for the sciences and arts, your inferiority will appear and you will become truly oppressed.

Guy de Maupassant, *Les Dimanches d'un Bourgeois.*

Such sympathetic recognition by humanists of the handicap which nature imposes on woman for man's work, and of the unmistakable way in which nature marks woman for her own more important racial work, is obnoxious to devout feminists. Miss Thomas witnesses that she felt a feeling of humiliation and degradation on reading Dr. Hall's quiet, scholarly account of those physiological and psychical differences between men and women which appear during adolescence.

Similarly, the disability for man's work which motherhood imposes upon women is dismissed by Feminism as due mainly to artificial civilisation. Stories of savage women who drop aside for an hour or two on their march and presently catch up with the caravan, carrying their new-born babe, are consoling to those who, in their eagerness to minimise the pangs and exhaustion of maternity, overlook the medical testimony that the increased difficulty of birth is due in large part to the increasing size of the baby's head under civilisation. [According to E.S. Chesser,] "The fact remains that more and more women require surgical aid, if they are to become mothers. Even within one generation, according to hospital statistics, the numbers requiring operative aid have enormously increased."

Even the greater muscular strength of man is not accepted by Feminism as inherent in the constitution of things. Jealous that Samsons are males, Feminism points with pride to the fact that "Japanese women will coal a vessel with rapidity unsurpassable by man and the pit-brow women of the Lancashire collieries are said to be of finer physical development than any other class of women workers." Such instances of the performance, under semi-savage conditions, of strenuous, brutalising physical toil by females do not shock the feminist.

In further denial of man's natural muscular superiority, some pleaders, following Lester Ward, take huge delight in the inferior size and relative unimportance of the male in the lowest reaches of the animal kingdom, away down below the vertebrates. At the beginnings of life, it appears that the male cell "was an afterthought of nature devised for the advantage of having a second sex," indicating that "the female is of more importance than the male from nature's point of view," [writes C.G. Hartley]. It is clearly, then, the height of impudence for the male, nowadays, to claim superiority.

Examples from the Animal World

Husbands among rotifers, cirripedes, menatodes and the like are usually pigmies, attached to the female and parasitic upon her. Cases have been found (and are seriously quoted in authoritative works for their significance in determining the relation of woman to man) in which seven little complemental males were attached to one female cirripede, and lived upon her juices, being tolerated by their host exclusively for their possible use in fertilising her.

"Here, indeed, is a knock-down blow to the theory of the natural superiority of the male," exclaims a woman apologist of unusual learning and poise.

If any twentieth-century man can stand upright again after this knock-down blow, Feminism invites him to contemplate the exploits of the female spider and the praying mantes, the conjugal antics of which are deliciously described by Jean-Henri Fabre. The female spider, huge, fat and ferocious, slays and devours her mate immediately she has received the conjugal embrace; but not quite with the same circumstance of ferocity as is displayed by the praying mantes. That small monster, with fiendish fury, devours limb by limb and piece by piece the body of her spouse as, driven by inexorable instinct, though shrinking in terror, he clasps her capacious body and offers himself a martyr to the continuance of his species. Literally, but a fleck of him remains when his fierce partner has finished her bridal repast. "For the female of the species is more deadly than the male."

These instances satisfy some feminist advocates that the female in nature may be more robust, more muscular, than the male and dominate him, and that muscular weakness in womankind is not, therefore, natural and unchangeable. It is not explained how, if the female started with this advantage and has lost it in the æons of development from spider to man, the difficulty can now be overcome of retracing that development or of reversing conditions.

However, return to spider and mantes is unnecessary, it is further implied, because, since man appeared on earth, he has passed everywhere through a matriarchal stage of government during which [according to C. G. Hartley], "the husband, without property right, with no—or very little—control over the woman and none over her children, occupying the position of a more or less permanent guest in her hut or tent," woman ruled the roost.

Matriarchal Societies

Some who find spider and mantes unsatisfactory examples for their imitation and doubtful proofs of any natural superiority of the female body (ethics being left out of account), yet discern in that period long since passed by civilised man, when children were known by the name of their mother, property descended through her and tribal rule was exercised by her, a demonstration that woman is naturally the head of the household, and that mother right has only been superseded by father right through the use of the brute force of brothers, uncles and husbands at a time when, warfare being well-nigh continuous, woman (who, it is admitted, is not the warrior partner) was fain to submit for the sake of protection.

That period of woman's rule and man's subordination gives great joy and hope to those who complain that woman in modern society is degraded and subjugated. "It is a period whose history may well give pride to all women," they aver.

If the historical existence of matriarchal societies in which women held social sway be admitted (though it is denied by Sir

John Lubbock, Letourneau, Joseph Chamberlain and other ethnologists), yet it remains to be explained how woman, having fatally permitted man by brute strength to dethrone her so long ago that the history of his usurpation can only be surmised, shall now undo that blunder and overcome the handicap of that difference of bodily strength which has been transmitted through the ages. If women once held sway and lost it, that is more damaging to their claim than if they had never possessed it. For, had they always been inferior in position, they might have contended that the inferiority of bodily strength was due to inferiority of position and would change with a change of *status*. But a monarch overthrown when she had the advantage of position can hardly reestablish herself, so long as her forces are weaker than her conquerors'.

It is indeed vain to deny the obvious. Woman is not identical with man, either in body, mind or feelings. As Havelock Ellis testifies: "The whole organism of the average woman, physical and psychic, is fundamentally unlike that of the average man. The differences may be often of a slight or subtle character, but they are none the less real and they extend to the smallest details of organic constitution." "A man is a man to his very thumbs and a woman is a woman down to her little toes."

Feminists Want to Eradicate the Best in Women

Women flatter men unduly when they deny their own natures and prefer masculinity. As Dr. G. Stanley Hall says: "The pathos about the leaders of woman's so-called emancipation is that they, even more than those they would persuade, accept man's estimate of their state, disapprove, minimise and perhaps would eliminate, if they could, the very best thing in their nature. In so doing, it is the feminists who are still apishly servile to man, even in one of his greatest mistakes, who have done woman most wrong."

Woman, then, is so distinct from man, in body and in mind, through and through, right down to the foundation of her nature, and such distinction is so precious to civilisation, so essential to that variety which is the mark of development and the charm of life that the approximation of woman's life and work to man's life and work is as hopeless as it would be disastrous.

"Many women have proved themselves capable of everything."

Women Are As Capable As Men

John Stuart Mill

John Stuart Mill (1806-1873) was one of the most influential philosophers of the nineteenth century. A strong advocate of women's rights and political and social reform, his ideas influenced economics, politics, and philosophy. In the following viewpoint, from his essay *The Subjection of Women*, Mill contends that women are as capable as men. Powerful and successful women such as Britain's Queen Elizabeth I attest to this fact, he maintains. Mill concludes that women have failed to achieve only because men have not allowed them to.

As you read, consider the following questions:

1. Why is it impossible to know the true nature of the sexes, in Mill's opinion?
2. Why does society still cling to the belief that women are inferior to men, in the author's opinion?
3. How are women's minds superior to men's, in Mill's opinion?

Excerpted from John Stuart Mill, *The Subjection of Women*, 1869.

The object of this Essay is to explain, as clearly as I am able, the grounds of an opinion which I have held from the very earliest period when I had formed any opinions at all on social or political matters, and which, instead of being weakened or modified, has been constantly growing stronger by the progress of reflection and the experience of life: That the principle which regulates the existing social relations between the two sexes— the legal subordination of one sex to the other—is wrong in itself, and now one of the chief hindrances to human improvement; and that it ought to be replaced by a principle of perfect equality, admitting no power or privilege on the one side, nor disability on the other. . . .

The social subordination of women stands out an isolated fact in modern social institutions; a solitary breach of what has become their fundamental law. . . .

No One Knows Woman's "True" Nature

Standing on the ground of common sense and the constitution of the human mind, I deny that any one knows, or can know, the nature of the two sexes, as long as they have only been seen in their present relation to one another. If men had ever been found in society without women, or women without men, or if there had been a society of men and women in which the women were not under the control of the men, something might have been positively known about the mental and moral differences which may be inherent in the nature of each. What is now called the nature of women is an eminently artificial thing—the result of forced repression in some directions, unnatural stimulation in others. It may be asserted without scruple, that no other class of dependents have had their character so entirely distorted from its natural proportions by their relation with their masters; for, if conquered and slave races have been, in some respects, more forcibly repressed, whatever in them has not been crushed down by an iron heel has generally been let alone, and if left with any liberty of development, it has developed itself according to its own laws; but in the case of women, a hot-house and stove cultivation has always been carried on of some of the capabilities of their nature, for the benefit and pleasure of their masters. . . .

However great and apparently ineradicable the moral and intellectual differences between men and women might be, the evidence of their being natural differences could only be negative. Those only could be inferred to be natural which could not possibly be artificial—the residuum, after deducting every characteristic of either sex which can admit of being explained [by] education or external circumstances. The profoundest knowledge of the laws of the formation of character is indispensable to entitle any one to affirm even that there is any difference, much more what the difference is, between the two sexes considered as moral and rational beings; and since no one, as yet, has that knowledge (for there is hardly any subject which, in proportion to its importance, has been so little studied), no one is thus far entitled to any positive opinion on the subject. Conjectures are all that can at present be made. . . .

Women and Occupations

On the other point which is involved in the just equality of women, their admissibility to all the functions and occupations hitherto retained as the monopoly of the stronger sex, I should anticipate no difficulty in convincing any one who has gone with me on the subject of the equality of women in the family. I believe that their disabilities elsewhere are only clung to in order to maintain their subordination in domestic life; because the generality of the male sex cannot yet tolerate the idea of living with an equal. Were it not for that, I think that almost every one, in the existing state of opinion in politics and political economy, would admit the injustice of excluding half the human race from the greater number of lucrative occupations, and from almost all high social functions; ordaining from their birth either that they are not, and cannot by any possibility become, fit for employments which are legally open to the stupidest and basest of the other sex, or else that however fit they may be, those employments shall be interdicted to them, in order to be preserved for the exclusive benefit of males. . . . When anything is forbidden to women, it is thought necessary to say, and desirable to believe, that they are incapable of doing it, and that they depart from their real path of success and happiness when they aspire to it. But to make this reason plausible (I do not say valid), those by whom it is urged must be prepared to carry it to a much greater length than any one ventures to do in the face of present experience. It is not sufficient to maintain that women on the average are less gifted than men on the average, with certain of the higher mental faculties, or that a smaller number of women than of men are fit for occupations and functions of the highest intellectual character. It is necessary to maintain that no women at all are fit for them, and that the most eminent women are inferior in mental faculties to the most mediocre of the men on whom those functions at present devolve. For if the performance of the function is decided either by competition, or by any mode of choice which secures regard to the public interest, there needs be no apprehension that any important employments will fall into the hands of women inferior to average men, or to the average of their male competitors. The only result would be that there would be fewer women than men in such employments; a result certain to happen in any case, if only from the preference always likely to be felt by the majority of women for the one vocation in which there is nobody to compete with them. Now, the most determined depreciator of women will not venture to deny, that when we add the experience of recent times to that of ages past, women, and not a few merely, but many women, have proved themselves capable of everything, perhaps without a single exception, which is done by men, and of doing it successfully and creditably. The utmost that can be said is, that there are many things which none of them have succeeded in doing as well as they have been done by some men—many in which they have not reached the very highest rank. But there are extremely few, dependent only on mental faculties, in which they have not attained the rank next to the highest. Is not this enough, and much more than enough, to make it a tyranny to them, and a detriment to society, that they should not be allowed to compete with men for the exercise of these functions? Is it not a mere truism to say, that such functions are often filled by men far less fit for them than numbers of women, and who would be beaten by women in any fair field of competition? What difference does it make that there may be men somewhere, fully employed about other things, who may be still better qualified for the things in question than these women? Does not this take place in all competitions? Is there so great a superfluity of men fit for high duties, that society can afford to reject the service of any competent person? Are we so certain of always finding a man made to our hands for any duty or function of social importance which falls vacant, that we lose nothing by putting a ban upon one-half of mankind, and refusing beforehand to make their faculties available, however distinguished they may be? And even if we could do without them, would it be consistent with justice to refuse to them their fair share of honour and distinction, or to deny to them the equal moral right of all human beings to choose their occupation (short of injury to others) according to their own preferences, at their own risk? Nor is the injustice confined to them: it is shared by those who are in a position to benefit by their services. To ordain that any kind of persons shall not be physicians, or shall not be advocates, or shall not be members of parliament, is to injure not them only, but all who employ physicians or advocates, or elect members of parliament, and who are deprived of the stimulating effect of greater competition on the exertions of the competitors, as well as restricted to a narrower range of individual choice.

Women's Right to Suffrage

It will perhaps be sufficient if I confine myself, in the details of my argument, to functions of a public nature: since, if I am successful as to those, it probably will be readily granted that women should be admissible to all other occupations to which it is at all material whether they are admitted or not. And here let me begin by marking out one function, broadly distinguished from all others, their right to which is entirely independent of any question which can be raised concerning their faculties. I mean the suffrage, both parliamentary and municipal. The right to share in the choice of those who are to exercise a public trust, is altogether a distinct thing from that of competing for the trust itself. If no one could vote for a member of parliament who was not fit to be a candidate, the government would be a narrow oligarchy indeed. To have a voice in choosing those by whom one is to be governed, is a means of self-protection due to every one, though he were to remain for ever excluded from the function of governing. . . . Under whatever conditions, and within whatever limits, men are admitted to the suffrage, there is not a shadow of justification for not admitting women under the same. . . .

Equal in Intellect

Will you tell us, that women have no Newtons, Shakespeares, and Byrons? Greater natural powers than even those possessed may have been destroyed in woman for want of proper culture, a just appreciation, reward for merit as an incentive to exertion, and freedom of action . . . ; and yet, amid all blighting, crushing circumstances—confined within the narrowest possible limits, trampled upon by prejudice and injustice, from her education and position forced to occupy herself almost exclusively with the most trivial affairs—in spite of all these difficulties, her intellect is as good as his.

Ernestine L. Rose, *History of Woman Suffrage*, Vol. I, 1881.

With regard to the fitness of women, not only to participate in elections, but themselves to hold offices or practise professions involving important public responsibilities; This consideration is not essential to the practical question in dispute: since any woman, who succeeds in an open profession, proves by that very fact that she is qualified for it. And in the case of public offices, if the political system of the country is such as to exclude unfit men, it will equally exclude unfit women: while if it is not, there is no additional evil in the fact that the unfit persons whom it admits may be either women or men. As long therefore as it is acknowledged that even a few women may be fit for these duties, the laws which shut the door on those exceptions cannot be justified by any opinion which can be held respecting the capacities of women in general. But, though this last consideration is not essential, it is far from being irrelevant. An unprejudiced view of it gives additional strength to the arguments against the disabilities of women, and reinforces them by high considerations of practical utility.

Let us first make entire abstraction of all psychological considerations tending to show, that any of the mental differences supposed to exist between women and men are but the natural effect of the differences in their education and circumstances, and indicate no radical difference, far less radical inferiority, of nature. Let us consider women only as they already are, or as they are known to have been; and the capacities which they have already practically shown. What they have done, that at least, if nothing else, it is proved that they can do. When we consider who sedulously they are all trained away from, instead of being trained towards, any of the occupations or objects reserved for men, it is evident that I am taking a very humble ground for then, when I rest their case on what they have actually achieved. For, in this case, negative evidence is worth little, while any positive evidence is conclusive. It cannot be inferred to be impossible that a woman should be a Homer, or an Aristotle, or a Michael Angelo, or a Beethoven, because no woman has yet actually produced works comparable to theirs in any of those lines of excellence. This negative fact at most leaves the question uncertain, and open to psychological discussion. But it is quite certain that a woman can be a Queen Elizabeth, or a Deborah, or a Joan of Arc, since this is not inference, but fact. Now it is a curious consideration, that the only things which the existing law excludes women from doing, are the things which they have proved that they are able to do. There is no law to prevent a woman from having written all the plays of Shakespere, or composed all the operas of Mozart. But Queen Elizabeth or Queen Victoria, had they not inherited the throne, could not have been entrusted with the smallest of the political duties, of which the former showed herself equal to the greatest.

Women Have Proved Themselves as Leaders

If anything conclusive could be inferred from experience, without psychological analysis, it would be that the things which women are not allowed to do are the very ones for which they are peculiarly qualified; since their vocation for government has made its way, and become conspicuous, through the very few opportunities which have been given; while in the lines of distinction which apparently were freely open to them, they have by no means so eminently distinguished themselves. We know how small a number of reigning queens history presents, in comparison with that of kings. Of this smaller number a far larger proportion have shown talents for rule; though many of them have occupied the throne in difficult periods. It is remarkable, too, that they have, in a great number of instances, been distinguished by merits the most opposite to the imaginary and conventional character of women: they have been as much remarked for the firmness and vigour of their rule, as for its intelligence. . . .

Women's Special Abilities

Looking at women as they are known in experience, it may be said of them, with more truth than belongs to most other generalizations on the subject, that the general bent of their talents is towards the practical. This statement is conformable to all the public history of women, in the present and the past. It is no less borne out by common and daily experience. Let us consider the special nature of the mental capacities most characteristic of a woman of talent. They are all of a kind which fits them for practice, and makes them tend towards it. What is meant by a woman's capacity of intuitive perception? It means, a rapid and correct insight into present fact. It has nothing to do with general principles. Nobody ever perceived a scientific law of nature by intuition, nor arrived at a general rule of duty or prudence by it. These are results of slow and careful collection and comparison of experience; and neither the men nor the women of intuition usually shine in this department, unless, indeed, the experience necessary is such as they can acquire by themselves. For what is called their intuitive sagacity makes them peculiarly apt in gathering such general truths as can be collected from their individual means of observation. When, consequently, they chance to be as well provided as men are with the results of other people's experience, by reading and education (I use the word chance advisedly, for, in respect to the knowledge that tends to fit them for the greater concerns of life, the only educated women are the self-educated), they are better furnished than men in general with the essential requisites of skilful and successful practice. Men who have been much taught, are apt to be deficient in the sense of present fact; they do not see, in the facts which they are called upon to deal with, what is really there, but what they have been taught to expect. This is seldom the case with women of any ability. Their capacity of 'intuition' preserves them from it. With equality of experience and of general faculties, a woman usually sees much more than a man of what is immediately before her. . . .

Women Focus on Reality

A woman seldom runs wild after an abstraction. The habitual direction of her mind to dealing with things as individuals rather than in groups, and (what is closely connected with it) her more lively interest in the present feelings of persons, which makes her consider first of all, in anything which claims to be applied to practice, in what manner persons will be affected by it—these two things make her extremely unlikely to put faith in any speculation which loses sight of individuals, and deals with things as if they existed for the benefit of some imaginary entity, some mere creation of the mind, not resolvable into the feelings of living beings. Women's thoughts are thus as useful in giving reality to those of thinking men, as men's thoughts in giving width and largeness to those of women. In depth, as distinguished from breadth, I greatly doubt if even now, women, compared with men, are at any disadvantage. . . .

Women's Oppression Harms All of Society

When we consider the positive evil caused to the disqualified half of the human race by their disqualification—first in the loss of the most inspiriting and elevating kind of personal enjoyment, and next in the weariness, disappointment and profound dissatisfaction with life, which are so often the substitute for it; one feels that among all the lessons which men require for carrying on the struggle against the inevitable imperfections of their lot on earth, there is no lesson which they more need, than not to add to the evils which nature inflicts, by their jealous and prejudiced restrictions on one another. Their vain fears only substitute other and worse evils for those which they are idly apprehensive of: while every restraint on the freedom of conduct of any of their human fellow creatures (otherwise than by making them responsible for any evil actually caused by it), dries up *pro tanto* the principle fountain of human happiness, and leaves the species less rich, to an inappreciable degree, in all that makes life valuable to the individual human being.

49

How Does Feminism Affect Women?

Feminism

Chapter Preface

Feminism has helped women make great strides toward equality. Without the efforts of feminists, there might not be women voters, physicians, executives, or Supreme Court judges. As writers Linda Gordon and Marla Erlien state, feminism "has transformed the lives and aspirations of the majority of women in ways unmeasurable by statistics and in areas unreachable by the law. These achievements include the raising of women's intellectual, economic, and political expectations, an increased intolerance of wife beating, rape, and other violence against women, and a redefinition of women's sexuality." Yet while feminism can be credited with many of the gains women have made in the twentieth century, there are critics—both feminists and nonfeminists—who blame the movement for some of the problems women face today.

One of the main criticisms is that, in an attempt to draw attention to women's oppression, some feminists portray women as constantly being victimized by men. As author and professor Jean Bethke Elshtain writes, "In the world of feminist victim ideology, women are routinely portrayed as debased, deformed, and mutilated. By construing herself as a victim, the woman, in this scheme of things, seeks to attain power through depictions of her victimization. . . . The voice of the victim gains not only privilege but hegemony—provided she remains a victim, incapable, helpless, demeaned." Elshtain and other feminists conclude that when women are portrayed as victims, men perceive them as weak and powerless—the very stereotypes most feminists are trying to eradicate.

While feminists attempt to purge society of its traditional perceptions of women, nonfeminists oppose feminism for undermining traditional values and the traditional family. These critics believe that by encouraging women to resist traditional roles, feminists have contributed to the increase in divorce and single-parent homes. These trends harm many women, who are now forced to raise children alone or to work two jobs: one at home and one at the office. As sociologist Steven Goldberg writes, "When women join the labor force, . . . [they] are forced into two full-time roles. These roles, each potentially life-satisfying in itself, can become back- and spirit-breaking when combined."

While most women have benefited in some way from the increased opportunities provided by feminism, the movement has generated both problems and critics. In the following chapter, the authors present differing views on how feminism has affected women.

51

"Women were better off before feminism."

Feminism Has Harmed Women

Kay Ebeling

Feminism can be credited with helping women gain access to education and career opportunities. But the harm it has caused women far outweighs these benefits, Kay Ebeling writes in the following viewpoint. She states that feminism has increased America's divorce rate and its number of single-parent families, and consequently is responsible for the demise of the traditional family. Ebeling concludes that women today face much more difficult lives as working mothers and wives than they did before the rise of feminism. Ebeling is a dance instructor, saleswoman, and freelance writer living in Eureka, California.

As you read, consider the following questions:

1. How has feminism harmed children, in the author's opinion?
2. What does Ebeling say concerning the "choices" that feminism has provided women?
3. How were women's lives better prior to feminism, according to Ebeling?

Abridged, with permission, from Kay Ebeling, "Feminists Are Not Funny," *The Human Life Review*, Spring 1991. Reprinted with permission.

In November 1990 *Newsweek* published a humorous essay of mine as a "My Turn" column. It chronicled what I see as the many ways feminism has backfired against women, and argued that women were better off before the "women's movement" of the sixties and early seventies took place. . . .

After the *Newsweek* article hit the newsstands I learned a new lesson: people who call themselves feminists don't want to hear anyone come out in the national media pointing out their mistakes. I learned that these women, and sometimes men, have a vise-like grip on what they believe is okay to say in print, and anyone who violates what feminists as a group think is "politically correct" is wide open for attack. I was called, among other things, an unenlightened reactionary who wants to lead men and women back into the dark ages. . . .

Life as a Single Mother

The last few years haven't been easy, and I was venting a lot of pent-up anger when I wrote that *Newsweek* piece. I work hard as a free-lancer from an office in my home. When my daughter was three months old, I picked up all our belongings and moved north, out of the smog and crime of the city. We live just a few steps above welfare in a small town, and my daughter Elizabeth is in day care more than I want her to be, even though I work only 75 percent of the time. Still, if she is sick, I keep her home with me. I don't have to explain things to a boss. As those dear feminists would say, I made my "choice" by switching to free-lance writing when I found out I was pregnant. I knew we'd live a simple, perhaps hungry life, but I can support my child and still be a nurturing, attentive mother. That's why I don't feel like a failure: I think I'm breaking new ground, maybe setting an example for other women who find themselves alone and raising children. In the *Newsweek* piece, I wrote: "The reality of feminism is a lot of frenzied and overworked women dropping kids off at daycare centers" so they can rush off to jobs they don't even like. I'm determined to find a way to avoid being a single mother who has to put her career above the needs of her child, and I think I'm doing a good job at it. . . .

The phone kept ringing for weeks after the article was published. Radio talk-show hosts across the country wanted me to go on their "live" shows, complete with call-in questions. I talked with people from Washington, D.C., to Maui, Hawaii. I was even on Tom Snyder's ABC Radio national network program. It amazed me that so many of the callers agreed with me. I kept hearing "I know exactly what she's talking about" as other women would give their life stories. Interestingly, on almost every show, a schoolteacher would call in to talk about the most blatant casualties of the feminist movement—the children who come home from school to houses where there is not even one parent. "You can tell which kids are latch-key," said one: "They're the wild ones, you can't get any control over them." Another teacher said that children with a mother at home are distinctly more self-confident than children who come home to empty houses.

©1991 P.C. Vey. Reprinted with permission.

As reactions poured in, I began to see that to make my monumental declaration that feminism had "failed" was an overstatement. The feminists have made some improvements. For instance, some letter-writers and callers pointed out that in the fifties a woman could not get credit, or even sign certain legal papers. It's true that doors have been opened for women in both education and the work force. So I modified my stand to say that feminism had completed its work, and is now "finished." If the "movement" is to keep going from here, it will have to move toward ludicrous extremes, like the new "eco-feminists" who want to mold our culture into a "matriarchy" based on pacifism and the worship of female goddesses. "Feminism is finished," I said on each talk show; "It's time now to go back and pick up the broken pieces.". . .

There must be many women like me, over 40 and raising children by ourselves. And there must be a direct correlation between this sad sociological fact and the rise of feminism. The "movement" opened the door for men to walk out of the responsibilities of marriage and child-raising, and the men walked out in droves. Now feminists insist that today's single mothers are single by "choice."

"CHOICE!" How that word gets thrown around these days! In one letter [in response to the *Newsweek* article] I circled the words "choice" seven times in just one paragraph. Another argument repeated in these letters is that feminism gave women the freedom to escape from marriages where they were being battered or otherwise abused. Well, that may be true in some cases, but I doubt that over 50 percent of women were in abusive marriages from which they escaped to become the enlightened feminist single parents of today. Yet the statistics, which have been reported in almost every women's magazine, show that over 50 percent of today's children will spend at least part of their childhood in a single-parent household. Feminists have got to start taking some responsibility for the ravaged condition of the American family: they advocated single parenthood as a way for women to live proud and fulfilled lives, but the result has been more broken homes. . . .

A high percentage of "pro" letters were from men. It seems feminism left many men perplexed and angry. One single father stopped mid-thought to write "Pardon me, I do not even know what women like to be called any more." One short note from a man in Indiana read "I could have told them all back then, when I would have been dubbed a chauvinist pig, that I knew this would eventually happen. I just never thought I would ever hear it before I died.". . .

Better Times

Feminists can't keep turning their backs on the life-damaging effects of their movement. I'm not alone in wanting the pendulum to swing back now, for a time, in the opposite direction.

My favorite letter came directly to me from a lady named Ida in Eureka, the big city near my small town. She wrote that she'd been married in 1937, and supported me in my position on "the sad state of the feminist movement." She described her life in the years before the feminist upheaval. Her housework would be finished by noon and she'd spend her afternoons in a beauty salon or with friends. Saturday and Sunday were "family days," not filled with the frenzied housework and errand-running of today's working mothers. Ida wrote: "I was shocked when women decided to trade their superior position for equality—the right to work in sewers or as highway workers. I don't remember ever feeling like a 'drudge' or victim of 'compulsive sex.' The real drudgery I see is single mothers struggling to raise kids. Whether on welfare or with a job, it must be hell for most of them." She closed with "I'm retired now and grateful to not be young in this age."

Ida's letter may summarize my entire "My Turn" and all the reactions, from the angry, bilious "anti" letters to the empathetic, sometimes sad stories in the pile of "pro" letters.

I think women were better off before feminism, and it will probably take them generations to realize they were misguided. I just hope it won't be too late to bring the sanity of tradition and family back into our lives.

"The afflictions ascribed to feminism are all myths."

Feminism Has Not Harmed Women

Susan Faludi

Susan Faludi is the author of the best-selling book *Backlash: The Undeclared War Against American Women*, from which the following viewpoint is excerpted. Faludi defends feminism, arguing that it is not responsible for the problems today's women face. Feminism has benefited women greatly in their family and work lives, the author states. The real cause of women's suffering is not feminism, but the continued lack of equality they face personally and professionally, she concludes.

As you read, consider the following questions:

1. What examples does Faludi give to show that women have still not gained equality?
2. According to surveys cited by the author, how do women themselves feel about feminism?
3. What does the author believe is feminism's agenda?

Excerpted from *Backlash* (pp. ix-xxiii) by Susan Faludi. Copyright ©1991 by Susan Faludi. Reprinted by permission of Crown Publishers, Inc.

To be a woman in America at the close of the 20th century—what good fortune. That's what we keep hearing, anyway. The barricades have fallen, politicians assure us. Women have "made it," Madison Avenue cheers. Women's fight for equality has "largely been won," *Time* magazine announces. Enroll at any university, join any law firm, apply for credit at any bank. Women have so many opportunities now, corporate leaders say, that we don't really need equal opportunity policies. Women are so equal now, lawmakers say, that we no longer need an Equal Rights Amendment. Women have "so much," former President Ronald Reagan says, that the White House no longer needs to appoint them to higher office. Even American Express ads are saluting a woman's freedom to charge it. At last, women have received their full citizenship papers.

And yet . . .

Behind this celebration of the American woman's victory, behind the news, cheerfully and endlessly repeated, that the struggle for women's rights is won, another message flashes. You may be free and equal now, it says to women, but you have never been more miserable.

All Sorts of Ailments

This bulletin of despair is posted everywhere—at the newsstand, on the TV set, at the movies, in advertisements and doctors' offices and academic journals. Professional women are suffering "burnout" and succumbing to an "infertility epidemic." Single women are grieving from a "man shortage." The *New York Times* reports: Childless women are "depressed and confused" and their ranks are swelling. *Newsweek* says: Unwed women are "hysterical" and crumbling under a "profound crisis of confidence." The health advice manuals inform: High-powered career women are stricken with unprecedented outbreaks of "stress-induced disorders," hair loss, bad nerves, alcoholism, and even heart attacks. The psychology books advise: Independent women's loneliness represents "a major mental health problem today." Even founding feminist Betty Friedan has been spreading the word: she warns that women now suffer from a new identity crisis and "new 'problems that have no name.' "

How can American women be in so much trouble at the same time that they are supposed to be so blessed? If the status of women has never been higher, why is their emotional state so low? If women got what they asked for, what could possibly be the matter now?

The prevailing wisdom of the past decade has supported one, and only one, answer to this riddle: it must be all that equality that's causing all that pain. Women are unhappy precisely *because* they are free. Women are enslaved by their own liberation. They have grabbed at the gold ring of independence, only to miss the one ring that really matters. They have gained control of their fertility, only to destroy it. They have pursued their own professional dreams—and lost out on the greatest female adventure. The women's movement, as we are told time and again, has proved women's own worst enemy.

THE INCREDIBLE SHRINKING WOMAN

©Kirk Anderson. Reprinted with permission.

"In dispensing its spoils, women's liberation has given my generation high incomes, our own cigarette, the option of single parenthood, rape crisis centers, personal lines of credit, free love, and female gynecologists," Mona Charen, a young law student, writes in the *National Review*, in an article titled "The Feminist Mistake." "In return it has effectively robbed us of one thing upon which the happiness of most women rests—men." The *National Review* is a conservative publication, but such charges against the women's movement are not confined to its pages. "Our generation was the human sacrifice" to the women's movement, *Los Angeles Times* feature writer Elizabeth Mehren contends in a *Time* cover story. Baby-boom women like her, she says, have been duped by feminism: "We believed the rhetoric." In *Newsweek*, writer Kay Ebeling dubs feminism "the Great Experiment That Failed" and asserts "women in my generation, its perpetrators, are the casualties." Even the beauty magazines are saying it: *Harper's Bazaar* accuses the women's movement of having "lost us [women] ground instead of gaining it.". . .

Finally, some "liberated" women themselves have joined the lamentations. In confessional accounts, works that invariably receive a hearty greeting from the publishing industry, "recovering Superwomen" tell all. In *The Cost of Loving: Women and the New Fear of Intimacy*, Megan Marshall, a Harvard-pedigreed writer, asserts that the feminist "Myth of Independence" has turned her generation into unloved and unhappy fast-trackers, "dehumanized" by careers and "uncertain of their gender identity." Other diaries of mad Superwomen charge that "the hardcore feminist viewpoint," as one of them puts it, has relegated educated executive achievers to solitary nights of frozen dinners and closet drinking. The triumph of equality, they report, has merely given women hives, stomach cramps, eye-twitching disorders, even comas.

But what "equality" are all these authorities talking about?

If American women are so equal, why do they represent two-thirds of all poor adults? Why are nearly 75 percent of full-time working women making less than $20,000 a year, nearly double the male rate? Why are they still far more likely than men to live in poor housing and receive no health insurance, and twice as likely to draw no pension? Why does the average working woman's salary still lag as far behind the average man's as it did twenty years ago? Why does the average female college graduate today earn less than a man with no more than a high school diploma (just as she did in the '50s)—and why does the average female high school graduate today earn less than a male high school dropout? Why do American women, in fact, face one of the worst gender-based pay gaps in the developed world? . . .

Nor do women enjoy equality in their own homes, where they still shoulder 70 percent of the household duties—and the only major change in the last fifteen years is that now middle-class men *think* they do more around the house. (In fact, a national poll finds the ranks of women saying their husbands share equally in child care shrunk to 31 percent in 1987 from 40 percent three years earlier.) Furthermore, in thirty states, it is still generally legal for husbands to rape their wives; and only ten states have laws mandating arrest for domestic violence—even though battering was the leading cause of injury of women in the late '80s. . . .

Women Do Not Feel Liberated

The word may be that women have been "liberated," but women themselves seem to feel otherwise. Repeatedly in national surveys, majorities of women say they are still far from equality. Nearly 70 percent of women polled by the *New York*

Times in 1989 said the movement for women's rights had only just begun. . . .

Seen against this background, the much ballyhooed claim that feminism is responsible for making women miserable becomes absurd—and irrelevant. The afflictions ascribed to feminism are all myths. From "the man shortage" to "the infertility epidemic" to "female burnout" to "toxic day care," these so-called female crises have had their origins not in the actual conditions of women's lives but rather in a closed system that starts and ends in the media, popular culture, and advertising—an endless feedback loop that perpetuates and exaggerates its own false images of womanhood.

Women themselves don't single out the women's movement as the source of their misery. To the contrary, in national surveys 75 to 95 percent of women credit the feminist campaign with *improving* their lives, and a similar proportion say that the women's movement should keep pushing for change. Less than 8 percent think the women's movement might have actually made their lot worse. . . .

What has made women unhappy in the last decade is not their "equality"—which they don't yet have—but the rising pressure to halt, and even reverse, women's quest for that equality. The "man shortage" and the "infertility epidemic" are not the price of liberation; in fact, they do not even exist. But these chimeras are the chisels of a society-wide backlash. They are part of a relentless whittling-down process—much of it amounting to outright propaganda—that has served to stir women's private anxieties and break their political wills. Identifying feminism as women's enemy only furthers the ends of a backlash against women's equality, simultaneously deflecting attention from the backlash's central role and recruiting women to attack their own cause. . . .

To blame feminism for women's "lesser life" is to miss entirely the point of feminism, which is to win women a wider range of experience. . . . Feminism asks the world to recognize at long last that women aren't decorative ornaments, worthy vessels, members of a "special-interest group." They are half (in fact, now more than half) of the national population, and just as deserving of rights and opportunities, just as capable of participating in the world's events, as the other half. Feminism's agenda is basic: It asks that women not be forced to "choose" between public justice and private happiness. It asks that women be free to define themselves—instead of having their identity defined for them, time and again, by their culture and their men.

The fact that these are still such incendiary notions should tell us that American women have a way to go before they enter the promised land of equality.

"The law ought to prohibit, penalize, or regulate pornographic materials because they cause harm."

Feminists' Attempts to Censor Pornography Benefit Women

Marianne Wesson

Pornography that portrays violence against women is a dangerous product that threatens women's safety and promotes sexual harassment and discrimination against women, Marianne Wesson asserts in the following viewpoint. By opposing such pornography, feminists protect women and their rights. Wesson is a law professor at the University of Colorado in Boulder.

As you read, consider the following questions:

1. Why does Wesson believe violent pornography is not protected by the First Amendment?
2. What four forms of speech are not given full First Amendment protection, according to the author?
3. How does pornography silence women, in Wesson's opinion?

Abridged from Marianne Wesson, "Sex, Lies and Videotape: The Pornographer as Censor," 66 *Washington Law Review* 913 (1991). Reprinted by permission of the Washington Law Review Association.

For some years now, the feminist project of transforming law into a phenomenon more consonant with the experiences of women, and more conducive to their welfare, has generated a body of "legal" materials in a variety of forms—including scholarship, judicial decisions, statutes, regulations, and teaching materials. Like any social movement, the feminist legal movement has generated its share of internal disagreements. Apart from the question of exactly what it means to be a feminist, no issue has generated more fierce disagreement than the question of pornography. As one woman put it, "Pornography is our Skokie."

Pornography and the First Amendment

The debate about pornography, together with the parallel debate about what the correct "feminist" position should be with regard to it, proceeds today in many forums, not all closely related to the law. But it is the legal debate about pornography that is haunted by the fourteen words that comprise a central portion of the first amendment of the United States Constitution: "Congress shall make no law . . . abridging the freedom of speech, or of the press. . . ." The first amendment is a formidable obstacle to those who believe that the law ought to prohibit, penalize, or regulate pornographic materials because they cause harm. Many voices, including some self-identified feminist voices, argue that such governmental intrusion is both unwise—in part because it might ultimately turn against other forms of expression, including feminist forms—and unconstitutional, because of the firm and inviolable dictates of the first amendment.

Many thoughtful and original thinkers have concluded that the suppression of pornography is too costly and dangerous a project for feminism to undertake. I take exception to that view, and argue that materials that equate sexual pleasure with the infliction of violence or pain, and imply approval of conduct that generates the actor's sexual arousal or satisfaction through this infliction, can and ought to be exempt from the protection of the first amendment. Those who create and disseminate such material should be susceptible to suits for damages by those who believe, and can prove, they have been harmed by the creation and dissemination of pornography. . . .

Any serious debate about the first amendment must begin by acknowledging that the first amendment is simply a collection of words—eloquent, moving, and venerable, but like all words, they require human interpretation and construction before they become useful in the resolution of constitutional disputes. Judges, scholars, students, and ordinary citizens continually grapple with the meaning of the first amendment. . . .

It is beyond dispute that courts have long recognized several varieties of speech or quasi-speech as deserving either no, or limited, first amendment protection. Some courts have begun to incorporate new varieties of speech into these categories. I suggest that violent pornography, of the sort defined here as "new hard core," has many features in common with four of these recognizably regulable categories of speech. A Supreme Court that allows the regulation of these other varieties of speech must at least explain why violent pornography cannot constitutionally be made the subject of suits for damages. . . .

The Analogy to Sexual Harassment

The first category of regulable speech that provides a useful analogy to pornography is in the law of sexual harassment. Sexual harassment is an especially interesting comparison for several reasons, among them that it was Catharine MacKinnon who proposed what has come to be the accepted law of sexual harassment in the United States, and that the authors of the FACT [Feminist Anti-Censorship Task Force] brief expressed agreement with the rationales underlying the law of sexual harassment. As recognized by the United States Supreme Court in a moment of rare unanimity, sexual harassment is illegal as a form of sex discrimination under Title VII of the Civil Rights Act of 1964. Hence it may be regulated and prohibited, and remedied by compensation. Moreover, sexual harassment includes not only the classic proposition-from-the-boss, but also the much more pervasive practices of creating or tolerating a "hostile or abusive working environment." It is thus potentially illegal for male workers in an office to affix to bulletin boards or illustrate weekly memos with *Playboy* centerfolds or cartoons that demean or insult women—even if the materials are not "obscene" under the prevailing definition of that term. The law of sexual harassment, on this interpretation, unquestionably constitutes a restriction on speech, enforced by the power of the courts to penalize not only the offender but also in some cases the supervisor or employer. These decisions interpreting Title VII have generated remarkably little first amendment-based criticism. They are based on a recognition that the effect of such "speech" in the workplace is to make it virtually impossible for women to be treated as equals and to have their work performance judged by the same standards used to evaluate that of males. If sexually harmful materials, some far less insulting and harmful to women than new hard core pornography, may be legitimately banned from the workplace in the interest of equality in employment, then such material should properly be excludable from other public places in the interest of equality in other spheres of life.

The second category of regulable speech that provides insights useful to the regulation of pornography is "clear-and-present-danger" speech. As every first-year law student knows, speech may be limited if there is a "clear and present danger" that it will provoke a harm that the government is empowered to prevent. If certain speech, for example words of conspiracy or solicitation, create a danger of bank robbery or arson, the words may be punished—not because they are not speech, but because they are very dangerous speech, *harmful* speech. To premise the regulation of violent pornography on this aspect of first amendment law requires, of course, some empirical reason to believe that its existence creates a danger of cognizable harm to women. That evidence exists in a more than sufficient quantity, although it is controversial.

Women as Second Class Citizens

Pornography is a violation of women's civil rights. By allowing such pornographic material to exist, society accepts and institutionalizes the idea that men have power and that women are powerless. By reinforcing the images of gender inequality and the idea of exploitation and subjugation of women in society, pornography perpetuates the view that women are second class citizens. This view is inconsistent with the Constitution and the values underlying a free society.

Marie-France Major, *Journal of Contemporary Law*, Vol. 19:1, 1993.

Rivers of ink have been spilled in the debate about what the empirical evidence demonstrates. Different commentators make diametrically opposing claims based on the same evidence. The best synthesis of the evidence can be found in the work of E. Donnerstein, D. Linz, and S. Penrod. Donnerstein is a trustworthy guide in an odd way because he has credentials on both sides of the question. He testified before the 1986 Attorney General's Commission on Pornography, and his findings were cited by that Commission as a basis for recommending increased prosecution of creators and purveyors of pornographic materials. On the other hand, he has publicly indicated that the Commission and others have exaggerated the link between pornography in general and violent behavior directed toward women. Although any discussion of the complexities of this issue deserves an article of its own, a quotation from the book provides a fair summary. Focusing on *violent* pornography (of the sort encompassed in my definition of new hard core), Donnerstein, Linz, and Penrod write:

[V]iolent pornography influences attitudes and behaviors. . . .
Viewers come to cognitively associate sexuality with violence,

to endorse the idea that women want to be raped, and to trivialize the injuries suffered by a rape victim. As a result of the attitudinal changes, men may be more willing to abuse women physically (indeed, the laboratory aggression measures suggest such an outcome).

Some critics have derided the effort to premise public policy on studies conducted in the artificial setting of the laboratory, but Donnerstein and his colleagues understand and explain why "better" data is not and cannot be available:

> The social scientist would have a difficult time asserting that the *immediate* outcome of exposure to sexual violence is *actual* violence to women because it is not possible to design an experiment in which subjects are exposed to sexually violent materials, then allow those individuals to engage in any behavior that may threaten public safety.

The conclusions of Donnerstein and his partners do not amount to a scientifically absolute statement of cause and effect, but as science, they are certainly as probative as the science that, for example, led the Supreme Court to conclude that separate-but-equal education causes low self-esteem among blacks. Donnerstein's data is more convincing than the virtually nonexistent data that led the Supreme Court to conclude that women who work as prison guards suffer a greater likelihood of sexual assault by inmates than do male guards, thereby justifying the exclusion of women from that job category. In short, if the Supreme Court were disposed to see it (and whether they are will most likely rest on extra-scientific considerations), the evidence of a link between violent pornography and cognizable harm is certainly visible. . . .

The Group Libel Analogy

Pornography represents a lie about women as a class, a form of collective defamation. Seen in that light, group libel seems a natural comparison for it. The concept of group libel was recognized by the United States Supreme Court in a 1952 decision that, although it has been questioned and criticized many times since, has not been overruled. Importantly, the decision, *Beauharnais v. Illinois*, considered the constitutionality of imposing a criminal penalty, not merely civil damages, on the disseminators of the libelous material. In that case an inflammatory leaflet alleged that blacks and civil rights organizations were bent on "mongrelizing the white race" and that blacks as a group were associated with "rapes, robberies, knives, guns, and marijuana. . . ." Moreover, the statute did not recognize truth alone as a defense, so Mr. Beauharnais was not permitted to present any evidence to establish the truth of the leaflet's claims. The Supreme Court upheld Beauharnais' conviction over his first amendment objections. Justice Frankfurter's opinion for the majority is very direct in its reasoning:

No one will gainsay that it is libelous falsely to charge another with being a rapist, robber, carrier of knives and guns, and user of marijuana. The precise question before us, then, is whether the . . . Fourteenth Amendment prevents a State from punishing such libels—as criminal libel has been defined, limited, and constitutionally recognized time out of mind—directed at designated collectivities and flagrantly disseminated. . . . We cannot say . . . that the question is concluded by history and practice. But if an utterance directed at an individual may be the object of criminal sanctions, we cannot deny to a State power to punish the same utterance directed at a defined group, unless we can say that this is a willful and purposeless restriction unrelated to the peace and well-being of the State.

In the face of . . . history and its frequent obligato of extreme racial and religious propaganda, we would deny experience to say that the Illinois legislature was without reason in seeking ways to curb false or malicious defamation of racial and religious groups, made in public places and by means calculated to have a powerful emotional impact on those to whom it was presented. . . .

. . . [W]e are precluded from saying that speech concededly punishable when immediately directed at individuals cannot be outlawed if directed at groups with whose position and esteem in society the affiliated individual may be inextricably involved.

Justice Frankfurter's powerful language provides a promising rationale for permitting the much milder sanction of damages against the purveyors of violent pornography. . . .

Pornography Promotes Inequality

Pornography, not alone but crucially, institutionalizes a subhuman victimized second class status for women in particular. If a person can be denigrated, and doing that is defended and legalized as freedom; if one can be tortured and the enjoyment of watching it is considered entertainment protected by the Constitution; if the pleasure that other people derive from one's pain is the measure of one's social worth, one isn't worth much, socially speaking. . . . Tolerance of such practices is inconsistent with any serious mandate of equality and with the reasons speech is protected.

Catharine MacKinnon, *Law & Inequality Journal*, Vol. 38, 1986.

In addition to the group libel analogy, opponents of racist speech often resort to the concept of "fighting words" as an argument for the constitutionality of suppressing such speech. It is "fighting words" that provides the fourth and in many ways most compelling analogy to pornography.

Understanding the relationship between "fighting words" and pornography requires the reader to make a paradigm shift in thinking about the first amendment, and to embrace what might be called feminist method. This shift is necessary because conventional explanations for the lack of first amendment protection afforded "fighting words" are either unconvincing or incomplete. . . .

When fighting words are uttered, the marketplace of ideas, to use a central metaphor of the first amendment, is transformed into a marketplace of fists or bullets, and speech is destroyed. Hence fighting words, although strictly speaking "speech," do not contribute to the sum total of speech in the marketplace because they operate to suppress other speech by provoking the next likely speakers to fighting instead of language.

This analysis has appeal, but begs for revision. Leaving aside the male-oriented nouns and pronouns, the world-view reflected when some are protected from having to listen to certain speech because it makes them so angry they are provoked to physical violence is unquestionably male. A feminist version of the "fighting words" exception would protect persons from exposure to speech—and from a marketplace saturated by that speech—if it would prevent the responsive speech of an average, intelligent *woman*. But that is far more likely to happen because she is thrust into silence than because she is provoked into violence. A gender-inclusive first amendment theory that values speech in the way that the "fighting words" exception seems to do would not protect speech that silences the voices of women.

Porn Silences Women

Silence, no less than fists and guns, can entail the end of speech. When one who has something to say is intimidated, derided or defamed into silence, speech is again the victim. Under these circumstances, the marketplace of ideas cannot be enriched by "more speech." It is my view that certain pornographic materials operate in precisely that fashion, silencing the voices of women, especially when they seek to speak their views pertaining to issues of sexuality and sexual freedom, ethics, and pleasure. . . .

Whether the work is called sexual harassment, clear and present danger, group libel, or the feminist equivalent of fighting words, it silences women. The pornographer and his defenders claim they fear censorship, the loss of their freedom to speak and their opportunity to be heard. But for women, the pornographer *is* a censor—he is the thought police, the slayer of words, the silencer, the burner of books, the killer of poets. He leaves in the wake of his creations a vast and terrible silence; he prevents us from saying and hearing important truths that we need to heal our troubled sexual spirits and our equally troubled world.

VIEWPOINT

"Censoring 'pornography' would have an adverse impact upon women's rights and interests."

Feminists' Attempts to Censor Pornography Harm Women

Nadine Strossen

Nadine Strossen is a law professor at New York Law School, president of the American Civil Liberties Union [ACLU], and a founding member of Feminists for Free Expression. In the following viewpoint, she contends that feminists who attempt to censor pornography threaten women's rights in many ways. All censorship threatens freedom of speech, she maintains, and censoring of pornography especially threatens women's right to sexual expression. In addition, censorship promotes the stereotype that women cannot make their own decisions concerning sex. Strossen concludes that feminists must oppose all censorship, including censorship of pornography.

As you read, consider the following questions:

1. What are five of the ten ways censorship of pornography harms women, in Strossen's opinion?
2. What does the author believe are the most significant causes of discrimination against women?
3. What is a "blame-the-book" attitude, and how does it relate to women's oppression, according to the author?

Abridged from Nadine Strossen, "A Feminist Critique of 'The' Feminist Critique of Pornography," 79 *Virginia Law Review* 1099 (1993). Reprinted with permission.

The radical message of feminism is the recognition that equality is not just a measure of equalization or fairness, . . . but . . . part of a larger struggle for social change. . . . Equal pay for work of equal value is no more or less important than the right of women to explore the range and depths of human experience, the diverse models of human relations as well as the psychological limits and beyond of acceptable behavior. If we are ever to find our own identity and give equality a social meaning, there is a process of cognitive reflection and emotional insight; we must be free to think about saints and sinners, . . . slavery and freedom, deviants and conformists, sadists and martyrs, Mother Teresa and Madonna.

State censorship denies us that experience. . . .

—Thelma McCormack

Sexual expression is perhaps the most fundamental manifestation of human individuality. Erotic material is subversive in the sense that it celebrates, and appeals to, the most uniquely personal aspects of an individual's emotional life. Thus, to allow freedom of expression and freedom of thought in this realm is to . . . promote diversity and nonconformist behavior in general. . . .

It is no coincidence that one of the first consequences of democratization and political liberalization in the former Soviet Union, Eastern Europe and China was a small explosion of erotic publications.

Suppression of pornography is not just a free-speech issue: Attempts to stifle sexual expression are part of a larger agenda directed at the suppression of human freedom and individuality more generally.

—Gary Mongiovi

Over the past decade, some feminists—led by Andrea Dworkin and Catharine MacKinnon—have had great influence in advancing the theory that certain sexually oriented speech should be regulated because it "subordinates" women. They have labeled this subset of sexually explicit speech "pornography" to distinguish it from the separate subset of sexually explicit speech that the Supreme Court has defined as proscribable "obscenity." This viewpoint counters the Dworkin-MacKinnon pro-censorship position with an argument grounded in feminist principles and concerns. It refers to objections that are based on traditional free speech principles only in passing. . . .

The Definition of "Pornography"

Because I am offering a feminist critique of the efforts by the Dworkin-MacKinnon faction of feminism to regulate the expression they label "pornography," I use the term as they do, which is to refer to sexually explicit speech that allegedly "subordinates" women. I emphasize that such speech "*allegedly*" is subordinating, because that subjective characterization is one with which many women, feminists, authors, and artists disagree. To highlight the problematic nature of the term "pornography," I put it in quotation marks throughout this viewpoint.

Many women who champion feminist values oppose the censorship of "pornography" specifically because they regard such censorship as undermining those values. . . . This Section elaborates upon ten major ways in which censoring "pornography" would have an adverse impact upon women's rights and interests. Pro-censorship feminists argue in rebuttal that censoring "pornography" would have the positive result of reducing discrimination or violence against women. However, as the next section shows, their argument is speculative at best. Indeed, evidence suggests that in some instances censoring "pornography" could well increase anti-female discrimination and violence. Accordingly, on balance, censoring "pornography" would do more harm than good to the women's rights movement.

Ten Negative Effects of Censoring Pornography

The principal negative effects that censoring "pornography" would have upon feminist values, which this Section discusses, are the following:

1. Any censorship scheme would inevitably encompass many works that are especially valuable to feminists.

2. Any censorship scheme would be enforced in a way that would discriminate against the least popular, least powerful groups in our society, including feminists and lesbians.

3. Censorship is paternalistic, perpetuating demeaning stereotypes about women, including that sex is bad for us.

4. Censorship perpetuates the disempowering notion that women are essentially victims.

5. Censorship distracts from constructive approaches to countering anti-female discrimination and violence.

6. Censorship would harm women who make their living in the sex industry.

7. Censorship would harm women's efforts to develop their own sexualities.

8. Censorship would strengthen the power of the religious right, whose patriarchal agenda would curtail women's rights.

9. By undermining free speech, censorship would deprive feminists of a powerful tool for advancing women's equality.

10. Sexual freedom, and freedom for sexually explicit expression, are essential aspects of human freedom; denying these specific freedoms undermines human rights more broadly.

The ACLU's brief in *American Booksellers Association v. Hudnut* noted the adverse impact of "pornography" censorship on feminist concerns. It explained that the Dworkin-MacKinnon model law, by proscribing sexually explicit depictions of women's "subordination," outlawed not only many valuable works of art and literature in general, but also many such works that are particularly important to women and feminists:

> Ironically, much overtly feminist scholarly material designed to address the same concerns prompting the [ordinance] would fall within [its] sweeping definition of pornography. Prominent examples include Kate Millett's *The Basement*, a graphic chronicle of sexual torture; . . . works on rape, wife beating and domestic violence; court testimony and photographic evidence in rape and sexual assault cases; works like [Susan] Brownmiller's *Against Our Will: Men, Women and Rape*; and psychiatric literature describing sexual pathologies and therapeutic modalities. Indeed, *Pornography: Men Possessing Women*, a work by Andrea Dworkin, one of the ordinance's original drafters, contains . . . so many . . . passages graphically depicting the explicit sexual subordination of women that it could easily be pornographic under the ordinance.

I have been told that Andrea Dworkin acknowledges that much of her own work would be censored under her model law, but that she considers this "a price worth paying" for the power to censor other works that would also be viewed as "pornography." Even assuming that Andrea Dworkin or other advocates of censoring "pornography" do in fact take this position, they certainly do not speak for all feminists on this point. Many may well believe that works such as Dworkin's, by depicting and deploring violence and discrimination against women, make invaluable contributions to redressing those problems. . . .

Discrimination Against the Least Powerful

Vague censorship laws always rebound against the groups that hope to be "protected" by them. This is because such laws are enforced by the very power structure against which the disempowered censorship advocates seek protection. Given that the laws' vague and open-ended terms require the enforcing authorities to make subjective, discretionary judgments, it should not be surprising that these judgments are unsympathetic to the disempowered and marginalized.

The phenomenon of disempowered groups being disproportionately targeted under censorship schemes that are designed for their benefit is vividly illustrated, for example, by the enforcement record of laws against "hate speech"—i.e., speech that expresses racial, religious, sexist, and other forms of invidious discrimination. In the U.S., recently implemented campus hate speech codes consistently have been used disproportionately to punish the speech of the very racial minority groups whose interests, according to the code proponents, should have been advanced by such codes.

This recent American campus experience typifies a more long-term, worldwide pattern. Censorship laws intended to "protect" minority groups have been enforced in a manner that penalizes disproportionately the speech of those very groups. . . .

Ironically, the Dworkin-MacKinnon effort to extirpate sexually explicit expression that, in their view, perpetuates demeaning stereotypes about women, itself perpetuates such demeaning stereotypes. One subordinating stereotype that is central to the feminist censorship movement is that sex is inherently degrading to women.

To emphasize that the feminist pro-censorship position rests upon traditional, stereotypical views disapproving sex and denying women's sexuality, anti-censorship feminists have characterized their own views as "pro-sex." . . .

Censorship Threatens Those Who Work for Change

Despite the ugliness of a lot of pornography, . . . I believe that censorship only springs back against the givers of culture—against authors, artists, and feminists, against anybody who wants to change society. Should censorship be imposed, . . . feminists would be the first to suffer.

Erica Jong, as quoted in *Ms.*, April 1985.

The "anti-sex" position of the pro-censorship feminists essentially posits a mutual inconsistency between a woman's freedom and her participation in sexual relations with men. For example, both Dworkin and MacKinnon have argued that, in light of society's pervasive sexism, women cannot freely consent to sexual relations with men. Dworkin makes this point in the most dramatic and extreme terms in her book *Intercourse*, which equates *all* heterosexual intercourse with rape.

Just as the pro-censorship movement views women as inevitably being victims in sexual matters, that movement also perpetuates the stereotype that women are victims in a more general sense. For example, feminist law professor Carlin Meyer has noted the pro-censorship feminists' "general tendency to view women as actually, not merely portrayed as, submissive—as acted upon rather than acting; as objects of male will rather than subjects able to challenge or change cultural norms." . . .

Reducing Discrimination Against Women

Like all censorship schemes, the feminist proposal to censor "pornography" diverts attention and resources from constructive, meaningful steps to address the societal problem at which the censorship is aimed—in this case, discrimination and violence against women. Feminist advocates of censoring "pornography"—along with feminist opponents of such censorship—are concerned about the very real, very disturbing societal problems of discrimination and violence against women. The focus on censoring "pornography," though, diverts attention from the root causes of discrimination and violence against women—of which violent, misogynistic "pornography" is merely one symptom—and from actual acts of discrimination and violence. . . .

By asserting that "pornography" is a central cause—or even *the* central cause—of sex discrimination, pro-censorship feminists deflect energy and attention from the factors that feminist scholars and the U.S. Commission on Civil Rights have found to be the most significant causes of such discrimination: sex-segregated labor markets; systematic devaluation of work traditionally done by women; sexist concepts of marriage and family; inadequate income-maintenance programs for women unable to find wage work; lack of day care services and the premise that child care is an exclusively or largely female responsibility; barriers to reproductive freedom; and discrimination and segregation in education. . . .

Distraction from Real Causes of Misogynistic Violence

Just as the focus on "pornography" distracts from the real causes of gender discrimination, it also distracts from the real causes of anti-female violence. A comprehensive analysis of the literature on this issue concluded:

> Leading feminists and the U.S. Commission on Civil Rights suggest that violence against women begins with educational and economic discrimination. . . . Men learn to consider women burdens, stiflers and drags on their freedom. Women, in turn, do not have the economic independence and access to day care that would enable them to leave abusive settings. Feminists also suggest that violence begins with the infantilization of women so that men hold them in contempt and see them as easily dismissed or lampooned and ready targets for anger.

By arguing that exposure to "pornography" causes violent crimes against women, pro-censorship feminists dilute the accountability of men who commit these crimes by displacing some of it onto words and images, or those who create or distribute them. . . .

"Blaming the Book" and "Blaming the Victim"

Censorship's "blame-the-book" attitude closely parallels a "blame-the-victim" attitude that has characterized some perceptions of female victims of sexual assault, and that until recently was enshrined in American law. While the assaulted woman herself used to be blamed for the assault if, for example, her skirt was "too short" or her sweater was "too tight," now it is the woman who poses for a sexually suggestive photograph or film

74

who is blamed.

What "blaming the book" and "blaming the victim" have in common is the creation of a scapegoat. They divert attention away from the real problem, which is the men who discriminate or commit violence against women, and they ignore the real solution, which is the imposition of measures to prevent and punish such actions. . . .

Censorship Would Harm Women in the Sex Industry

The Dworkin-MacKinnon approach to sexually oriented expression would undermine the interests of women who choose to make their living in the sex industry in several respects. Most obviously, by seeking to ban major aspects of this industry, the Dworkin-MacKinnon regime would deprive women of an option that many now affirm they have freely chosen.

Moreover, as even feminist censorship advocates recognize, the practical impact of their approach would not be to prevent the production of sexually explicit expression altogether, but rather simply to drive that production underground. In consequence, the women who participate in producing sexually oriented materials would be more subject to exploitation and less amenable to legal protection. The Dworkin-MacKinnon approach also deprives women who pose for sexually explicit works of an important tool for guarding their economic and other interests because it deems women incompetent to enter into legally binding contracts regarding the production of such works. . . .

Harming Women's Efforts to Develop Their Own Sexuality

As each successive wave of the women's movement has recognized, sexual liberation is an essential aspect of what has been called "women's liberation.". . . Dr. Leonore Tiefer, who believes that "women are in more danger from the repression of sexually explicit materials than from their expression," grounds that conclusion in large part on the fact that such materials are especially important for women's "struggl[e] to develop their own sexualities. . . ." She explains:

> We need the freedom for new female sexual visions to inspire our minds and practices away from the ruts worn by centuries of religious inhibition, fear of pregnancy and disease, compulsory heterosexuality, lies and ignorance of all kinds.
>
> . . . Female sexuality is a joke without freely available information and ideas.

Censoring "pornography" would also stultify discussions and explorations of female sexuality by women, including by female artists. As one woman artist stated: "Censorship can only accentuate the taboos that already surround women's open exploration of their sexuality. There are too many other obstacles now in place to women becoming artists or writers, or even speaking out publicly, without inviting the judicial control of censorship."

Censorship Would Strengthen the Religious Right

As discussed above, the traditional, right-wing groups that have exercised much political power since 1980 have lent that strength to the feminist pro-censorship faction by using its rhetoric in an attempt to justify various censorship measures. The feminist and right-wing advocates of censoring "pornography" have a symbiotic relationship. Thus, just as the right-wing activists have reinforced the influence of the pro-censorship feminists, so too, the pro-censorship feminists have strengthened the political power of the religious right. . . .

Advancing Women's Equality

Because free speech is a powerful tool for advancing women's equality, and because censorship consistently has been used to undermine women's rights, advocates of such rights have far more to lose than to gain from any censorship scheme. For example, free speech has proven to be an effective ally even of feminism's anti-"pornography" faction; they and others have successfully used "pornography" itself, as well as other expression, to counter misogynistic attitudes. . . .

Viewing Pornography Should Be an Individual Choice

Women do not require "protection" from explicit sexual materials. It is no goal of feminism to restrict individual choices or stamp out sexual imagery. Though some women and men may have this on their platform, they represent only themselves. Women are as varied as any citizens of a democracy; there is no agreement or feminist code as to what images are distasteful or even sexist. It is the right and responsibility of each woman to read, view or produce the sexual material she chooses without the intervention of the state "for her own good." We believe genuine feminism encourages individuals to make these choices for themselves. This is the great benefit of being feminists in a free society.

Ad Hoc Committee of Feminists for Free Expression, letter to the U.S. Senate Judiciary Committee, February 14, 1992.

In light of the numerous adverse effects that censoring "pornography" would have on women's rights and interests, those who advocate such censorship ostensibly on feminist rationales have a heavy burden of proof indeed. The only alleged justification they offer is the claim that censoring "pornography" will reduce violence and discrimination against women. This claim rests on three assumptions, all of which must be established to substantiate the asserted justification: 1) that the effective suppression of "pornography" would significantly reduce exposure to sexist, violent imagery; 2) that censorship would effectively suppress "pornography"; and 3) that exposure to sexist, violent imagery leads to sexist, violent behavior. In fact, each of these assumptions is fatally flawed.

First, given the pervasive presence of sexist, violent imagery in mainstream American culture, most such imagery would remain intact, even if "pornography" could be effectively suppressed. Moreover, because the mainstream imagery is viewed by far more people than is "pornography," and because it has the stamp of legitimacy, it has a greater impact on people's attitudes. Therefore, if it is true—as the feminist censorship advocates assert—that exposure to sexist, violent imagery leads to sexist, violent conduct, such conduct would still be triggered, even if "pornography" could be effectively suppressed.

Second, "pornography" could not be effectively suppressed in any event. As feminist censorship advocates themselves have recognized, any censorship regime would simply drive "pornography" underground, where it might well exercise a more potent influence on its viewers.

Costs of Censorship Outweigh Benefits

For the foregoing reasons, even assuming for the sake of argument that exposure to sexist, violent imagery caused anti-female discrimination and violence, censoring "pornography" would make, at best, an insignificant contribution to reducing these problems. At worst, censorship could actually aggravate these problems, since some evidence indicates that censorship could augment any aggressive responses that some viewers might have to "pornography." The conclusion that the costs of "pornography" censorship outweigh its putative benefits, in terms of women's rights, is reinforced by the lack of evidence to substantiate the alleged causal link between exposure to "pornography" and misogynistic discrimination or violence. . . .

As is true for all relatively disempowered groups, women have a special stake in preserving our system of free expression. . . . Government power to censor "pornography" would predictably be unleashed against feminist messages and perspectives. The power the government would assume in censoring "pornography" would pose a far greater threat to women's rights than the alleged power of "pornography" itself. In the memorable words of journalist Ellen Willis, "How long will it take oppressed groups to learn that if we give the state enough rope, it will end up around our necks?"

*"A variety of strategies has been used to increase
the responsiveness and the efficacy of legal
institutions to the concerns of women."*

Feminism Improves Women's Legal Rights

Diane Crothers

In the following viewpoint, Diane Crothers describes how
women have benefited from changes in America's laws in recent
decades. Crothers states that because of the work of women's
groups, laws now exist that make sexual harassment, domestic
violence, and gender discrimination illegal. Crothers concludes
that women must continue to work to ensure that the legal system protects women's rights. Crothers is social science advisor
and legislative analyst for the Women's Bureau of the U.S.
Department of Labor in Washington, D.C.

As you read, consider the following questions:

1. How did the 1991 Thomas-Hill hearings affect women's
   perception of sexual harassment, according to Crothers?
2. How has the women's movement affected family life, in the
   author's opinion?
3. What changes is the legal profession making to expand
   women's role in society, according to Crothers?

The move toward women's legal literacy argues that we must get beyond what has been for centuries a government of *men's* laws.

All rights depend upon knowledge of the law and the means to exercise and enforce such rights by an enlightened citizenry. Barred for so long by the legal system itself from participating in the creation and maintenance of legal institutions as voters, lawyers, judges, and legislators, the current generation of women are the first to assume this responsibility.

During the past 30 years, a variety of strategies has been used to increase the responsiveness and the efficacy of legal institutions to the concerns of women.

Today, criminal law in cases such as rape, incest, and physical abuse; domestic relations law, such as divorce, child support, and child custody; and employment law, such as job discrimination and workers' compensation, more accurately reflect the actual circumstances of women's lives than ever before in this country.

Unlike 30 years ago, major statutory protections against employment discrimination on the basis of gender exist today at the national, state, and local level.

The perception of what constitutes the most urgent employment issue for working women has changed as new legislation, court cases, and media information shape cultural expectations of how women should be treated on the job.

Pregnancy discrimination, maternity leave, and protecting job rights when working parents need to care for sick children have been focal points since the late 1970s. These concerns have culminated in the Pregnancy Discrimination Act of 1978 and the Family and Medical Leave Act of 1993.

Women today are encouraged to raise new and innovative fairness issues in the courts, legislatures, and at the work place. In addition, women are now putting before the public the question of the fitness for leadership roles of those individuals who have behaved unjustly to women workers.

Sexual Harassment and the Legal System

It wasn't until the late 1980s, as more women entered the work force and the U.S. Supreme Court ruled sexual harassment was a form of sex discrimination, that sexual harassment received more attention by working women.

Sexual harassment became one of the most talked-about issues in late 1991, thanks in large part to the televised Anita Hill-Clarence Thomas controversy.

Prior to these hearings, a national study of sexual harassment in the federal work force reported that only 5 percent of victims filed a complaint. In the last quarter of 1991, sexual harassment claims filed with the Equal Employment Opportunity Commis-

79

sion were 71 percent higher than in the same quarter of 1990, suggesting that not only did the public discussion make women more aware of sexual harassment as unlawful, but also instilled faith in the legal system's ability to address these wrongs.

An acceptable definition of sexual harassment has been developing over the past 10 years. In the legal arena, Catharine MacKinnon's books, *Sexual Harassment of Working Women: A Case of Sex Discrimination* (1979) and *Toward a Feminist Theory of the State* (1989), have been instrumental in formulating the concepts of power and sexuality in the work place.

©John Trever/*The Albuquerque Journal*. Reprinted with permission.

Freada Klein, a consultant on sexual harassment in Cambridge, Massachusetts, made public her 1984 study of 20,000 federal government workers and their experiences with sexual harassment in the work place.

Klein reminds us that efforts to end sex discrimination in employment first focused on the most blatant examples of disparate treatment: unequal pay for equal work and occupational segregation.

Twenty years after passage of the Equal Pay Act and Title VII of the Civil Rights Act of 1964, improvement in the ratio of pay between men and women remained comparatively minor, shifting attention to the subtle forces that maintain occupational segregation.

Simultaneously, the social mythology about rape and other sexual assaults was unraveling. The use of physical and sexual violence in the family came under scrutiny, challenging the accepted notion of family life. In turn, this added fuel to the quest for ending employment discrimination; women needed access to economic independence to extricate themselves from violent homes. It also led to a quest for better understanding of violence, its causes, and adequate remedies.

Has the Work Place Changed?

It was the civil rights movement that provided a model for systematic analysis of sexual harassment, which could then be seen as a discriminatory work condition, an extension of spheres in which male violence is exercised, and as a method to enforce the primary definition of women as sexual beings.

The general theory of sexual harassment law rests upon earlier court decisions holding employers liable under civil rights laws in which the harassment creates psychologically damaging work environments.

In addition, with innovative arguments by women of color, courts have begun to recognize a special class of harassment aimed specifically at them. In *Hicks v. Gates Rubber Co.*, the court held that racially hostile treatment combined with sexual harassment would create a hostile work environment toward a black woman employee.

Even with all of the current dialogue about sexual harassment, much about sex discrimination at work remains hidden. Victims often fear that they will be further isolated, or that the harassment will be discounted or minimized, or that they will be held responsible.

A Gap in Perception

A decade ago, a study in the *Harvard Business Review* reported that although corporate men and women agree on an abstract definition of harassment, there is a real and significant gap in perception of what actually happens in the work place.

Increasingly, some experts think that without a new view of the power and communication gap that exists between women and men, significant sexual harassment will continue. Women workers will quit rather than complain; a few lawsuits will recover substantial damages; bitterness and incomprehension between the sexes will escalate; and employees will be unable to focus on doing their jobs.

On the homefront, many women's groups focus today on both the development and enforcement of women's legal rights within the family. Laws regarding domestic violence, child custody, child support, marriage, and divorce have all been redefined over the past three decades.

Women have taken on the challenge of transforming the laws regarding domestic violence. Lobbying efforts at the state and federal level have resulted in laws that now see the eviction of the aggressor, child support enforcement, and civil protection orders that trigger criminal penalties when violated. . . .

Women have moved forward in redefining the ways in which the legal system prosecutes incest. There has been successful civil litigation in which the woman recovers damages for acts of incest she recalls only after many years have passed. And efforts are under way to extend the statute of limitations for incest from the time the victim first remembers the incident.

The Legal Profession

Demographic pressures within the legal profession are encouraging systemic changes as to women's legal status. According to the ABA's [American Bar Association] Commission on Women in the Profession, women now constitute 43 percent of current law graduates, 31 percent of all attorneys, and close to 23 percent of ABA members.

The association's statistics clearly show that it needs to attract newly graduating women attorneys in order to grow. However, as of 1992, only four of 58 chairs of ABA standing committees are women and 27 states have no women representatives in the ABA's House of Delegates.

Clearly the legal profession itself is struggling to redefine itself along more inclusive gender lines. This movement will affect how the substantive law is developed and applied by practitioners.

Law schools also are engaged in similar redefinitions of women's roles in the law. . . . Some law schools now offer advanced feminist legal theory courses.

The judiciary, too, has had to focus on what some see as a systemic gender bias on the part of the entire court system, including judges, prosecutors, juries, and court personnel.

The National Judicial Education Program to Promote Equality for Women and Men in the Courts, a project sponsored by the National Organization for Women Legal Defense and Education Fund in cooperation with the National Association of Women Judges, was established in 1980 and pioneered the introduction of continuing judicial education programs on the way gender bias affects decision making and court interaction.

Ten years ago, the term "judicial gender bias" had not yet been coined. As of 1993, special task forces established in more than half the states are investigating gender bias in the state judicial systems and proposing and implementing a wide range of reforms.

Once women exercise their rights to participate at all levels of the legal system, both the substantive law and its enforcement will move closer toward protecting the legal rights of all citizens.

"The legitimate gains achieved on behalf of all women . . . are seriously diminished by the self-anointed high priestesses of women's rights."

Feminism Often Harms Women's Legal Rights

Kenneth Lasson

Feminists have helped women gain rights in many areas, Kenneth Lasson writes in the following viewpoint. But today feminism threatens to erode much of the progress women have made, he argues, especially in the area of family law. Lasson believes that because of their extreme views, feminists no longer represent the needs and wishes of most women. He maintains that if feminists are not challenged, they will continue to harm women's legal rights. Lasson is a law professor at the University of Baltimore School of Law.

As you read, consider the following questions:

1. What criticisms does Lasson make concerning the writings of radical feminist legal scholars?
2. What are the differences between liberal, cultural, and radical feminists, according to the author?
3. How might the radical feminists' goals concerning family law harm women's rights, in the author's opinion?

Abridged from Kenneth Lasson, "Feminism Awry: Excesses in the Pursuit of Rights and Trifles," *Journal of Legal Education* vol. 42, no. 1 (March 1992). Copyright ©1992, Association of American Law Schools. Reprinted with permission.

From virtually any perspective, liberal and conservative feminists in the twentieth century have improved the quality of life for many women in a number of noteworthy ways. They have helped win the right to vote, to own property, to make contracts, to serve on juries, to use contraceptives. They have succeeded in asserting the need for enhanced economic opportunities: equal pay for equal work, maternity leave, flex-time for mothers. They have made significant advancements against both domestic battery and sexual harassment in the workplace. As a consequence of all these efforts, there are more women now than ever before in professional schools, city halls, state houses, and courts.

Such well-deserved victories, however, have been achieved at the cost of a goodly number of Pyrrhic ones, not the least of which have been wholesale changes in the language and literature of the law—most of it force-fed to the silent majority of women everywhere and to a lesser extent the hapless readers of law reviews. Good people of both sexes have been stampeded into corners of stilted parlance and tortured logic by self-appointed thought police. Big Sister has imposed herself on us all; nowadays she throws no pots and burns no bras but brandishes instead a sacred and unabridgeable Lexicon of Political Correctness.

How Feminism Threatens Society

It is not just labeling lawyers who apply the "reasonable *man*" standard as profoundly sexist or forcing substantial expenditures to render the text of codes and constitutions "gender-neutral"— or even likening the first movement of Beethoven's Ninth to the murderous rage of a rapist. The vernacular required by Feminist Newspeak is as inconsequential as it may be silly or supercilious.

Nor does it cause anything more than a mild ripple among the *cognoscenti* when feminist professors demand removal of a Goya nude from a university lecture hall or loftily lump male law professors in with all the other licensed lechers seen to saturate the legal establishment.

These are but the piddling quibbles.

More serious and wasteful—and ultimately more dangerous— is the inordinate attention paid to abstruse rantings by radical feminist theorists by the media and in political arenas, and the even more obsequious homage accorded the obscure ravings of their academic counterparts, the radical feminist legal scholars. Whether on the hustle or the hustings their words are often virtually incomprehensible, their writings filled with shrill jargon and polysyllabic gibberish—their voices as outraged as their messages outrageous. Whatever they lack in clarity is made up for in volume: they dominate the discussion of the agenda they so stridently dictate, lashing out against all those who do not accept their world view with the same unadorned scorn they heap upon tellers of off-color jokes. In so doing they serve to obfuscate the legitimate gains of the women's movement, shrouding it in the clothes of shrill revolutionary discourse. Many women have thus come to see the feminist movement as antimale, antichild, antifamily, and antifeminine.

A Challenge to Feminists

What we know as radical feminist jurisprudence has been with us for at least twenty years now. It is part of the curricula of many law schools, and the focal point of an increasing number of law review articles. If this is "scholarship," what is it all about? Does the virtual absence of any meaningful challenge mean that the majority of male scholars tacitly agree with their radical feminist colleagues? Or are they too intimidated, bored, amused, or confused to respond? How much does the current literature continue to reflect a plaintive cry for equality by a sex unjustly scorned—and how much of it is strewn with the petty mewlings of pouty prima donnas who are intellectually dishonest to boot? Which are the rights, and which the trifles?

Such quaeres themselves, of course, can be criticized as gender-biased, and it is a virtual certainty that the answers suggested by this viewpoint—that the best-known feminist legal scholars have unfairly arrogated to themselves the right to speak for all women, that their advocacy is confounded by their language, and that what they can or should get is more often limited by logic and the natural human condition than by an oppressive masculine society—will be dismissed as reflecting the misguided misogyny of a society dominated by male chauvinists.

So be it. The time is past due for an intellectually responsible challenge to the radical feminists who have assumed command of the Ivory Tower and the world beyond to which it beckons. Abdication of that responsibility—whether because it is felt that the feminists in question are unfathomable, or their agenda illogical, or that fighting them could be career-threatening— amounts to endorsement of an authoritarian ideology that runs roughshod over the few scholars who dare to question its merits. Just ask the handful of outspoken women who have had the temerity to denounce radical feminist scholarship in its own terms, calling it "a travesty of the intellect" [Brigitte Berger], "bald ignorance," and "pop fascism" [Maureen Mullarkey].

In truth, the thesis is a simple one: the legitimate gains achieved on behalf of all women—largely by the Herculean efforts of both latter-day Lysistratas *and* their high-minded male colleagues—are seriously diminished by the self-anointed high priestesses of women's rights who minister their metaphysics from behind the protective walls of an unquestioning academy. . . .

Sometimes called liberal feminists or rational empiricists, those who reason on the basis of equality seek to minimize the differences between men and women and focus upon issues of equality. Proponents of this point of view argue that it is arbitrary and irrational to make any distinction between the sexes; their primary goal is passage of an Equal Rights Amendment; their principal voice is the National Organization for Women. . . .

But liberal feminists are sometimes faced with the practical problem that equality can work *against* women. Consider various areas of the law in which women once had a certain favored status. For example, the National Organization for Women has helped quash legislation that would allow adoption of out-of-wedlock children only by the mother's consent, void statutes requiring that only a husband need pay alimony, and oppose the male-only draft. In so doing, NOW clearly does not speak for all women. . . .

Cultural Feminism

Cultural feminists take a more chauvinistic tack. Differences between men and women, they say, are profound and immutable. Further, the "different voice" of women—a truer, more caring nature—is one on which a superior feminist jurisprudence can be based. . . .

Cultural feminists maintain that all legal theory is male-oriented because all legal theory is based on the notion that each individual is separate. Women, however, are not separated but connected; they reason differently from men; they are more sensitive to situations in context; they emphasize practical results over abstract justice; they resist universal principles and generalizations. The attack on the male-oriented theory emphasizes the distinctive way in which women approach problems—advocating negotiation rather than conflict, making the most of feminine mystique, rising above principle.

In other words, women are nurturing and altruistic, men individualistic and (it may be inferred) insensitive.

Radical Feminism

Radical feminists (the primary focus of this viewpoint) go even further than their cultural counterparts, beginning with the explicit assumption that men by their very nature consciously and systematically *oppress* women, who in turn are depicted as the primary victims of the male-hierarchic society. The differences between men and women are not just biological, say the radical feminists, but diabolical as well. The radicals do not hide how they feel. They are *angry*. And because the shrill voice is often the one that is most heard, they dominate both the popular media and the academic literature. . . .

Radical feminists often vociferously oppose both liberal and cultural feminists, asserting that all women will be sold short by anything less than a cosmically changed social order. Neutral criteria, say the radicals, deprive women of the few protections they once had; they now lose more child-custody battles than before; they do not get as much alimony as they used to. Women do not need a declaration of equality, because it would inhibit the law from recognizing that men *start* with an unfair advantage. What women do need, say the radicals, is an aggressive affirmative action program—an Anti-Subordination Amendment rather than an Equal Rights Amendment.

Conservative Digest, May 1982.

Cultural feminists are likewise attacked by the radicals on the ground that those qualities traditionally ascribed to females—for example, compassion and empathy—are in truth neither natural nor inherent, but simply an adjustment to the social subordination of all women by all men. The differences that exist between the sexes are not to be celebrated, but deplored.

Radical feminists thus align themselves with lesbian-rights groups, which likewise attack the notion of a male's right of access to women (and ultimately a rite of passage and conquest). The radicals see sexual coercion as the root of the whole "women problem." It is this mindset that empowers their forays into the legislative and jurisprudential arenas, especially in the areas of sexual harassment and pornography. . . .

Attacking the Law

Another common characteristic of radical feminist legal theory is that it is antimainstream and ever-more-often revisionist and revolutionary. By definition it regards the existing order as oppressive to women. Its primary attack is against contemporary law itself, whose rules and methodology conceal and perpetuate oppression. The radicals take aim at the basic verities of all institutions and traditions, starting with religion and ending with the family. God the Father is anathema. The family is the principal focal point of oppression—perpetuating as it does a sexual hierarchy and promoting heterosexuality as the norm. Because they regard marriage as a form of prostitution, radical feminists have a detailed program for ridding the world of the nuclear family. They would like to see the term "family law" changed to "household law," so that they could have individual benefits and tax allowances. They would abolish all sorts of immunities from suit.

For them, solving "the women's problem" is usually not enough: the "women's problem" must be seen as part of a larger injustice. Their articles therefore attack all the ills of the world: poverty, discrimination, social and economic exploitation, or as one feminist scholar puts it, the whole range of "racist, misogynist, homophobic, patriarchiac and economic hierarchies." In seeking a holistic theory of justice, feminist legal scholars conclude that *all* of our values have to be transformed. The code word is "empowerment"; political power is what radical feminists seek above all else—their agenda unmodified. Though "feminist theorizing is never far removed from 'political struggle,'" the radicals have little patience for conjecture about the nature of law, for precedent or jurisprudence. For them power is at the core of legal decision making. The radicals view the world as a male-dominated engine of oppression, which they would like to shift into reverse. Women would give the orders. It is They Who Must Be Obeyed.

How Feminism Harms Women

But shifting gears runs the risk of stripping them. Consider, for example, the feminist legal scholars' current criticism of typical marital property laws. When such laws were first passed in the 1970s, feminists strongly supported them as necessary to deal with a "women's problem," men who did not pay court-ordered alimony. Under the marital property acts the spousal assets would be divided at the time of divorce, with the woman getting a lump sum. Usually there is no alimony, and so no need to enforce monthly payments. Lobbyists supporting the acts persuaded legislators that the new laws would also solve a "men's problem"—that is, divorced women refusing to get a job or remarry because they could live better on their ex-spouses' alimony payments. These days, though, radical feminists *attack* marital property acts as unjust, because older untrained women, wealthy when married, are now being denied alimony and forced to take minimum-wage jobs. Judges are likewise criticized for abusing their discretion, particularly when financial awards appear to favor the male party. The radicals' remedy is to increase the number of female judges. Left unaddressed is the possibility that increasing the number of female judges might only throw the bias toward the females or bring about inconsistency in how the law is applied. . . .

And it is with strident revolutionary declarations that radical feminists skewer themselves, ignoring what could be much more persuasive arguments. For example, they could (but do not) assert that the changes they advocate would benefit men as well as women, in that working wives and mothers take some of the strain off men to provide for families. They should (but do not) emphasize the universal merits of a system in which *everyone* places a greater value on raising children, friendly relationships in the workplace, or the care of the elderly. They would do well to recognize (but do not) that men have human frailties as well. . . .

For their part, men (especially male academics) must reaffirm their commitment to equality of choice and opportunity for women, while at the same time overcoming the apathy (or chauvinism, or chivalry, or chagrin, or whatever it is) that causes them to avoid confronting radical feminist effronteries to the intellect.

"We need to reject the very concept of surrogacy."

Feminists' Attempts to Outlaw Surrogacy Would Benefit Women

Barbara Katz Rothman

Barbara Katz Rothman is an assistant professor of sociology at Baruch College of the City University of New York. A noted opponent of surrogacy, Rothman is the author of the book *Recreating Motherhood: Ideology and Technology in a Patriarchal Society*. In the following viewpoint, Rothman states that surrogacy harms society, women, and children. Because surrogacy involves men's paying women to bear children, Rothman believes it perpetuates a system in which men control women's reproductive choices. In addition, it creates an oppressive class system in which poor women bear children for the wealthy. She concludes that feminists must continue to oppose surrogacy to protect women.

As you read, consider the following questions:

1. How does Rothman define "patriarchy," and what role does she believe it plays in surrogacy?
2. How have men always gotten what they wanted in terms of keeping or rejecting children, in Rothman's opinion?
3. Why does the author believe it is helpful to view infertility as a disability?

Abridged from Barbara Katz Rothman, "Reproductive Technologies and Surrogacy: A Feminist Perspective," 25 *Creighton Law Review* 1599 (1992). Reprinted with permission.

During the "Baby M" case, I found myself caught up in the media circus surrounding the case and spent an amazing amount of time in green rooms with Noel King, the man who had brokered the surrogacy contract between Mr. and Mrs. Stern and Mr. and Mrs. Whitehead. I think I spent more time putting on my makeup for that particular surrogate broker than I did with my husband that year. I found that one of the interesting things that happened was the way that the media used me for something it called balance. The media would have a carefully groomed "surrogate" and her broker on one side and then on the other side, it would usually have a rabbi or a priest or minister, and then me. The little tag that appeared in white letters on the television screen under me sometimes read "author" and sometimes read "sociologist," but usually it read "feminist," and so I was there to be the feminist balance. My family and friends time and again agreed with the viewpoint of the rabbi, the priest, or the minister. Today, I find myself in the same general mode of opposition to this arrangement we call surrogacy, proving the point that surrogacy does, indeed, in every possible way, make for very strange bedfellows.

The Ideology of Patriarchy

Although I and others who are critical of the development of surrogacy from a feminist perspective may be on the same side of this particular fence as the religious leaders, we are coming from a very different place, and we are going to a very different place. We just happen, for the moment, to be in agreement on a particular issue. I think it is important not to merely say, "Yes, I, too, oppose surrogacy because it demeans women," and let it go at that. I believe it is important to look at some of the underlying assumptions that make my opposition to surrogacy so different from the religious opposition. Each of the religious traditions, . . . which *are* related to our legal tradition, stemming as it does from some of that Judeo-Christian religious tradition, is based on a fundamental assumption of relationships between people that comes from an underlying ideology of patriarchy. The word "patriarchy" is often used as a synonym for sexism or men's rule or any system in which men rule. This common usage is inaccurate. "Patriarchy" has a specific technical meaning, and the technical meaning becomes important here. "Patriarchy" refers to a system in which men rule as fathers. A patriarchy is a rule of fathers. Men rule all over the world. In some places they rule as fathers and in some places they rule on other authority. . . .

I think it is important to look at the way that modified patriarchy works in the legal history of the custody of the family. The case of "Baby M" is the pivotal case that got people thinking about these issues. A couple of great privilege who decided that the wife should not have a pregnancy hired themselves a woman of considerably less privilege to bear their child for them. Had that man gone into a bar and picked up a devout seventeen-year-old Catholic girl who would not have an abortion, seduced her, sent her two maternity smocks, a layette, and a basket of flowers, he could then claim paternity and take the baby from her in a custody battle. He would have been exactly where he ended up—with custody of a child even though the mother is still legally the mother. That is something that I think a lot of us did not fully appreciate until that case broke upon us.

What Makes a Mother

We need to reject the notion that any woman is the mother of a child that is not her own, regardless of the source of the egg and/ or of the sperm. Maybe a woman will place that child for adoption, but it is *her* child to place. Her nurturing of that child with the blood and nutrients of her body establishes her parenthood of that child.

Barbara Katz Rothman, *Creighton Law Review*, Vol. 25, 1992.

We realized that even if you invalidate the surrogacy concept and say that the woman is still the mother, this makes little difference. Women do not have particular rights to their children; they have half rights at best, just as many rights as the father has. Those half rights become weakened dramatically by the position women find themselves in within our society. We have this notion, a very recent historic notion, that women get custody of children. Women only came to routinely get custody of children in recent industrial times in which children were more of a liability than an asset. This developed at a time when a large number of men, once their marriages had ended, did not want the responsibilities or burdens of these children and could not afford huge household staffs of other women to raise those children. Consequently, the men wanted the women to take the children. Men would write minimal child support checks and did not want custody. . . .

In modern times, when men of a certain class have decided that children are an asset, a status item, then men wanted to keep these babies. Babies became a status item of the 1980s as expensive acquirements that complemented things like the fancy stroller. When men wanted to keep these children, men kept these children. Men repeatedly win custody battles at much higher rates than women do. When men want custody, they get custody. Men often have acquired wives subsequent to divorce, so that they can offer a child a two-parent family.

Women are less likely to be able to remarry and, therefore, cannot offer the child a two-parent family. Men usually have higher incomes and other assets that women do not have. Consequently, men win custody when they want custody.

Women as Fertile Soil

Reproductive technology has developed within this context. The fundamental ideas were that children were the children of men and that men have certain rights to "their" children. Noel King, who brokered the contract between the Sterns and Whiteheads in the "Baby M" case repeatedly asked how anyone could talk about Mr. Stern buying the child? King answered that the child *was* Mr. Stern's. Whitehead just gave the baby back to the father, Mr. Stern. Mr. King's viewpoint expresses the age-old idea that the man carries the seed, the homunculus, that the little person is curled up inside the sperm and women are, as Caroline Witpick puts it, just the flowerpot in which men plant it. The daddy plants the seed in mommy, and mommy is simply dirt, in which one plants seeds. A lot of our religious tradition builds upon the idea of women as unclean, dirty houses for the pure seed.

When one analyzes the language used by members of a society, the assumptions of that society are often revealed. The language we use and the assumptions it embodies are the perspectives of men. One of the places the importance of language struck me was in the recent description of the woman in South Africa who served as a "surrogate" for her daughter. She explained that you do what you have to do for your children. Her daughter needed this, and she did it for her so that the daughter could have her children. That surrogate was described as the "mother-in-law" for her daughter and "son-in-law." The role of the son, the father of the child, is the perspective one takes, as demonstrated by the language chosen. The surrogate acted for her daughter; she did not say that you do what you have to do for your son-in-law, your son-in-law must have his children. The woman, who acted in a mother/daughter relationship at great personal sacrifice for her *daughter*, is described in terms of her relationship to the son-in-law, who is the parent of importance. It is important that he has his children. The religious focus does this also; it puts us in a man's perspective and then asks what motherhood means from the perspective of men.

Surrogacy and reproductive technologies also cause us to think about inheritance. Inheritance has been entirely a male problem. Until very recently, religious traditions and our legal tradition did not recognize women's property rights, let alone the ability to pass property on. If you could not own property, then you could not pass it on. Property is not the only thing that is being passed on. The purity of a male line is also passed down,

93

and most religious traditions are based on the purity of a male line in which property descend. . . .

The perspective that the religious traditions have adopted made them tend to reject many of the reproductive technologies, not just this particular use of women as "surrogates." If one examines the Catholic tradition, various aspects of the Protestant, and the Jewish traditions, or the Islamic tradition, there has been a real hesitation to make use of any kind of donor gamete, whether it is donor insemination or the use of donor eggs. Religions have hesitated about any kind of "artificial" procreation at all. I think it is important to know that this hesitation comes from the leadership down. What does it mean, then, that devout religious women, believing religious women, women who follow their traditions, use this technology? Catholic women are over-represented among the users of *in vitro* fertilization. Women disobey the teachings of their religions because the real messages are the importance of having children and that women are not worthy unless they are the mothers of children. In many traditions, women are not worthy unless they are the mothers of sons. This explains why the need to use reproductive technologies is very powerful even among those who otherwise adhere to the teachings of their religious communities. From the perspective of religious leaders, however, it looks a little different. The leaders can ban all forms of surrogacy and reproductive technologies as defying the exclusivity of marriage or the sanctity of the family, raising concerns over adultery and bastardism.

If one starts from a perspective which does not include as its focal points the sanctity of the male-dominated family and the notion of illegitimacy, then some very different ideas become possible. I do not reject any and all treatments for infertility that make use of "high technology," though our high technology is pretty low when you are on the receiving end of it. Many of these technologies cause cancers in women. These technologies can be very dangerous to the women users, and that danger has barely been explored.

How to Address Infertility

I regard infertility as a disability and, like every other disability, people cope with it in different ways. Some people who learn they are going to go blind will sacrifice their home, their financial security, the whole family; they will move heaven and earth to retain their sight. Other people will learn braille and go on. People have different ideas about what constitutes wholeness for themselves. There are deep psychological reasons for that, and I have to be supportive of people doing what they need to do to feel whole. But one's fears about going blind do not entitle one to purchase corneas from living donors who do not want to give them, or sign people to contracts and then hold them to it if they change their minds on the way to the operating room. But I can understand why one might be tempted to do it.

Viewing infertility as a disability opens us up to thinking about mechanical, social, medical, and biological approaches to dealing with infertility. It becomes easier to understand that different approaches are going to be acceptable for different people. Some people accept the disability of infertility in different ways. It has a different meaning to each of them. Given the diversity of women's feelings on this subject, I think it is unfair for us to say that the uniform solution for every person unable to have children is to adopt. The most typical rationale for this "solution" is that we need to have more adoptions anyway because so many unwanted children exist today. The response to this "solution" is that blocked tubes do not make one morally responsible for the unwanted children of the world. If there is some sort of moral obligation to adopt among those who can afford children and are at all good at parenting children, then that moral obligation does not depend upon the condition of your fallopian tubes or your sperm count. The solution is not to make all infertile persons adopt, solving two problems at once and getting us off the hook. Infertility demands more serious treatment than that.

The bottom line is that from a woman's perspective, none of this discussion of surrogacy and reproductive technologies sounds the same. . . . From a woman's perspective, every woman has her own child. We do not bear the children of other people. We do not bear our husband's children. We do not bear a purchaser's children. We do not bear the children of the state. It is very dangerous to speak of the needs of society for fewer children or for more children, because this characterizes women's procreation as a societal resource. When society needs fewer children, the conclusion would be not to help women get pregnant; when society needs more children, the conclusion is to prevent them from avoiding pregnancy. This "societal viewpoint" leads to the control of women's bodies as if they were a kind of mechanism that society owns to produce the number of children a society wants at a given moment.

Pregnancy is an intimate social relationship. Our language discards that. Our language says babies "enter the world." From where? We say babies "arrive." Women do not feel babies "arrive," they feel them "leave." Parenthood itself is an intimate social relationship wherever it develops and between whomever it develops. We need to find a perspective as a society that does not discard the intimacy, nurturing, and growth that grows between generations, but a perspective that supports, develops, and encourages that intimacy. We need to reject the very concept of surrogacy.

95

"If surrogacy were made illegal, there is a well-founded fear that the practice would go underground and there would be no recourse for the parties involved."

Feminists' Attempts to Outlaw Surrogacy Could Harm Women

Katherine B. Lieber

While some feminists support surrogacy as one of many reproductive choices for women today, others believe it oppresses women by making them baby factories. In the following viewpoint, Katherine B. Lieber maintains that surrogacy is a complex issue that cannot be resolved simply by making it legal or illegal. Feminists who attempt to outlaw surrogacy could potentially harm women in the long run, Lieber believes, by causing surrogates to operate without legal protection and by threatening women's reproductive rights. Lieber, a 1993 graduate of Indiana University School of Law in Bloomington, is an attorney with an Amherst, Massachusetts, law firm.

As you read, consider the following questions:

1. Some feminists believe that hormonal changes make it impossible for a surrogate to predict her feelings concerning her pregnancy. How does the author respond to this belief?
2. How can the potential harm surrogacy poses to society and children be minimized, in Lieber's opinion?

Abridged from Katherine B. Lieber, "Selling the Womb: Can the Feminist Critique of Surrogacy Be Answered?" 68 *Indiana Law Journal* 205 (1992). Copyright ©1992 by the Trustees of Indiana University. Reprinted with permission.

Since the emergence of the feminist movement around 1910, women have attempted to gain control over their bodies. For centuries, their bodies and reproductive capacities were used to control and oppress them. The feminist movement has attempted to break this mold. Women sought to control their bodies so as not to be prisoners of their biological capacity. An important step towards liberation was the legalization of abortion on demand, which gave women a choice of whether or not to bear children without having to ask anyone's permission. With the emergence of new reproductive technologies, however, women are faced with new challenges and choices. Some regard these choices as new reproductive freedoms while others view them as other ways for society to continue to control women through their reproductive capacities.

Among these new reproductive technologies, surrogacy in particular has alarmed many commentators, especially feminists. Although they have been fighting for years to enable women to gain control over their bodies, many feminists believe that surrogacy is a form of oppression and that the choice for a woman to become a surrogate is really no choice at all. This viewpoint examines feminist perspectives of surrogacy and analyzes whether these concerns are ameliorated by recent legislative activity regulating the practice. It attempts to answer whether or not a legislature, typically dominated by males, can adequately respond to feminist concerns regarding surrogacy and whether it is possible to establish adequate safeguards to answer the concerns of feminists without effectively eliminating surrogacy arrangements. . . .

Feminist Perspectives

It is impossible to identify one unified feminist perspective on surrogacy because feminists are as varied in their views as they are in their identities. Some feminists believe that surrogacy is one of the many reproductive choices that women should be free to make. However, most feminist writers see surrogacy as a form of slavery or prostitution in which the surrogate is exploited through the enticements of money, the social expectation of self-sacrifice, or both.

One of the main tenets of feminism is that women should not have their destiny controlled by their biology. Historically, the social roles of women have been defined by the fact that only women can become pregnant. In Western society, women not only bear the children, but are also given the primary responsibility for rearing them. However, control over women's bodies, and particularly over their reproductive capacities, has been largely in the hands of men. This control is cited by feminist scholars as one of the main factors in the domination and oppression of women.

For centuries women were considered little more than the property of their fathers or husbands. Surrogacy conjures up many of the same fears of women's bodies being controlled by men for their own ends. As sociologist Jalna Hanmer has observed, "in a system characterized by a power imbalance, the greater the asymmetry, the greater the potential for abuse of the less powerful group." Thus, when analyzing surrogacy, the fact that contemporary U.S. society is still largely patriarchal is relevant—most of the power is possessed by men and arguably used to further their own needs and desires.

Should Surrogates Be Paid?

Is it possible to reconcile feminist concerns with a statute that allows surrogates to receive a fee? The concerns of feminists could be meaningfully eliminated only if payment to surrogates were prohibited. Yet, if effective legislation is desired, payment needs to be part of the package. Although payment to surrogates is not the first choice of many feminists, outlawing payment and driving the practice underground is an unacceptable alternative.

Katherine B. Lieber, *Indiana Law Journal*, Vol. 68, 1992.

Many feminists contend that once women gain control of their reproductive capacities, women will have made an essential first step in gaining the much-needed control over their bodies and thus their destiny. Feminists have made great gains in their fight for the right to reproductive choice. Women have established significant reproductive rights, including the right to avoid pregnancy through the use of contraceptives; the right to become pregnant through artificial insemination; the right to control their bodies during pregnancy by choosing, for example, not to have Caesarean sections; and the right to terminate their pregnancies through abortion. "According to feminist arguments, these rights should not be overridden by possible symbolic harms or speculative risks to potential children," [according to Lori B. Andrews, a noted legal scholar on reproductive technologies].

Early on in the surrogacy debate, feminist principles "provided the basis for a broadly held position that contracts and legislation should not restrict the surrogate's control over her body during pregnancy (such as by a requirement that the surrogate undergo amniocentesis or abort a fetus with a genetic defect)," [Andrews states]. This argument is based on the notion of gender equality. It rests on common law principles that protect a person's bodily integrity, and contract law principles which reject the remedy of specific performance for personal service contracts. Currently, however, many feminists are seeking to ban surrogacy entirely. "The rationales being used," says Andrews, "fall into three general categories: the symbolic harm to society of allowing paid surrogacy, the potential risks to the women of allowing paid surrogacy, and the potential risks to the potential child of allowing paid surrogacy."

Harm to Society

The symbolic harm to society posed by surrogacy is that surrogacy may be characterized as baby selling, a practice that demeans all of society. Some argue that surrogacy treats children as commodities that can be bought or sold for a price. Others contend that surrogacy should be prohibited for the same reasons that the sale of organs for transplantation is prohibited. Shari O'Brien states that "the law deters people from relinquishing nonregenerative parts of themselves for mere money. . . . [W]hen an organ or an infant is being marketed the seller experiences pain and substantial risks, the buyer may pay a hefty or even an extortionate fee, and the commodity sold is unique and irreplaceable.". . .

Many feminists have also likened surrogacy to prostitution, in which reproductive capacity becomes a commodity. . . . In turning the womb into a commodity, many feminists fear that society will once again value women primarily for their reproductive capacities. This fear is exacerbated by the strong possibility that, because of economic coercion, surrogacy will occur for the benefit of the rich at the expense of poorer women. Many feminists additionally fear that surrogates will be turned into a class of breeders and that, as Gena Corea states, a "reproductive brothel" will emerge. . . .

Some feminists, however, argue that what is being sold is not the resulting child but [as Andrews states] the "pre-conception termination of the mother's parental rights" and the use of the surrogate's time, energy, and womb. They analogize this practice with the pre-conception sale of a father's parental rights through the donation of sperm and artificial insemination. If a man has a right to sell his sperm, a woman should have a right to sell her ovum and reproductive capabilities as well.

Harm to Women

Another major rationale against the legalization of surrogacy is the potential for actual psychological and physical harm to women. Proponents of surrogacy argue that it is a woman's choice to use her body any way she sees fit. Many feminists believe, however, that commercial surrogacy will lead to the exploitation of women, not only through economic pressures but through societal ones as well. . . .

With surrogacy, the psychological risks women face and the

potential for regret are thought by some to be enormously high. Visions of babies being ripped from their mothers' arms are extremely disturbing to say the least. It is assumed that many surrogates will feel the same regret that biological mothers feel in traditional adoption cases. But, "[w]hile 75 percent of the biological mothers who give a child up for adoption later change their minds, only around 1 percent of the surrogates have similar changes of heart" [as Andrews states].

Women's Ability to Make Decisions

Feminists generally agree that women should be able to enter into potentially risky behavior as long as they have given their voluntary and informed consent. But [Andrews writes that] "a strong element of the feminist argument against surrogacy is that women cannot give an informed consent until they have the experience of giving birth." Some believe that hormonal changes during pregnancy make it impossible for the surrogate to predict how she will feel about relinquishing her parental rights at the time of birth. Other feminists argue that . . . if feminists are not careful, this type of rationale could come back to haunt women in other areas. [As psychologist Joan Einwholer argues,] "It would seem to be a step backward for women to argue that they are incapable of making decisions. That, after all, was the rationale for so many legal principles oppressing women for so long, such as the rationale behind the laws not allowing women to hold property."

The third major argument in opposition to surrogacy is the potential harm to children. Just as baby selling is harmful to society's notion of children, it may also be harmful to the children themselves. [As Einwholer argues,] "Baby selling is prohibited in our society, in part because children need a secure family life and should not have to worry that they will be sold and wrenched from their existing family." But, [she continues,] the child born of a surrogate is never in a state of insecurity because "[f]rom the moment of birth, he or she is under the care of the biological father and his wife, who cannot sell the child."

An additional argument states that the effects on the surrogate's existing children could be harmful. "All children may be burdened by special fears and insecurities in a society where their parents may obtain money for family necessities by giving away newborn siblings" [Anita L. Allen argues]. This may cause the surrogate's children to believe that they too may be sold. The fears of these children, however, may be unfounded. Andrews believes that if the surrogate were to explain to her own children that she is helping another couple and that the child she is carrying is not part of their own family, they would "realize that they themselves are not in danger of being relinquished." . . .

Feminist scholarship reflects many of the tensions and conflicting concerns that surround the issue of surrogacy. On the one hand, women producing babies for a fee makes many feminists particularly uncomfortable. On the other hand, allowing the government to restrict women's choices may result in diminishing all other strides women have made in the area of reproductive rights. This prospect also makes many feminists very uneasy.

So where does this leave us? Women, as independent economic beings, should be allowed to decide whether or not they wish to become surrogates. However, there should also be some form of government intervention that would hopefully reduce the perceived harms associated with surrogacy. This can and should be done, but legislatures and courts need the guidance and wisdom which only women can provide in the area of reproductive technologies. Of course, no single statute would be able to answer all of the various concerns that feminists have about surrogacy, but, arguably, certain statutory provisions may lessen the concerns of many feminists.

If surrogacy were made illegal, there is a well-founded fear that the practice would go underground and there would be no recourse for the parties involved. Like prostitution, without regulation, many of the opponents' worst fears of surrogacy could come true. If our society has reached the point where this type of arrangement will happen with or without the state's involvement, it would be better for the state to make the practice legal and to set up a regulatory scheme to protect those involved. . . .

Minimizing the Harm to Women

A woman's right to control her body is fundamental in the struggle for control over her life. This control is evidenced in many ways but the main element of control is choice—the choice not to become pregnant, the choice to become pregnant, and the choice to abort. The choice to become a surrogate or to hire a surrogate is a natural evolution of the right of reproductive choice. Limiting women's choices regarding surrogacy may lead to limiting choices which have already been legally guaranteed to women. . . .

The harm to society and children alike in viewing children as commodities could be minimized not only by controlling the amount paid to a surrogate, but by examining that for which the surrogate is paid. Surrogacy is unlike any other contract, and the price of it should not be controlled by market forces. If the legislature sets a mandatory surrogacy fee, the intended parents will not be able to shop around for a better bargain. This would differentiate surrogacy from commodities available on the open market. It would further give legislatures some control over the supply and demand of surrogacy.

The surrogate should be paid for the gestation and birth of the child, but payment should never be conditioned on relinquishing the child to the intended parents. If the surrogate is paid for delivery of the child to the intended parents, it looks like baby selling, which is, and should be, prohibited. If, however, the surrogate is paid for her services in carrying the child for nine months and giving birth to the child, baby selling is not implicated. The intended parents are not buying physical custody of the child because the surrogate can always elect to keep the child. The intended parents are paying for their use of the surrogate's womb and not the child. If the surrogate elects to keep the child, however, she could not keep the fee. Although the services of carrying the baby to term were performed by the surrogate in this case, they were for the benefit of the surrogate and, thus, were never provided *to* the intended parents. . . .

Surrogates Should Be Given Control

The choice is not an easy one to make, but giving the surrogate as much control as possible in the surrogacy contract minimizes the risk of exploitation. Mandatory counseling would provide the potential surrogate with the opportunity to consider her decision. Giving the surrogate the right to terminate the contract and keep the child ensures that performance of the contract is a voluntary act. Thus, while the economic incentive inherent in permitting the surrogate to receive a fee cannot be avoided, measures could be enacted that would help ensure that the surrogate makes the right decision for the right reasons.

It is unrealistic to believe that all of the harms associated with surrogacy can be eliminated. However, the harms associated with either the legalization or banning of surrogacy will be felt by society as a whole. Women as a group need to explore any and all possibilities which can minimize the harm to women. Women are identified by their ability to reproduce because, up to this point, only women can do so. The only way for women to seize and stay in control of any existing or new reproductive technology is to present viable legislation for the decision-making bodies of government to act upon. If women, as a group, do not allow themselves to compromise they may end up with an unbearable situation completely out of their control rather than a tolerable situation they helped develop.

Periodical Bibliography

The following articles have been selected to supplement the diverse views presented in this chapter.

Rozanne M. Brooks — "How Far Women Have Come: Women on Campus," *Vital Speeches of the Day*, July 1, 1991.

Diana Hochstedt Butler — "Between Two Worlds," *The Christian Century*, March 3, 1993.

Betty Carter — "Stonewalling Feminism," *The Family Therapy Networker*, January/February 1992. Available from 7703 13th St. NW, Washington, DC 20012.

Jean Bethke Elshtain — "Women and the Ideology of Victimization," *The World & I*, April 1993. Available from 3600 New York Ave. NE, Washington, DC 20002.

Susan Faludi and Gloria Steinem, interviewed by Nancy Gibbs and Jeanne McDowell — "How to Revive a Revolution," *Time*, March 9, 1992.

Kari Jenson Gold — "Getting Real," *First Things*, January 1994. Available from 156 Fifth Ave., Suite 400, New York, NY 10010.

Gertrude Himmelfarb — "Self-Defeating Feminism," *The Human Life Review*, Winter 1990.

bell hooks — "Out of the Academy and into the Streets," *Ms.*, July/August 1992.

Julia Hughes Jones — "A Greater Voice in Action," *Vital Speeches of the Day*, December 1, 1992.

Elizabeth Kaye — "What Women Think of Other Women," *Esquire*, August 1992.

Robin Morgan — "The Politics of Silence," *Ms.*, September/October 1992.

Eloise Salholz — "Did America 'Get It'?" *Newsweek*, December 28, 1992.

Urvashi Vaid, Naomi Wolf, Gloria Steinem, and bell hooks, interviewed by *Ms.* — "Let's Get Real About Feminism," *Ms.*, September/October 1993.

Cathy Young — "Victimhood Is Powerful," *Reason*, October 1992.

How Does Feminism Affect Society?

Feminism

Chapter Preface

When the women's movement was revived in the 1960s, even though women were entering the workforce in growing numbers, the roles of men and women still seemed well defined. The "women's liberation" movement aimed, among other goals, to change the boundaries of those roles. The new feminists asserted equality with men in political, economic, and social spheres—indeed, in every area except the biological role of childbearing. Gender roles became less distinct, a change some people welcomed and others bitterly opposed.

Some critics, such as Steven Goldberg, a sociologist and author of *Why Men Rule*, believe that by blurring the traditional definitions of gender roles, feminism has harmed relationships between men and women:

> The contemporary urge to refuse to acknowledge sex differences has rendered impossible our giving respect to men and to women on the basis of the characteristics rooted in their respective physiologies. . . . This new attitude is the effective opposite of acknowledging the specialness of the other sex. And if maleness and femaleness are not qualities seen as special and inherently worthy of respect, our respect for our spouse or lover—indeed our respect for ourselves—is diminished.

But others view traditional male and female roles not as natural, but as suffocating and restricting for both men and women. Changing and expanding the roles available to each sex, they point out, gives people more choices in life. Many women who are now enjoying the benefits of these expanded horizons urge that the next step is to include men in these broader roles. As Gloria Steinem, looking back at the beginnings of the current women's movement, said in 1993:

> Well, we spent the first 20 years demonstrating that women can do what men can do, and most of the country believes that now. But we have not demonstrated that men can do the reverse—what women can do.

> Until children are raised by men as well as by women, until men aren't burdened by this compulsion to be in control or even violent, we won't have [further] change.

How feminism has affected male and female roles is one of the intriguing issues discussed in the following chapter. Feminism has brought tremendous changes to Western society. Whether these changes are positive or negative is debated by the authors in the chapter.

"Half *of everything taught should be about women.*"

Feminist Teachings Would Improve Higher Education

Dale Spender

Dale Spender is the author of the books *Man Made Language, Women of Ideas,* and *Nattering on the Nets: Women, Information, and Power.* In the following viewpoint, she expresses her belief that colleges fail to teach students about women: their history, their accomplishments, and their concerns. Spender concludes that if students studied these topics, more women would consider themselves feminists and would be motivated to fight for equality with men.

As you read, consider the following questions:

1. What are some of the examples the author gives showing that education as taught today is male-centered?
2. In what positive ways has feminism changed society, in Spender's opinion?
3. What does "gender equity demand," according to Spender?

Dale Spender, "An Alternative to Madonna," *Ms.*, July/August 1993. Reprinted by permission of the author.

It is reasonable to expect that those who work for a better world should be written up in history books as decent human beings who warrant our thanks for the contribution they make to our quality of life. Right? Well, not quite. Because being praised for a commitment to social justice applies only to some people, and *feminists* aren't among them. On the contrary, feminists—whose primary goal has been to provide a better deal for women and children—have been mocked and maligned throughout history. They are the recipients of some of the worst press that there has ever been; and this raises many questions—about power, about men, and about education. No books have been written on the failure of educational institutions—charged with the role of combating prejudice and presenting truth—to challenge this distorted view of women and their history. "The history of men's opposition to women's emancipation is more interesting perhaps than the story of that emancipation itself," mused Virginia Woolf in 1928 in *A Room of One's Own*.

Men's Mistreatment of Women

If the laws men had made in relation to women were the subject of study, few would be impressed with the male performance. They made women chattels who could legitimately be punished (wife beating was legal); who could be raped (conjugal rights were enshrined in the law and the "disobedient" wife who tried to escape was returned to her husband). Women in marriage were deprived of their identity, were not allowed to own property, and in the event of children, not allowed to be their guardians. Men even passed laws against contraception on the grounds that it would be an end to civilization if women could control their own fertility and men's conjugal and impregnating rights were curtailed. Not a pretty story. No wonder there is such reluctance to relate it.

Failing also to include information on the *triumphs* of women across the centuries, in spite of the treatment handed them by men, adds insult to injury. And it isn't just that the aspirations and attainments of women have been excised from the knowledge that is encoded in our institutions. The attempts being made by women *today* to reclaim and to pass on this history to a new generation of women (and men) *continue* to be discredited.

Most of the politics we teach relates to males (we concentrate on national/international rather than local levels where women are likely to be represented). We teach about the evolution of democracy as it relates to men, and men's struggle for the vote. (In Australia we rarely make it clear that women and men stand in a different relationship to the franchise: while men's *right* to vote is enshrined in the constitution, women have only the *privilege* of voting.)

Most sociology we teach is about males (urban man, rural man, man at work, man at sport—and these days with ostensible male-role changes—man at home).

Most of the laws we teach relate to males (we don't teach laws men have passed to prevent women from behaving in particular ways; we don't teach the campaigns women have embarked on or the battles won in repealing, and changing, laws passed exclusively by men and intended to restrict women's liberty).

Darkow. Reprinted by special permission of North America Syndicate.

We don't teach the history and philosophy of ideas to show how with the scientific revolution women's wisdom was replaced by men's institutionalized knowledge—although there are books that deal with this transformation, and with the role played by witch-hunting in the "politics of knowledge." (We might know how Copernicus and Galileo were persecuted for their ideas—but what about the millions of women who suffered similar fates and were burnt at the stake for being knowledgeable?)

The history we teach concentrates overwhelmingly on wars and revolutions, rather than on peace and conciliations, and while it is replete with male victories there are very few texts—inside or outside educational institutions—that are critical of male power and masculinity.

Even such ostensibly neutral subjects as math and science have assumed the centrality of the male; the examples relate to males, the illustrations take males as the standard, and while women have a splendid history of achievement as mathematicians, it would be possible for students to graduate from advanced mathematics classes without knowing that women ever participated, let alone excelled, in this area.

Women Are Portrayed Negatively

When women do get a mention, it is as a problem. Information presented in educational institutions has women as a poor and despised footnote. Nowhere is this more obvious than in relation to feminism.

So commonplace is this occurrence that it inspires what has become a joke in feminist circles: the individual who appears to be perceptive and unintimidated—and who blithely and sometimes belligerently declares, "Oh, I am not a feminist!" This person may then say, "I just believe in social justice, in equality between the sexes, in an end to discrimination, and in equal domestic duties and equal pay, and so forth."

In Brisbane, Australia, which now has become my hometown, I have a wonderful friend and mentor, Dr. Janet Irwin. Born a New Zealander, she was a medical doctor (she ran the University of Queensland Health Service); she was a commissioner on the Criminal Justice Commission, and has a record of fighting for justice and equality; she also has a warm face and soft white hair. And she is proudly and publicly *a feminist*.

From her I have learned a great deal. For example, whenever she meets someone who says, "Oh, I'm not a feminist," she smartly says: *"Why? What's your problem?"*

Feminism has fought no wars. It has killed no opponents. It has set up no concentration camps, starved no enemies, practiced no cruelties. Its battles have been for education, for the vote, for better working conditions for women and children; for property rights for women, for divorce, for custody rights, for the right to safety on the streets. Feminists have fought for child care, for social welfare, for greater visibility for people with disabilities. And feminists have had to fight for rape crisis centers, women's refuges, reforms in the law. Feminists have also devised some of the most spectacularly successful strategies to achieve these great goals.

Everyone Will Want to Be a Feminist

If we start teaching feminism, the history of social justice, of gender equity, of the campaigns for a sane and humane world, not only will we have a society that provides a better place to live—but *all the socially responsible members will want to sign up as feminists*. They will see being a feminist as an honorable way to live their lives. And all the excitement, the intellectual joys, the emotional satisfactions, and the sense of commitment that have been open to me as a feminist—will be available to them.

My first premise would be that *half* of everything taught should be about women. This is about the most radical demand that one could make; and there is no way that it could currently be met, because the curriculum materials simply have not been constructed to provide students with such a balance.

Gender equity demands nothing less than half the curriculum space; women comprise half the population, have half the human experiences, and have contributed half of the energies to our society, so reason demands that they constitute half the knowledge base. This means that half the authors taught should be women, half the mathematics examples should relate to females, and half the mathematical models should be women as well. Half the science should relate to females, and the increasing prestige of biology, ecological studies, and environmental science makes this a very realistic proposition. Half the sociology, politics, and geography/anthropology disciplines should be concerned with women's lives. And of course, half the history should be about women.

An Alternative to Madonna

Whenever I teach such information to young women, countering the misinformation they are given, there is no problem about "feminism." Offered an alternative to Madonna, they seize on it with excitement.

Until the day I hear young women talking about the way they were taught feminism in school, and how wonderful the women of the past have been; until I hear them say, "You must be really proud to be a feminist," and, "How can we get to do the same thing as you?"—until I hear such words spoken, I will know that education is not providing equal opportunity for women.

"Women's studies should stop treating women as an ensemble of victimized identities."

Feminist Courses Often Weaken Higher Education

Karen Lehrman

Since the 1970s, many universities have created women's studies courses and departments to promote the study and understanding of women's issues. In the following viewpoint, Karen Lehrman argues that, while these courses are well intentioned, many do not promote independent, critical thinking in students. Lehrman, who visited the women's studies programs of four universities, found that in many of the courses students were expected to simply divulge their feelings about issues without any intellectual analysis, or were only encouraged to spout pro-feminist attitudes. Lehrman supports the study of women's issues, but concludes that changes must be made in the existing programs. Lehrman, an editor at the *Wilson Quarterly* in Washington, D.C. has written articles for *Mother Jones* and other magazines.

As you read, consider the following questions:

1. How does the structure of women's studies courses differ from that of other, more traditional courses, according to Lehrman?
2. In the author's opinion, why do many women's studies professors teach students about unremarkable women, as opposed to famous women?
3. How have feminist politics harmed women's studies, according to Lehrman?

Abridged from Karen Lehrman, "Off Course," *Mother Jones*, September/October 1993. Copyright ©1993 by the Foundation for National Progress. Reprinted with permission.

It's eight o'clock on a balmy Wednesday morning at the University of California at Berkeley, and Women's Studies 39, "Literature and the Question of Pornography," is about to begin. The atmosphere of the small class is relaxed. The students call the youngish professor by her first name; the banter focuses on finding a man for her to date. She puts on the board: "Write 'grade' or 'no grade' on your paper before turning it in." Students—nine women and one man—amble in sporadically for the first twenty minutes.

Today's discussion involves a previous guest speaker, feminist-socialist porn star Nina Hartley. The professor asks what insights the students gained from Hartley's talk. They respond: "She's free with her sexuality. . . . I liked when she said, 'I like to fuck my friends.'. . . No body-image problems. . . . She's dependent in that relationship. . . ." The professor tries to move the discussion onto a more serious question: have traditional feminists, in their antiporn stance, defined women out of their sexuality? After a few minutes, though, the discussion fixes on orgasms—how they're not the be-all and end-all of sexual activity, how easy it is to fake one. The lone male stares intently at a spot on the floor; occasionally he squirms.

I never took a porn class when I went to college ten years ago. In fact, I never took a women's studies class and don't even know if the universities I attended offered any. Women's studies was about a decade old at the time, but it hadn't yet become institutionalized (there are now more than six hundred programs), nor gained notoriety through debates over the canon and multiculturalism. But even if I had been aware of a program, I'm certain I would have stayed far away from it. It's not that I wasn't a feminist: I fully supported equal rights and equal opportunities for women. But I was feminist like I was Jewish—it was a part of my identity that didn't depend on external affirmation.

Perhaps more important, as a first-generation career-woman, I felt a constant need to prove my equality. I took as many "male" courses—economics, political science, intellectual history—as I could; I wanted to be seen as a good student who happened to be a woman. There were a couple of problems, though: I didn't learn much about women or the history of feminism, and like most of my female peers, I rarely spoke in class.

What Are Women Discussing?

In 1992 I toured the world of women's studies, visiting Berkeley, the University of Iowa, Smith College, and Dartmouth College. I sat in on about twenty classes, talked to students and professors at these and other schools, amassed syllabi, and waded through the more popular reading materials. I admit to having begun with a nagging skepticism. But I was also intrigued: rumor had it that in these classes, women talked.

And they do. The problem, as I see it, is what they're often talking about. In many classes discussions alternate between the personal and the political, with mere pit stops at the academic. Sometimes they are filled with unintelligible post-structuralist jargon; sometimes they consist of consciousness-raising psychobabble, with the students' feelings and experiences valued as much as anything the professor or texts have to offer. Regardless, the guiding principle of most of the classes is oppression, and problems are almost inevitably reduced to relationships of power. "Diversity" is the mantra of both students and professors, but it doesn't apply to political opinions.

Not every women's studies course suffers from these flaws. In fact, the rigor and perspective of individual programs and classes vary widely, and feminist academics have debated nearly every aspect of the field. But it seems that the vast majority of women's studies professors rely, to a greater or lesser extent, on a common set of feminist theories. Put into practice, these theories have the potential to undermine the goals not only of a liberal education, but of feminism itself. . . .

Classroom Therapy

"Women's studies" is something of a misnomer. Most of the courses are designed not merely to study women, but also to improve the lives of women, both the individual students (the vast majority of whom are female) and women in general. Since professors believe that women have been effectively silenced throughout history, they often consider a pedagogy that "nurtures voice" just as, if not more, important than the curriculum.

Women's studies professors tend to be overtly warm, encouraging, maternal. You want to tell these women your problems—and many students do. To foster a "safe environment" where women feel comfortable talking, many teachers try to divest the classroom of power relations. They abandon their role as experts, lecturing very little and sometimes allowing decisions to be made by the group and papers to be graded by other students. An overriding value is placed on student participation and collaboration: students make joint presentations, cowrite papers, and use group journals for "exploring ideas they can't say in class" and "fostering a sense of community." Because chairs are usually arranged in a circle, in a couple of classes taught by graduate students I couldn't figure out who the teacher was until the end.

To give women voice, many professors encourage all discourse—no matter how personal or trivial. Indeed, since it is widely believed that knowledge is constructed and most texts have been influenced by "the patriarchy," many in women's

113

studies consider personal experience the only real source of truth. Some professors and texts even claim that women have a way of thinking that is different from the abstract rationality of men, one based on context, emotion, and intuition. Fully "validating" women, therefore, means celebrating subjectivity over objectivity, feelings over facts, instinct over logic.

The day I sat in on Berkeley's "Contemporary Global Issues for Women" (all women except for one "occasional" male), we watched a film about women organizing in Ahmadabad, India. The film was tedious, but it seemed like grist for a good political/economic/sociological discussion about the problems of women in underdeveloped countries. After the film ended, though, the professor promptly asked the class: "How do you *feel* about the film? Do you find it more sad or courageous?" Students responded to her question until the end of class, at which point she suggested, "You might think about the film in terms of your own life and the life of your mother. Women are not totally free in this culture. It just might come in more subtle ways."

Self-Revelation

A previous discussion was apparently not much better. "We had to read an enormous amount of interesting material on reproductive rights, which I was very excited to discuss," Pam Wilson, a women's studies sophomore, told me. "But all she did in class was ask each of us, 'What forms of birth control have you used, and what problems have you had?' We never got to the assigned readings."

Self-revelation is not uncommon to women's studies classes. Students discover that they're lesbian or bisexual, for example, and then share it with the class. In a group journal (titled "The Fleshgoddesses") from last year's porn class, B. wrote: "There is still something about a [man] eating a [woman] out . . . that freaks me out! I guess I'm such a dyke that it seems abnormal." G. recalled that her father used to kiss her on the mouth "real hard" when she was eight or nine.

Of course, self-discovery and female bonding are important for young women, and so, one might argue, are group therapy and consciousness-raising. Indeed, I wish I had had some when I was that age; it might have given me the courage to talk in class and to deal with abusive bosses later in life. But does it belong in a university classroom?

Many of the professors I talked with (including the chair of Berkeley's women's studies department) viewed the more touchy-feely classes as just as problematic as I did. I saw a couple of teachers who were able to use personal experience, either of historical figures or students, to buttress the discussion, not as an end in itself. But even these classes were always on the verge of slipping into confession mode.

This pedagogy does get women talking. But they could do much of this type of talking in support groups at their schools' women's centers. Young women have many needs, and the college classroom can effectively address only one of them: building their intellects. As Ruth Rosen, who helped start the women's studies program at the University of California at Davis, puts it, "Students go to college to be academically challenged, not cared for."

Women's Studies Handicap Female Students

Women are equal in numbers to men on college campuses, making up half the undergraduates at the best schools. But they're setting up a new system of handicaps for themselves.

The new obstacles are called women's studies, written by women, for women, about women. The classes are taught by middle-class, educated women, the new oppressors of women.

Originally created as fringe courses for feminists to hyperventilate about their frustrations with men, women's studies have become institutionalized at some of our most famous universities, wasting valuable educational time (not to speak of parents' money) on intuitional, angry rhetoric about victimhood and validating the worst stereotypes of women as the weaker (thinking) sex.

Suzanne Fields, *Insight*, October 18, 1993.

But the problem with a therapeutic pedagogy is more than just allowing students to discuss their periods or sex lives in class. Using the emotional and subjective to "validate" women risks validating precisely the stereotypes that feminism was supposed to eviscerate: women are irrational, women must ground all knowledge in their own experiences, etc. A hundred years ago, women were fighting for the right to learn math, science, Latin— to be educated like men; today, many women are content to get their feelings heard, their personal problems aired, their instincts and intuition respected. . . .

Politics as Usual

Most women's studies professors seem to adhere to the following principles in formulating classes: women were and are oppressed; oppression is endemic to our patriarchal social system; men, capitalism, and Western values are responsible for women's problems. The reading material is similarly bounded in political scope (Andrea Dworkin, Catharine MacKinnon, bell hooks, Adrienne Rich, and Audre Lorde turn up a lot), and opposing viewpoints are usually presented only through a feminist critique of them. *Feminist Frontiers III*, a book widely used in intro courses, purports to show readers "how gender has shaped your life," and invites them to join in the struggle "to reform the structure and culture of male dominance."

Although most of the classes I attended stopped short of outright advocacy of specific political positions, virtually all carried strong political undercurrents. Jill Harvey, a women's studies senior at Smith, recalls a feminist anthropology course in which she "quickly discovered that the way to get A's was to write papers full of guilt and angst about how I'd bought into society's definition of womanhood and now I'm enlightened and free."

Sometimes the politicization is more subtle. "I'm not into consciousness-raising," says Linda K. Kerber, a history professor at Iowa. "Students can feel I'm grading them on their competence and not on their politics." Yet in the final project of "Gender and Society in the United States," she asked students: "Reconsider a term paper you have written for another class. How would you revise it now to ensure that it offers an analysis sensitive to gender as well as to race and class?"

Politicization is also apparent in the meager amount of time the classes devote to women who have achieved anything of note in the public sphere. Instead, students scrutinize the diaries and letters of unremarkable women who are of interest primarily because the patriarchy victimized them in one way or another.

According to professors and students, studying "women worthies" doesn't teach you much about oppression. Moreover, some added, these women succeeded by male, capitalist standards. It's time for women's traditional roles and forms of expression to be valued.

This may be true, but you don't need to elevate victimized women to the status of heroes to do that. It should also be noted that over the past twenty-five years feminists have been among those who have devalued women's traditional roles most vigorously. I bet not many women's studies majors would encourage a peer's decision to forgo a career in order to stay home and raise children. More important, examples of women who succeeded in the public sphere, possibly even while caring for a family, could be quite inspiring for young women. Instead, the classes implicitly downplay individual merit and focus on the systematic forces that are undermining everything women do.

Are "Practicums" Practical?

In general, "core" women's studies courses are more overtly political and less academically rigorous than those cross-listed with a department. The syllabus of Iowa's "Introduction to Women's Studies" course declares: "As we make our collective and individual journeys during this course, we will consider how to integrate our theoretical knowledge with personal and practical action in the world." "Practicums," which typically entail working in a women's organization, are a key part of many courses, often requiring thirty or more hours of a student's time.

Volunteering in a battered-women's shelter or rape crisis center may be deeply significant for both students and society. But should this be part of an undergraduate education? Students have only four years to learn the things a liberal education can offer—and the rest of their lives to put that knowledge to use.

Courses on women don't have to be taught from an orthodox feminist perspective. Smith offers a biology course that's cross-listed with women's studies. It deals with women's bodies and medical issues; feminist theory is not included. Compare that to the course description of Berkeley's "Health and Sex in America": "From sterilization to AIDS; from incest to date rape; from anorexia to breast implants: who controls women's health?" Which course would you trust to be more objective?

Many women's studies professors acknowledge their field's bias, but point out that all disciplines are biased. Still, there's a huge difference between conceding that education has political elements and intentionally politicizing, between, as Women's Studies Professor Daphne Patai puts it, "recognizing and minimizing deep biases and proclaiming and endorsing them." Patai, whose unorthodox views got her in hot water at the University of Massachusetts, is now coauthoring a book on the contradictions of women's studies. "Do they really want fundamentalist studies, in which teachers are not just studying fundamentalism but supporting it?"

A still larger problem is the degree to which politics has infected women's studies scholarship. "Feminist theory guarantees that researchers will discover male bias and oppression in every civilization and time," says Mary Lefkowitz, a classics professor at Wellesley. "A distinction has to be made between historical interpretation of the past and political reinterpretation." And, I would add, between reading novels with an awareness of racism and sexism, and reducing them entirely to constructs of race and gender. . . .

Women as Individuals

As the status of women in this country evolves, so should the goals of women's studies. It's for its own sake that women's studies should stop treating women as an ensemble of victimized identities. Only when the mind of each woman is considered on its own unique terms will the minds of all women be respected.

"Ecofeminism proposes a new relationship with the Earth and with the entire cosmos."

Ecofeminism Can Benefit Women and the Earth

Ivone Gebara, interviewed by Mary Judith Ress

Most of the traditional religions are patriarchal—that is, they emphasize the power of men over women and the power of a male God over the universe. These beliefs have led men to oppress both women and the environment, Ivone Gebara states in the following viewpoint. She believes an ecofeminist view of the world would emphasize the feminine aspects of God and would help people to consider the earth as something to be card for and treasured, not exploited. Gebara is a feminist theologian from Brazil. In the viewpoint, she is interviewed by Mary Judith Ress, a lay minister and founding editor of *Con Spirando*, a Latin American quarterly that focuses on ecofeminism, theology, and spirituality.

As you read, consider the following questions:

1. What does the author believe are the two main goals of ecofeminism?
2. What are Gebara's views concerning the nature of God?
3. How does the author regard the Bible and the gospel of Jesus?

Abridged from Ivone Gebara, interviewed by Mary Judith Ress, "Cosmic Theology: Ecofeminism and Panentheism," *Creation Spirituality*, November/December 1993. Reprinted with permission.

What is "holistic ecofeminism"? It doesn't sound very Latin American!

No, what I call holistic ecofeminism or critical feminism comes out of a worldwide critique of modernity. It comes from a growing suspicion that the sciences, both social and physical, may not have the solutions to carry us into a safe, more life-giving future. But let us be clear here: this thinking is not a Latin American native flower—just as, if we are honest, liberation theology is not native, but was highly influenced by European thinking. Both have been given different shades and hues by Latin Americans, but let us not fall into a naive nationalism when speaking of theologies! And here, besides the feminist theologians such as Dorothee Solle, Rosemary Radford Ruether and Mary Daly, I must recognize the influence of people like Teilhard de Chardin, Fritjof Capra, Thomas Berry, Brian Swimme, among others.

Holistic ecofeminism questions a theology that sees God as above all things. God has always been used by both the left and the right to justify particular political programs. There simply is no pure God!

Weary of the Struggle

There is also a growing suspicion that the age-old conviction that "redemption comes through suffering" might not be true. There is growing dissatisfaction with liberation theology. The promise of a new society founded upon justice and equality just hasn't happened. We are tired of the struggle, which is often violent and which promises our liberation at the end. All we have seen is destruction and death, never victory. So we are suspicious of this approach, tired of yet another document. Analysis on the political and economic situation of our people is very important, but it is not everything!

Instead, we look at the air, the water, the Earth. We look at all the garbage surrounding us, and we sense deep within ourselves that our planet is not just a place—it is our own body. Ecofeminism proposes a new relationship with the Earth and with the entire cosmos.

For me, "holistic ecofeminism" has a double purpose. First is the fundamental concern for the oppressed—the voiceless of history—who when they are born are *de facto* excluded from the chance to live a full life because of their economic situation. It is the poor who are the greatest consumers of patriarchal religion because of the consolation it provides! They are caught in a vicious circle here, but for me it is absolutely key to avoid distancing myself from these voiceless ones. Second is the commitment to put an end to patriarchy in all its forms.

But what are you proposing when you say we must change the anthropological basis upon which Christianity is built?

I suggest that we must first change our image of men and women within the cosmos. And when we change that image, our image of God changes. Any image of God is nothing more than the image of the experience or the understanding we have of ourselves. We must re-situate the human within—not above—the cosmos. This is diametrically opposed to a Christian anthropology that insists humanity is "Lord of Creation" ordered by the Creator to "increase and dominate the Earth." In the current anthropology, the human's right to dominate, control, and possess has been legitimatized by the Creator and thus becomes part of human nature, pre-established—and therefore impossible to change.

We must break with our dualistic constructs of God and of the world—constructs that are hierarchical and tend to exclude the "other" as less valuable; for example, God is separated from the world; man from woman; heaven from Earth; good from bad. If one is good, one cannot be bad; if one is master, one cannot be a slave, and so on.

Discovering Our "Connectedness" to the Earth

Yet, I am convinced that this way of thinking is shifting. Today we are beginning to experience who we are in a different way—more holistically. Why? Because we are beginning to suffer because our water is dirty, our rivers and oceans are dirty, because our food isn't very good anymore. We feel great pain at such destruction. We sense at a gut level that we too are "dirty," somehow "polluted" as well. Our intuition tells us what many so-called primitive peoples have always held: that we are all in all.

The scientists are also showing us how our very "power over" is tragic because it is not only causing our own destruction as human beings, but it is destroying life itself! We humans cannot live if we destroy the rest of our body.

And so we are beginning to discover our inter-connectedness. We humans are not "Lords of Creation." Instead, we are the Earth's thought, the Earth's reflection of itself; one type of consciousness present on the planet.

Therefore, when we behold the sick body of the poor, and see the injustice they suffer, we see it as our own body. There is no other. The other is myself. We are part of one immense, pulsating body that has been evolving for billions of years—and is still evolving.

But then are you saying that there is no God, no Lord of history, no Yahweh or loving father?

I am saying that our understanding of God must change. We can no longer posit a God who is Being-unto-himself, omnipotent, above all. This image of God is no longer adequate; we can no longer give obedience to someone "up there." This is the God built by patriarchy!

Instead, our intuition tells us that we dwell in Mystery larger than ourselves. We are part of this Mystery, which, like us, is evolving. This Mystery is what we call the Divine. But this Mystery is not a being, not a person. There is no God sitting on a throne who will judge us when we die. Our brothers and sisters on this Earth are our only judges!

New Religious Traditions

Ecofeminism . . . celebrated women's values. During the eighties, women's spirituality groups sprang up all over the country. The women who formed them were intrigued by archaeological indications that long before the Judeo-Christian tradition took root, people worshiped a nurturant goddess. The women met to explore the histories of male-dominated religions and assess their impact on women's lives—a form of consciousness-raising for the eighties and nineties. . . . In every generation of feminists, there have been women who felt the need to purge religious traditions of their misogyny and reclaim them for women.

Flora Davis, *Moving the Mountain: The Women's Movement in America Since 1960*, 1991.

But is there a personal God?

If God were a person, God would be an autonomous being, which is the same thing as the patriarchal concept of God who is "above" and "over" life itself. God is not a person, but we humans are persons so this is how we tend to relate to Divine Mystery. Because we are persons, we are able to initiate a dialogue, and we personalize all our relationships. Therefore, analogously, I speak to God as a person. It is as if I were talking or praying to my double. I attribute the qualities of a person to my double, but it is my "I" talking to my "I."

But what is the fear here? There is no "one God" to manipulate, as the "mono" theists have done, by making God "one," "universal," as well as "masculine." This God is an entirely political God, a God whose main job is to *dominate* and *control*.

Holistic ecofeminism holds that God is in all—and therefore all is sacred. We speak of pan-en-theism. This is much closer to what primitive peoples have believed; there are many different ways to express our experience of Divine Mystery.

Then we have no source of revelation? The Bible is not the word of God?

We must remember that sacred books like the Bible are human productions. The Bible is not "the Word of God." It is the word

121

of humans about God. But some texts in the Old Testament and in the New Testament recount experiences so profound, so essential to us that we say "this is the word of God." For instance, those texts that speak to us of sharing, forgiving, mercy, and compassion.

Changing Christianity

The Gospel is the story of the Jesus movement, a movement of resurrection. It is a collection of stories that recount *actions of resurrection*, of giving people life in many different ways. We are told to love our neighbor as ourselves. We are invited to love ourselves, which is relatively easy; but then we are asked to step outside our individual "I" and realize that we are not separate from our neighbor, something that is harder because it doesn't come as naturally as loving ourselves does. But we do so because we are moved to compassion to do so, not because we will be rewarded in heaven.

What you are suggesting is certainly very radical, in the sense of returning to roots. But in stripping Christianity of its patriarchal structure, what is left?

What we are trying to do is to *relativize* Christianity. It is *one* experience of how human beings explain Divine Mystery. The Jesus movement offers one response to humanity's search for meaning. But the Christian experience is only one response, not *the* response. It is just one small key. But even if we could unite all the keys, all the responses, we still wouldn't be able to fathom the Mystery in which we live.

Patriarchy is a development of human evolution—whether or not we had to develop this way is beside the point—but we did develop patriarchy and it has been the overriding way we have organized society for over 5,000 years. Christianity is marked by patriarchy; it was born and has flourished in a patriarchal society. But the other great religions are also riddled with patriarchy: Buddhism, Islam, Hinduism are all marked with patriarchy. It is not a question of throwing out these religions, but stripping them of their patriarchal constructs.

We are speaking here of a change in paradigms. The patriarchal paradigm has lasted for more than 5,000 years. But everywhere that paradigm is falling apart. These old clothes no longer fit. We must look for new clothes, new constructs which we probably won't live to see firmly in place. But we are called to do so by the future, by our grandchildren.

VIEWPOINT

"The ecofeminist movement can be dangerous and warrants close scrutiny."

Ecofeminism Is Dangerous

Kay Ebeling

Ecofeminism, a branch of feminism, is a broad movement that has many definitions. While some ecofeminists simply focus on solving environmental problems, others combine this goal with pagan spiritual rituals and traditions. In the following viewpoint, Kay Ebeling warns that ecofeminists, especially those who practice pagan rituals, are strange and threaten society. Ebeling writes that many ecofeminists hate men and want women to control the world. Ebeling is a dance instructor, saleswoman, and freelance writer living in Eureka, California, and a frequent contributor to *Human Life Review*.

As you read, consider the following questions:

1. What practices of ecofeminism does the author find bizarre?
2. What environmental policies of ecofeminism does Ebeling disagree with?
3. Why does Ebeling dislike what she sees as ecofeminism's anti-male stance?

Abridged, with permission, from Kay Ebeling, "Eco-Feminists and Pagan Politics," *The Human Life Review*, Summer 1991. Reprinted with permission.

At first I thought I'd stumbled across The Total Woman from Mars. I was attending a workshop titled "Shamanic Woman-craft" at a center for New Age practices in a northern California town. Women arrived in long print dresses with shawls and sat on mats in a circle on the floor. Many carried babies, and nursed them casually. The silver-haired Shaman woman in mystical clothing entered and set up a centerpiece for the circle, placing dolls, candles, and artifacts at precise angles. Among the little statues was a Madonna and an African goddess of fertility. As the woman laid out herbs with a thick aroma, her husband walked around the room waving incense, much like a priest, then exited.

Jeannine Parvati Baker then began the ritual, swaying to a chant that could have been American Indian. She called out, "Our goddesses who art in heaven and upon this earth, we celebrate the divine feminine within and without.". . .

At times Parvati Baker made the sound "Ho—!" and the women in the circle responded "—Mmm," creating the word "Home." She passed out medicine cards; she taught us rituals we can do in our own living rooms. As the third hour began, she asked the women to share the contents of their "sexuality bundles" which they'd packed for the workshop. First Baker reached into her own little bag, and pulled out a piece of cloth diaper, "the best things to use as menstrual pads, aren't they? Ho—" "Mmmm." Her cloth was "spotted with a pattern that shows the six bleeding hearts of my six children," she said with pride. I started to squirm. Baker then pulled out the umbilical cords of all her six children, and the room began to swirl. The next woman reached in her bundle and pulled out a picture with a baby's hand in a flame saying that it represented "how many of us were burned at the stake in past lifetimes," but I couldn't stay to hear the rest. I was losing my dinner in the ladies' room outside.

What Is "Ecofeminism"?

As weird as she is, Jeannine Parvati Baker is one of the more sane voices rising up under the aegis of "Ecofeminism," a nascent movement, part ecology, part self-made religion. . . .

Mainline ecofeminists insist the ecology movement should be run by more women because, with our monthly biological cycles, we are somehow more in tune with the earth and the cosmos than men. They talk of a time, 5,000 years ago, when the earth was led by a matriarchy, and we had a thousand years with no war. . . .

Ecofeminism is more than a political movement; it is the creation of a new religion, and a mandate to believe or perish. To define their new theology, these women reach handily into Buddhism, Hinduism, Native American and Greek mythology—

it's a kind of ABC approach to spirituality: Anything But Christian. They are especially preoccupied with Gaia, the earth goddess in Greek myths, and they identify with the Minoan Crete civilization which took place from about 3000 to 1200 BC. Ecofeminists know that they are God themselves. They pray, "All is One, all forms of existence are comprised on one continuous dance of matter/energy arising and falling away. . . . The union with the One has been called cosmic consciousness, God consciousness, knowing the One Mind" [from Charlene Spretnak's *The Politics of Women's Spirituality*]. It's an easygoing religion as Starhawk explains in "Feminist, Earth-based Spirituality and Ecofeminism," her contribution to ecofeminist Judith Plant's book *Healing the Wounds: The Promise of Ecofeminism*. "We have no dogma, no authorized texts or beliefs and no authoritative body to authorize anything; nor do we want one." Would you want to live in a nation founded on these principles? . . .

The Man-Hating Anger of Ecofeminists

Ecofeminists are angry. Whether they realize it or not, they are following in the footsteps of the sixties and seventies feminists. In the anti-Vietnam war movement, many women got frustrated by their subjugated role in protest organizing and leadership. They did not want to run the offices and make coffee—in the feminist movement they could be leaders. . . . Ecofeminists are even angrier at men than Germaine Greer or Gloria Steinem when they wrote in the sixties and seventies. . . . Indeed, as I read more of [ecofeminists'] words, I never find a place for men to fit into their hierarchy.

Kay Ebeling, *Human Life Review*, Summer 1991.

Ecofeminists in the western American continent tie their politics to the preservation of all trees, at all costs. Their quasi-religion and passive philosophy brings many wiccas and pagans to anti-timber-industry rallies and blockades. Judith Plant lives and works with a "publishing collective" in British Columbia. She describes the peacefulness of their knoll overlooking a narrow valley, then gets angry as it is disrupted again by the roar of an 18-wheeler. They've moved into a timber industry corridor, a roadway between the forest and the sawmill, "a path beaten hard from the weight of dead trees," Plant laments.

"It is no accident that the Minister of Forests is a man," Plant writes with typical ecofeminist open-mindedness. "The logging company is owned and run by men, the logging truck driver is a man." Men are all "voraciously trying to control all that is natural, regarding nature as a resource to be exploited for the gain of a very few." Like most radical ecologists, the members of this movement give no credit to the changes in timber harvest practices that have taken place since 1980, as the timber industry has incorporated environmental concerns into its management practices. They hoot, hiss, and holler at rallies if a timber-industry representative tries to speak. Ecofeminists would rather look to ancient cultures and rituals for the answer to problems currently facing the earth. Plant reveres the Kung Bush People, who spent about 20 hours a week gathering and hunting food, so the rest of the day could be spent in leisure, "recreating their culture." Ecofeminists want to take man back to a tribal existence, where everyone hunts and forages for food that is not planted in disruptive rows but grows wild, as a gift from goddess Earth. Somehow this would bring an end to all wars as well as solve our environmental crisis.

I looked up the Greek Goddess Gaia (aka "Ge"); she was a female entity, sort of floating in space. She wanted a baby so badly that she got pregnant without needing to involve a male entity. She gave birth to her son Uranus and proceeded with him to have more children. They dispensed with the mutants and cyclopses in various ways, then parented the Titans and others. Meanwhile Gaia, the ultimate working mother, created the earth and all life on it. One of their children, the Titan Cronos, eventually helped Gaia get rid of Uranus. She seduced her son/husband into her room and Cronos castrated him viciously with a jagged stick. From his body parts on the ocean sprang Aphrodite—a kinder, gentler woman.

Gaia doesn't sound like a peaceful, loving goddess to me, but then I don't claim to be an expert in Greek mythology. I'm also no Biblical scholar, but I do know that ecofeminists, Earth First!, and other New Age weirdness is predicted in the Bible. For example, the apostle Paul writes in a letter to Timothy that, "In later times some will abandon the faith and follow deceiving spirits and things taught by demons. Such teachings come through hypocritical liars, whose consciences have been seared as with a hot iron. They forbid people to marry and order them to abstain from certain foods." (I Timothy 4:1-6) Sounds a lot like the New Age vegetarian ABC theological mystics who live near me. The first Book of Romans 1:22-23 says of an ancient culture, "Although they claimed to be wise, they became fools and exchanged the glory of the immortal God for images made to look like mortal man and birds and animals and reptiles.". . .

Man-Hating

If ecofeminism were all innocent frolicking in the trees, it would not be so frightening. Ecofeminism in its original conception may have had only the highest of motives, a true concern for the future of the earth. But why reject everything American or Judeo-Christian? Why blame everything that's wrong with the earth on men? The deification of everything female is to me dangerous. "This conversion will demand a new form of human intelligence," writes Rosemary Radford Ruether. "Patterns of left-brain (i.e., masculine or linear) are, in many ways, ecologically dysfunctional. This rationality screens out much of reality as 'irrelevant,'" Ruether continues, and she is serious.

Man-hating, like Gaia's treatment of Uranus, permeates these writings. "This 'man's world' is on the very edge of collapse, because there is no respect for the 'other' in patriarchal society," writes Judith Plant. "The war of the sexes is done so brilliantly by ecofeminists," writes Sharon Doubiago. Any reference to God as He or Him is followed by a (*sic*). All the world's problems can be traced to the patriarchy, which rules in a dominating authoritative way, not harmoniously, as would a matriarchy.

Ecofeminists believe that women, left to run the world without any nettlesome patriarchal interference, would end nuclear power, nuclear weapons, any further development of the wilderness, military adventurism, industrial control over nature as it destroys the environment, racism, violence, and the wealth and greed that come inherently with business. There we'll all be, merrily picking berries and nursing our babies, back in paradise. . . .

Ecofeminists are not fairy princesses with peace and harmony as their innocent goals. The ecofeminist movement can be dangerous and warrants close scrutiny. For one thing, I don't want to live in a world run by dominating women, where the men wear skirts.

Perhaps Moses was the most eloquent critic of the ecofeminist movement: he told the Jews in the desert (Deuteronomy 18:10-12): "Let no one be found among you who practices divination or sorcery, interprets omens, engages in witchcraft, or casts spells, or who is a medium or a spiritist or who consults the dead. The Lord your God will drive out those nations."

"If the extreme feminist thesis is correct, there is no hope for anything but an ongoing battle of the sexes."

Feminism Harms Women's Perceptions of Men

Tibor R. Machan

Feminists who blame men for intentionally oppressing women only harm the relationship between the sexes, Tibor R. Machan states in the following viewpoint. Machan argues that women will gain equality only when they stop blaming men and start working with them to change society. Machan teaches philosophy at Auburn University in Alabama.

As you read, consider the following questions:

1. What does Machan view as the worst claim by extreme feminists?
2. What comparisons does Machan make between the traditional roles played by men and women?
3. What does the author mean when he says that women's oppression has chiefly been caused by negligence?

Tibor R. Machan, "Sex, Lies, and History," *The Freeman*, May 1992. Reprinted with permission.

For the last couple of decades, feminism has been a major force in American politics. This, in itself, is lamentable: Why should every movement become a matter of politics?

But we should not dismiss feminism. After all, John Stuart Mill, one of the intellectual heroes of classical liberalism, was a feminist. He argued forcefully against the subjugation of women, for universal suffrage and other sound feminist objectives. And there have been plenty of injustices against women; when feminists call this to our attention, they should be congratulated. Women are human beings, first; and whatever a human being has a right to, women have a right to as well. Any system of law that denies this—and there are many such around the world—needs improvement.

However, we also should consider some of the feminists' more extreme positions. These tend to center around the theme that males have waged a deliberate vendetta against women throughout human history. In several academic disciplines—English, history, philosophy, sociology, psychology, and economics—we find the forceful development of this thesis.

The Truth Is the Same for Men and Women

In my own field, philosophy, there are feminists claiming that the prominent role of men has involved deliberate distortions in established doctrines. Even in the philosophy of scientific method there are feminists who claim that men have put forth a lopsided view of how science should be conducted. Feminist ethics, in turn, often amounts to the thesis that since most of the moral philosophers have been men, the ethical theories we have offered for consideration have favored male domination. Great composers, playwrights, and novelists have come under similar indictment—that they put men first and distorted the worth of women.

No doubt there is something to the claim that men have been the focus of much of our cultural activity. Yet, if men and women are basically equal, this should not have amounted to a major distortion. Except for issues relating specifically to sexuality, whatever matters or is true should be as easy to reveal through our understanding of males as it is from our understanding of females.

But the worst claim by extreme feminists is not that there has been a bias in favor of men but that it has been perpetrated deliberately, so as to deprive women. Keeping women down is supposed to be a major objective behind the bias.

There are several things wrong with this position. First, if it were true, we would have to believe that males are indeed very different from women, for better or for worse. In that case there is no justice in the call for equal treatment of the sexes.

129

Second, this implies that men have been much better off than women in how they lived their lives. Is that credible? Men went hunting, to war, to the office, to government, to business—women were left in the home, in the nurturing professions, and so on. Is that such a break for men?

"You're too aggressive."

Third, if the extreme feminist thesis is correct, there is no hope for anything but an ongoing battle of the sexes. We can look forward to continued strife, hostility, misunderstanding, and power struggles. What is the point of seeking solutions when, supposedly, the nature of the human animal makes it im-

possible to find any? If men are bent on hurting women and if women cannot escape this, where is the point to any proposed remedy? Any gesture of goodwill from males to females would have to be dismissed as subterfuge.

A Fear of Change

However, there is a more reasonable view of how things have turned out between men and women. Briefly, certain job specializations that made sense in the past have been extended beyond their usefulness, and we are struggling to catch up with new possibilities and, thus, with the need for new sensibilities. Human beings generally don't change rapidly. We shouldn't be appalled when outmoded traditions aren't immediately rejected as soon as we see they are pointless. Just think how tough it is for someone to follow up on the realization that smoking, lack of exercise, or a fatty diet may be harmful. Clearly, our unwillingness to change, including in our relationships between the sexes, is not usually a matter of deliberate misconduct. More often it is inertia, negligence, or fear of novelty.

I am not arguing that these are innocent practices. Negligence can be destructive. But just as in the law, there is much difference between misconduct stemming from negligence as opposed to premeditation. Feminists who claim that our problems stem from the latter are misjudging the situation to the detriment of us all. And they fail to acknowledge that the negligence involved in keeping up with new developments that would warrant changes in attitudes and conduct is something of which both men and women are guilty. There would be no need for sexual scapegoating if such an acknowledgment were made up front and were to moderate the rhetoric of feminism.

"Men can find common cause with feminist women."

Men Should
Support Feminism

R.W. Connell

R.W. Connell is a sociology professor at the University of California, Santa Cruz, and the author of the books *Gender and Power* and *Schools and Social Justice*. In the following viewpoint he describes how pro-feminist men have worked to improve women's status. Connell believes that by making changes in their personal and professional lives, men can further the women's movement and improve their own lives.

As you read, consider the following questions:

1. Why are many men uncomfortable with the thought of supporting feminism, in the author's opinion?
2. What steps have a small number of men taken to escape conventional masculinity, according to Connell? What results does he see from these steps?
3. What steps does the author suggest men take to help end women's oppression?

R.W. Connell, "Men and the Women's Movement," *Social Policy*, Summer 1993, published by Social Policy Corporation, New York, NY 10036. Copyright ©1993 by Social Policy Corporation. Reprinted by permission.

What place should men have in feminist politics? Given the record of men's violence against women, abusive attitudes and speech, relentless sexism in high culture and the mass media, it's not hard to justify the notion that men have no place at all in the women's movement.

Yet, while we undeniably live in a sexist culture, men are far from monolithic in support of its sexism. There are significant resources among men that can be tapped for the resistance. Some men want to support feminism, and some men—not always the same ones—have been *useful* to feminism (for instance, in passing anti-discrimination laws, introducing women's studies programs in universities, and so on). Yet after a generation of continuous feminist mobilizing, men's support is erratic, contradictory, and mostly small-scale. Why, and what can be done about it?

Men and Anti-Sexist Politics

Anti-sexist politics for men is difficult at a personal level. Feminism (especially feminism concerned with violence) often reads to men as an accusation. If the accusation is accepted, the result is sometimes a paralyzing guilt. For sympathetic men, the encounter with feminism can easily be more disabling than energizing.

Nonetheless, some men do get energized—such as those who have gone to work with abusive men to reduce domestic violence. But for others, the encounter leads to a turn inward, in which men focus on reconstructing their own personalities and lose their impulse to reform social relations. There is a small but steady flow out of politics into therapy. . . .

In the 1970s, some men's "consciousness-raising" groups began in the United States and in Britain. Anti-sexist politics among men thrived for some years, declined in the 1980s, but still persists today. Left-wing men in Britain produced a lively and intelligent magazine called *Achilles Heel*, pooling anti-sexist men's experience, and discussing principles. The most impressive movement has been in Canada, in the wake of the Montreal killings of 1989 [in which a man massacred fourteen female students at the University of Montreal]. The "White Ribbon" movement about violence against women, which saw men campaigning alongside feminists, gained widespread support and had a considerable impact on mass media and conventional politics.

Since patriarchy works in "private" life as much as in public affairs, households and sexual relations also form a political arena. Some men have been part of the reconstruction of domestic life: sharing childcare, cleaning and cooking, and decisionmaking. Among some groups of young people this is now common sense: a claim to precedence by men just because they are men would appear grotesque.

133

A few men have embraced feminism at a deeper emotional level, and have attempted to reconstruct their personality in total to escape conventional masculinity. This has elicited a variety of responses—becoming noncompetitive, taking a supportive rather than dominating position in conversations, engaging only in nonpenetrative sex, refusing careers and power in organizations. But the numbers trying in these ways to exit from mainstream masculinities are small, and it is difficult to see this approach becoming widely popular. Its emotional costs (at least in the short term) are high; it attracts ridicule from more conservative men and may not be attractive to women either.

A New Gender Order

It does not require a complete demolition of hegemonic masculinity to democratize gender relations. The many forms of patriarchal ideology point to many ways of contesting it—in sexual life, in mass media, in the workplace, in formal politics, in conversation, in raising children. If conventional gender is, as sociologists call it, an "accomplishment"—something made by the way we conduct ourselves—then we can certainly accomplish something better.

This is happening in a number of settings where gay or straight men have worked productively with feminist women. Green politics, where there is a strong feminist presence, is perhaps the most obvious case. Similarly, in certain university departments, men have supported setting up and staffing feminist courses. In certain unions, men have allied themselves with militant women to break the traditions of exclusion and male dominance, and have worked for the needs of women workers—equal pay, work-based childcare, freedom from sexual harassment, and other issues.

How Feminism Benefits Men

I strongly suspect that feminism has done fathers and sons a favor. With its emphasis on individualism rather than stereotypes, on communication rather than hierarchy, on self fulfillment rather than role fulfillment, feminism probably has made it easier for fathers and sons to detoxify their relationships, to purge away the Oedipal competitiveness that can foul the springs of generational affection. In that respect, anyway, feminism may make my relationship with Garner (my son) more easygoing and empathetic.

James H. Andrews, *The Christian Science Monitor*, February 21, 1990.

In such work, men can find common cause with feminist women without falling into the "me-too" mold as the Men's

Auxiliary To Feminism. What is required is not a yen for self-immolation, but, quite simply, a commitment to social justice. Under our current social arrangements women are, as a group, massively disadvantaged; and men as moral and political agents ought to be involved in changing that.

There are many ways men can do this. Share the care of young children equally, and change working hours to make this possible. Work to put women into office—until at least 50 percent of decision-making positions are held by women. Confront misogyny and homophobia in workplaces and media. Work for pay equity and women's employment rights, until women's earnings are equal to men's. Support the redistribution of wealth, and universal social security and health care. Talk among men to make domestic violence, gay bashing, and sexual assault discreditable. Organize political and monetary support for battered women's shelters, rape crisis centers, domestic violence intervention. Change curricula in schools and colleges to include women's ideas and experiences, and to open up issues about men.

These are political strategies that can operate on a large scale, although they are based on particular workplaces, neighborhoods, and other settings. They offer a way past the general interest that men have in defending patriarchy by building on the specific interests particular groups of men share with women—as parents needing childcare, workers needing improved conditions, lesbians and gays fighting discrimination, for example. I find these strategies hopeful, not least because they offer some dignity to men involved in the highly undignified task of dismantling their own privileges.

Periodical Bibliography

The following articles have been selected to supplement the diverse views presented in this chapter.

Kathleen Barry	"Deconstructing Deconstructionism," *Ms.*, January/February 1991.
Thomas Droleskey	"Dressed to Kill," *The Wanderer*, May 13, 1993. Available from 201 Ohio St., St. Paul, MN 55107.
Elizabeth Fox-Genovese	"Feminist Rights, Individualist Wrongs," *Tikkun*, June 1992.
Tad Friend	"Yes," *Esquire*, February 1994.
Steven Goldberg	"Can Women Beat Men at Their Own Game?" *National Review*, December 27, 1993.
William Norman Grigg	"Feminist Reconstruction," *The New American*, September 20, 1993. Available from PO Box 8040, Appleton, WI 54913.
Steven Hill	"To Choose or Not to Choose: A Politics of Choice," *The Humanist*, May/June 1993.
E. Michael Jones	"Femi-Nazis?" *Fidelity*, June 1992. Available from 206 Marquette Ave., South Bend, IN 46617.
Jack Matthews	"Feminist Censorship," *The Freeman*, January 1992. Available from 30 S. Broadway, Irvington-on-Hudson, NY 10533.
Dwight D. Murphey	"Feminism and Rape," *Journal of Social, Political, and Economic Studies*, vol. 17, no. 1, Spring 1992.
Richard John Neuhaus	"Feminism and Feminism," *First Things*, June/July 1992. Available from 156 Fifth Ave., Suite 400, New York, NY 10010.
Richard John Neuhaus	"The Feminist Revolution," *First Things*, December 1991.
Katha Pollitt	"Are Women Morally Superior to Men?" *The Nation*, December 28, 1992.
Vicki Quade	"Redefining Notions: Feminist Legal Theory Pushes into the Mainstream," *Human Rights*, Fall 1993.
Leora Tanenbaum	"The Feminist Mistake," *In These Times*, December 13, 1993.
Michael Weiss	"Crimes of the Head," *Reason*, January 1992.
Noami Wolf	"Radical Heterosexuality," *Ms.*, July/August 1992.

Is Feminism Obsolete?

Feminism

Chapter Preface

The modern feminist movement that began in the 1960s is entering its fourth decade, and feminists celebrate the progress the movement has made for women. Life for most women in the 1990s is far different from life in the 1950s. Women have access to the same education as men, and by and large to the same career choices. Society is increasingly aware of sexual harassment and domestic abuse, and women can take legal action against such offenses.

This success of feminism has led some women to believe that the movement has outlived its purpose and is obsolete. So, while "a majority of American women agree that feminism has altered their lives for the better," according to author Wendy Kaminer, many women no longer see the need for the feminist movement. Other critics, like columnist John Leo, maintain that feminism is obsolete because it no longer addresses the needs and problems of mainstream women. The movement, he writes, has moved "away from its core constituency. Instead of focusing primarily on the problems of mainstream women and jobs and family," feminism has become "overly mesmerized by lesbian rights, radical chic and what we would today call the politics of victimization."

But many feminists contend that, while women have made tremendous progress in the last three decades, there is still much room for improvement, and feminism is necessary to catalyze further progress. "We live in a transitional age when some women can and do achieve great things, but where millions of women struggle with economic unfairness, physical terror, and psychological stress," charges Helen Neuborne, executive director of the NOW Legal Defense and Education Fund. Neuborne believes that as long as women still earn only sixty-one cents for every dollar earned by a man, perform 80 percent of the household duties, and are threatened by physical violence and sexual harassment, there is still a need for the women's movement.

Some of the authors in the following chapter echo Neuborne's belief in feminism. Others, however, maintain that feminism is obsolete. Together the authors present a series of compelling debates on the usefulness of feminism and its future in society.

> *"Is it possible that feminism as we have known it is dead? I think so."*

Feminism Is Obsolete

Sally Quinn

Feminism has failed to address the needs and problems of most women and has become an ineffectual fringe movement, Sally Quinn maintains in the following viewpoint. She argues that feminists portrayed a false image of women's lives, ignoring the importance and role of husbands and children and the difficulties most women face in juggling work and family life. Because of this, the movement failed to appeal to most women and is consequently obsolete. Quinn is an author and columnist in Washington, D.C.

As you read, consider the following questions:

1. How were feminists hypocritical, in Quinn's opinion?
2. Why does the author believe that many women perceive feminism as a fringe movement of extremists?
3. What is the legacy of feminism, according to Quinn?

Sally Quinn, "The Death of Feminism," *The Washington Post National Weekly Edition,* January 27–February 2, 1992. Reprinted with the author's permission.

There were several amazing revelations in the weeks preceding the 25th anniversary of the National Organization for Women:

• Gloria Steinem, in her new book, admits falling in love with someone who treated her badly. She had seduced him, she says, by playing down the person she was and playing up the person he wanted her to be. When he did fall in love with her, "I had to keep on not being myself."

• Jane Fonda, talking to *Time* magazine about her new husband, Ted Turner, announces that she's given up acting. "Ted is not a man that you leave to go on location," she explains. "He needs you there all the time."

• Barbra Streisand, in an interview with *Washington Post* TV critic Tom Shales, says that "even though my feminist side says people should be independent and not need to be taken care of by another person, that doesn't necessarily work that way. There's the human factor, you know."

• Washington Mayor Sharon Pratt Dixon marries a man named Kelly and, instead of reverting to Sharon Pratt, she changes her name to Sharon Pratt Kelly.

• Patricia Ireland, the new president of NOW, tells a gay magazine that, in addition to her husband, she's had a female "companion" for the last four years.

So. What are we to make of all this?

Is it possible that feminism as we have known it is dead? I think so.

Like communism in the former Soviet empire, the movement in its present form has outlasted its usefulness. There are no true feminists in the strictest sense of the word just as there probably were never any "pure" Communists.

Feminists Lied

The "feminists," and by that I mean the people who spoke for the movement, were never completely honest with women. They didn't tell the truth. They were hypocritical. Not surprisingly, when Steinem used to say, "A woman needs a man like a fish needs a bicycle," the women who believed her felt ashamed and guilty.

Like the Communists who denied the existence of God and the right to worship, leaders of the feminist movement have overlooked the deepest, most fundamental needs of their constituency.

The fact is, they have never been able to separate the workplace from the bedroom.

About 15 years ago, a woman named Marabel Morgan wrote a book called "The Total Woman," which sold 3 million copies and attracted the ire of feminists all over the country.

She said at the time, to a great deal of ridicule, "I think men and women are equal in status. They're just different in function in a marriage relationship. I believe women have the edge on men with brains, but they don't have the physical strength. I also believe that one of my functions is to create a happy atmosphere in the home. I believe that falls to the woman. I can't explain it. I just know that's the way it is. My 8-year-old daughter says it's not fair. And I say, 'Honey, you've got it. It's not fair.'"

Marabel Morgan obviously touched a nerve, though in those days it was not politically correct to admit it, especially among "enlightened" women. By then, the movement was so intent on achieving the legitimate goal of equality in the office that they tried to regulate people's behavior in their personal lives.

And that's where the feminist movement ran into problems.

Extremists Are No Longer Needed

Many of us have made enormous strides in the past 20 years, thanks in part to NOW, the movement and women like Gloria Steinem. The question is, are these same people and groups the ones to lead the next generation?

I don't think so. Not if they continue down the same path.

Any revolution needs extremists to get it off the ground, and the women's movement was no exception. But often the people who are responsible for change outlive their effectiveness, and a new group must take over.

What's happening in this country now is that more and more women are falling away from "feminism" because it doesn't represent, or more importantly, they *feel* it doesn't represent, them or their problems. Feminism is defined as the "principle that women should have political, economic and social rights equal to those of men." The problems arise over the "social" rights—and nobody knows what that means.

Betty Friedan wrote *The Second Stage* several years ago, a courageous book espousing the concept of motherhood. This was something which, unbelievably, had gotten lost on many of the feminists who felt having babies was not the politically correct thing to do. She was roundly criticized by many movement women who felt her book was a distraction from the main agenda.

For most women, equality and justice are at the head of any agenda. What most women don't want, though, is being told how to live. It's still not correct to say it too loudly, but many women believe they're better understood by the Helen Gurley Browns of the world than by the Germaine Greers.

They feel betrayed and lied to because trying to live a politically correct personal life doesn't always work, as Steinem, Fonda, Streisand, Kelly and others have demonstrated. If the feminists could say they were wrong about women needing men or men needing women, what were they right about? If they were living one life and espousing another, wasn't that corrupt?

There was always the suspicion that, like the commissars who preached sacrifice to their comrades and bought their caviar at the party store, feminist leaders were publicly telling mothers of three it was great to leave their husbands and be independent—and then secretly dressing up in Fredericks of Hollywood for their guys. It was the hypocrisy that turned off the mainstream women. Trusting themselves and their own instincts, they began rejecting the notion that they had to think and feel in a way that is unnatural.

Ideological Dead End

What kind of shape is American feminism in when its leading journal (*Ms.*) is edited by a woman who thinks most of the "decently married bedrooms across America are settings for nightly rape" and its leading organization (NOW) is headed by a woman with a husband in Miami and a female "companion" in Washington? Is this out of touch, or is NOW quietly banking on a sudden surge of bisexual adultery chic among its membership? . . .

Consider the voice of a successful mainstream woman trying to come to grips with the out-of-touchness of feminism: "I am skeptical about the women's movement. I find myself increasingly saying, 'Yes . . . but.' *Yes*, there may be a war between the sexes, *but* I am doubtful that it's the one the women's movement is currently fighting." The speaker is Margaret O'Brien Steinfels, editor of *Commonweal*, the liberal Catholic magazine. . . .

Since she does not feel oppressed by "the patriarchy," since her experiences with males, good and bad, do not fit the victim-oppressor mode, she feels the movement has little to do with her life.

John Leo, *U.S. News & World Report*, February 10, 1992.

The leaders of the movement, though, never blinked. Instead of helping women fulfill their needs, helping the "total woman," they acted as if women had but one side and ignored the reality of husbands and children. *You can do it all, look at us*, was the message. The poor average woman, struggling to make it work and failing, was often hurt more than helped by these phony examples of how wonderful life could be if only they would take charge and discard the men. Women felt ashamed to be housewives, ashamed to be full-time mothers.

Ultimately, this phoniness is what has hurt the feminist movement and, more importantly, hurt the very cause they're advocating—creating a negative reaction, the sort of thing Susan

Faludi talks about in her book, *Backlash*. Abortion rights, earning power and job promotion in the workplace are only some of the crucial issues that are being threatened today.

And people today trivialize the really important issues in the movement because the movement trivializes the important issues in people's personal lives. By dismissing what really goes on in the hearts and minds of women, the movement offered a target for its enemies—including the "antifeminists" who say, among other things, that they don't believe in equal pay.

The sad part is that the movement today is more and more perceived as a fringe cause, often with overtones of lesbianism and man-hating. This notion was hardly dispelled by Patricia Ireland's announcement of a "love relationship with a woman" and a declaration that she saw no reason to give up either that relationship or the one with her husband.

NOW's leader also said that she has never been anything but honest—an extremely odd choice of language. What are we talking about here? We are not just talking about open relationships or honesty or even lesbianism for that matter. Rather, what Ms. Ireland is talking about is, to my mind, adultery.

Most women I know are turned off by her boastful revelation, though they're reluctant to admit it. You can be absolutely sure that if she were having an affair with a man, we would never hear about it. But what kind of standards is she espousing? Would we elect anyone to a political office who announced they were having an affair? Can you imagine George Bush telling the world that he was having a homosexual relationship with another man and it was just swell with Barbara?

It is impossible to read the Ireland declaration and argue that the movement she leads is still in touch with the majority of women. How many women are going to tell their daughters that Patricia Ireland is a role model? The truth is that many women have come to see the feminist movement as anti-male, anti-child, anti-family, anti-feminine. And therefore it has nothing to do with us.

Confusion over Roles

Today, 25 years after the birth of NOW, the legacy of the feminist movement—beyond its vision and agenda—is a lot of confusion. So many women, and men too, are confused about what their roles are. For so long, they have been taught to pretend, to hide, to conceal their real feelings and their real beliefs about each other. You were either a good feminist or sexist, and the demands were rigid.

But life is more complicated than that, as the nation saw during the William Kennedy Smith rape trial and the debate over whether Clarence Thomas ever sexually harassed Anita Hill.

The women who believed Hill were outraged at her treatment by the Senate Judiciary Committee. But they were not without doubts. For a "pure" feminist, though, it was not politically correct to express them. The same kind of problem arose with the Smith trial, where, if you believed Smith's version, you were judged to have betrayed the movement.

All of these sexual issues are especially confusing to men. It's good for them, says the party line. But most women are confused too. Beyond the obvious cases (and everybody knows what they are), there's no simple test of what sexual harassment is. As one extremely liberated and politically sensitive male friend of mine said to me, "If you work for me and I ask you out, and you say no, that's sexual harassment, and if you say yes, it isn't."

The point is that such issues fall out of the strict confines of the workplace. And once in the bedroom, things can get very murky, even among the most clear-thinking.

Feminists Must Address the "Human Factor"

Most of us have husbands and sons and brothers and fathers that we love. We don't want them to be chauvinist pigs or wimps. We want them to be people who care about justice and equality as much as we do. And we don't need somebody else to tell us who should do the dishes.

We need leaders, like Betty Friedan, who will speak to those needs as well as the other issues that are so important. A friend of mine asked her college-age daughter the other day about feminism. Her daughter said she wasn't really a feminist but truly believed that there was no job she couldn't have, no profession she couldn't aspire to. For that alone, the feminist movement should be proud.

But that's not enough.

Whoever the new leaders are, whoever emerges to speak to the real issues confronting most women, will not succeed unless they are willing and able to acknowledge and address the basic question—the "human factor."

"People [are] becoming more aware and concerned about women's rights."

Feminism Is Not Obsolete

Paula Kamen

Through feminism, women can gain power and change society, Paula Kamen states in the following viewpoint. She believes that young women especially are drawn to feminism and will continue to make it a powerful, influential force in society. Kamen, a 1989 graduate of the University of Illinois in Urbana, is a journalist whose articles have appeared in publications such as the *Chicago Tribune*, the *New York Times*, *Ms.*, and *New Directions for Women*.

As you read, consider the following questions:

1. What does the author believe is the greatest key to feminism in the 1990s?
2. Why should women not abandon feminism for humanism, in Kamen's opinion?
3. How can feminists help to unite America's diverse, multicultural society, according to Kamen?

The first expressly feminist piece of writing I ever read was "Diving into the Wreck," a poem by Adrienne Rich, which has come to my mind while writing this and thinking about the future. Freshman year of college, I first examined, in a paper, the meaning of some of the imagery, which is as relevant now as it was when the words were written in 1972.

The narrator of the poem is on a treacherous and unguided journey: "I came to explore the wreck," she says. She is bravely diving into the ocean to investigate an old and deteriorating ship. Her equipment is a knife, perhaps for fighting; a camera, for recording what she finds; and a "book of myths," as a journal.

To get a clear view, she has to struggle to get deep, deep, deep, beyond the surface of the water:

> I go down
> Rung after rung and still
> the oxygen immerses me
> the blue light
> the clear atoms
> of our human air.
> I go down.
> My flippers cripple me,
> I crawl like an insect down the ladder
> and there is no one
> to tell me when the ocean
> will begin

In my paper, I said Rich was taking the initiative to inspect the tired and unneeded parts of society, exposing its myths. A central source of the myths seemed to be sexism, which has kept women from achieving their potential.

Now younger feminists are calling for women and men to embark on another difficult mission: a continued exploration of these myths—and others—that still requires plunging way beneath the surface. . . .

The Importance of Social Commitment

The greatest key to feminism in the Nineties is perhaps the neglected element of social consciousness. It involves making a commitment to women—a most basic and fundamental principle of feminism.

This transforms feminism from an exclusive, self-centered, individualist struggle to one for women. It also acts as an insurance policy for the movement to survive and develop. People know the work isn't done when their own personal goals have been realized. . . .

The period of pronounced activism of the 1960s can still provide some powerful lessons. Then, social consciousness was a part of popular dialogue, and people seemed to cultivate more confidence in their abilities to effect change for themselves and for others.

The 1960s also seemed to encompass more of a collective vision. I agree that individual battles are essential, such as in becoming a teacher or a social worker, being philanthropic, volunteering. But while working in one's niche, the feminist must also keep an eye on the big picture. This means being a watchdog of social policy and voting according to one's beliefs.

Young women must also do their own revision of some 1960s concepts. They need to temper grand, idealistic visions with some realism and cautiousness. . . . Activists in the Sixties almost collapsed under the weight of their own ambition. Social-justice activists seemed to run a long-distance race to achieve the Utopian Society with the drive and speed of sprinters. But the runners appeared spent after the first lap.

Feminism Is Power

In the Nineties, feminists have to pace themselves and keep their eyes down to see barriers that must be confronted. Meanwhile, they must also always be looking far enough ahead to see the finish line.

Making this commitment is difficult because it goes against the way young people have generally been socialized. Especially for white middle-class people, it requires a special effort to look beyond one's own experience. This involves initiative in learning about others and the risk of journeying into the unknown, being awkward and hitting snags.

Obliterating all these myths and building this social consciousness and sisterhood sounds like a lot of work. Is it worth the struggle? Why don't we just call ourselves humanists and abandon the feminist critiques? Why do we want to continue the women's movement?

The reason to break all these myths? I can summarize it in one word: power.

Feminism is one model for empowering the individual and then harnessing that collective energy for change. For the movement, more people acting on their beliefs can mean new life. This common goal of power for all women can give dialogue new freshness and drive. In political terms, a result is to stop and reverse the feminization of poverty, and accelerate and transform the feminization of power.

The motivation for power was most forcefully demonstrated by Anna Padia, director of human rights for the Newspaper Guild. A thunderous speaker, she drew rapt attention at an ambitious conference in October of 1990, planned by young women and the Institute for Women's Policy Research in Washington, D.C., with the following:

The reason for a diverse East Coast network—why? The answer is power. Both the individual power and the collective power to make the changes you want personally, professionally on the job, in the community and in every institution that you are now in or will be involved in during the future.

This is not to underestimate the power of one individual, for surely we know of individuals who have accomplished great things. Nor is this view to underestimate the tremendous power that already exists and that each of you now possesses, whether you know it or not.

But take your one hand, make that into a fist. Take that fist and magnify that a thousand fold and you have a very different kind of power. If you take that single one articulate voice of yours and you add it to a choir of a million, you have power.

Send that one postcard to that president, or the Congress or the manufacturer that makes products that are not healthy to your life . . . and you will be heard.

You will persuade. You will compel the attention to effect and implement the policies, the programs, and the very important young women's perspectives that only you can define.

To get at that power, women must visualize themselves as having the right to it. Susan Denevan, twenty-three, the 1990-1991 student body president at the University of Minnesota, said that sexism—both in self-image and in how women are treated—keeps women from achieving power. In this realm, women still basically have the myth of themselves as "the second sex."

"Due to sexism, the system of power distribution has made women not want to be involved with the process of policy-making. When we include classism, sexism, ableism and hetero-sexism, we see how many people have been locked out of decision-making and our reluctance grows even greater," she said, speaking at NOW's [National Organization for Women] First Young Feminist Conference in 1991.

Women Promote a Sense of Community

Denevan also stressed that through traditional and available channels, women can invent the future and transform institutions. "What kind of power do we as women bring to traditional politics? We bring an emphasis on community and interdependence. And not on hierarchy or self-promotion. What does this mean? It means that we see how our survival is linked with the survival of others and of our environment.

But, she added, survival is not enough, and the real source of power must be self-determination, a basic feminist goal.

"Self-determination for all peoples will only be achieved when our current system of power distribution is overthrown. Overthrown does not necessarily mean violent revolution, but it does mean directly confronting the assumptions and actions that disenfranchise all but those conforming to the white male model of leadership."

This myth-breaking of all types of sexism and stereotypes is a weighty, unsettling challenge. It involves unraveling countless assumptions about oneself and about others. It involves confrontation, feeling uncomfortable, taking risks.

The Movement Is Still Strong

Pundits have predicted the short-order demise of the women's movement throughout most of its history. By the mid-1980s many observers had begun declaring us to be in the "post-feminist era"; interestingly, the term was first used in 1919, the year before the women's suffrage amendment to the U.S. Constitution was ratified. The women's movement has clearly not died. . . .

The potential for mobilization in support of a women's movement seems, if anything, more widespread than ever. . . . No one would seriously argue that women speak with one political voice, but as we near the twenty-first century, the dominant opinion among women—and, indeed, a substantial view among men—still sees room for improvement in the situation of women as women and holds that one route to that improvement is a social movement organized for women.

Virginia Sapiro, *The Annals of the American Academy of Political and Social Science,* May 1991.

But these tremendous challenges also make feminism thrilling. This is groundbreaking work! Nothing could be more revolutionary than breaking down these barriers and empowering ourselves and others. In this country, in a growing multicultural society, looking at issues of diversity is the road to future success in every area: economic, social, in personal relationships. Now feminists are at the forefront of this struggle and are pioneering concepts of understanding and overcoming and celebrating difference.

Commitment Is Growing

The waters seem to be at just the right temperature for entry. In traveling across the country, I have noticed a phenomenon of people becoming more aware and concerned about women's rights and other social issues. In unison, people are telling me the same ideas, using almost the same language to describe how they are feeling. Different professors of women's studies across the country have told me that they sense the pendulum swinging back slightly from the right and students becoming more committed to working for others.

Everyone's help is needed to turn any current trends into serious dialogue to propel a movement. These feelings have the potential to result in more than just influencing the looks of the new spring fashions. Instead of continuing to look back to the beat of the Sixties with nostalgia, young people can take their energies and build on past work and make something they can be proud of. The innovative work of the activists profiled gives proof that young people can bring about change.

This work can also teach outsiders a lesson in defining a feminist. In building solidarity, feminists can transcend the popular myth that they are part of a fringe group.

The issue is not just who opens the door for women.

The issue is opening the doors of opportunity and empowering all people—certainly not a trivial matter.

"On the brink of the twenty-first century, the second wave [of feminism] was alive and well—broader, more deeply rooted, and more diverse than it had ever been."

Feminism Will Continue to Be Influential

Flora Davis

Feminism is a broad movement that has made great gains for women and that will continue to influence society in the future, Flora Davis asserts in the following viewpoint. Davis refutes the idea that feminism has accomplished its job and is no longer useful. As long as women are discriminated against and women's issues are ignored by those in power, feminism will play an important role in society, Davis concludes. Davis has taught writing and journalism at the New School for Social Research and at Fordham University in New York City. She writes frequently about women's issues for national magazines, and is the author of the book *Moving the Mountain: The Women's Movement in America Since 1960*, from which this viewpoint is excerpted.

As you read, consider the following questions:

1. What were women's lives like prior to the feminist movement, according to Davis?
2. According to the author, what are some of the many diverse coalitions that make up the women's movement today?
3. What do most women think of the women's movement, according to Davis?

The second wave of the women's movement accomplished an enormous amount during its first thirty years—Americans had only to look back to add up the score. At midcentury, women were limited in the courses they could take in high school; discouraged from considering any but the most traditional, feminine careers; kept out of graduate schools, medical schools, and law schools by quotas; barred from many occupations; automatically fired when they became pregnant; routinely denied credit; and forbidden by law to sit on juries in some states. Most Americans, male and female, took it for granted that as breadwinners, men had a right to earn more than a woman who was doing the same job. Battered wives had nowhere to turn; sexual harassment was a dirty secret; abortion was illegal; and a woman who was raped had to produce a witness if she wanted the rapist brought to justice. The list could go on, but the message is clear: Feminism in the last half of the twentieth century produced at least half a revolution.

A Diverse Movement

On the brink of the twenty-first century, the second wave was alive and well—broader, more deeply rooted, and more diverse than it had ever been. It encompassed older organizations such as the YWCA and the Girl Scouts of America, as well as an alphabet soup of second-wave groups such as NOW [National Organization for Women], NARAL [National Abortion Rights Action League], OWL [Older Women's League], and MANA [Mexican American Women's National Association].

Even to begin to describe the women's movement in 1990, one would have to list all the shifting, overlapping coalitions in Washington and in various state capitals that brought together feminist lawmakers, attorneys, and lobbyists to work on legislation for women. Then there were the women's PACs [political action committees], the feminist legal services, the women's policy institutes, and the women's caucuses and committees within most professional groups and many unions.

The movement had also branched out into global networks; it was linked to the women's peace movement, to the revived welfare rights movement, and to activists who had recently organized to fight for better treatment for women with AIDS. There had been an explosion of organizations for women of color and of groups focused on women's health or women's spirituality.

Meanwhile, a feminist subculture survived in women's bookstores and feminist publications and small presses. *Ms.* magazine had been reborn after a near-death experience. There were women's art galleries, including a National Museum of Women in the Arts in Washington, D.C. On college campuses around the country, women's studies programs were thriving, and student groups had organized to defend abortion rights. There were battered women's shelters, anti-rape hotlines, and much, much more.

Rumors of Feminism's Death Were Exaggerated

Contrary to suggestions in the media, the movement was not about to fade away. Although there would undoubtedly be some temporary setbacks in the future, there could be no going back for a generation of women used to seeing female police officers, doctors, and lawyers, used to women in the military, in the pulpit, in space, and almost everywhere else; a generation who simply assumed they could control their own fertility through birth control and—if need be—through abortion. Though they might take women's gains for granted, they weren't likely to surrender them without a fight because they believed that women had a right to them. Whether they knew it or not, that belief was a gift from the women's movement.

Feminism Has Helped Women

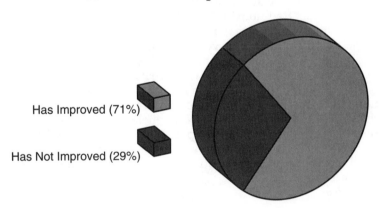

Has Improved (71%)

Has Not Improved (29%)

Percent of women who said feminism has/has not improved their lives.

Source: *Newsweek*, 1986.

Feminists had raised the consciousness of the nation and that was probably their most significant achievement. Many of the ideas introduced by the second wave had diffused into every corner of society, leaving no one untouched, and had been so thoroughly absorbed that they now shaped most people's beliefs about what women were like and what they could expect to do with their lives. Much of the time, those ideas were so commonly accepted that they were no longer even labeled "feminist."

If the image of women had changed, so had the image of the women's movement. By 1986, a *Newsweek* survey reported that 56 percent of the women polled said yes when they were asked, "Do you consider yourself a feminist?" Seventy-one percent said that the movement had improved their lives. In 1990, almost 60 percent of 3000 women surveyed said that they are discriminated against in getting top jobs. Women had become more savvy about the obstacles they faced, and they were also more ambitious.

In the nineties, there is still much work to be done. Activists have proved that the mountain can be moved, but they haven't yet been able to move it far enough. . . . The tasks that remain . . . are many and varied—they range from passing a family leave bill to reforming the health care system, achieving the ERA [Equal Rights Amendment] and fighting to preserve legal abortion.

The Threat from the Right

Unfortunately, feminists must still spend too much time and energy defending their gains. Right-wingers are as determined as ever to reverse social change: they'd like to confine women once again to their traditional role and at the same time put a lid on the advances made by men of color. Probably the greatest challenge for the women's movement—and the brightest promise—lies in the efforts white feminists and women of color are making to work together toward mutual goals.

In short, American women have pulled off just half a revolution, and it has taken the combined energy and determination of thousands of activists to do it. Nevertheless, given the enormous resistance to change over the past thirty years and what feminists have been able to accomplish in spite of it, prospects are good. As long as there's a strong women's movement, further progress is inevitable.

"Most women . . . have no need for a movement to speak on their behalf."

Feminism Has Lost Its Influence

The Washington Times

In the following viewpoint, the author maintains that most women no longer need feminism, and that the movement has lost any influence it once had in society. Because feminism portrays women as victims, women who are strong and successful are not attracted to the movement and find it unnecessary, the author argues. The author concludes that women today can speak and act for themselves—they do not need feminists to represent them. The author is the editorial columnist for the *Washington Times*, a daily newspaper.

As you read, consider the following questions:

1. What is the author's opinion of the "backlash" theory?
2. How has feminism changed in the 1990s, according to the author?
3. Why does the author disagree with feminism's portrayal of women as victims?

Editorial, *The Washington Times*, March 8, 1992. Reprinted by permission.

Is there a new resurgence of feminism? Well, judging by the covers of three distinguished magazines, one could be pardoned for thinking so.

Here's Gloria Steinem and Susan Faludi looking profound and chicly defiant out of the cover of *Time*. Here's Patricia Ireland, the new user-friendly face of the National Organization for Women, beaming a smile on the front page of the *New York Times* Sunday magazine. Not to be outdone, the *New Republic* features a raised fist with a studded black leather bracelet—and a string of pearls, a diamond ring and neatly polished red nails. The *New Republic* may not be subtle in its symbolism, but the picture certainly does match the cover line "The New Feminists."

The implication of all three covers is clear: The new feminism is very different from feminism of the old battle-ax variety. Would Molly Yard, she of the dowdy skirts and the unfashionable bun, have been caught dead with red nails or the sexy black tights that Ms. Steinem is sporting? Or Betty Friedan? There's a thought to blow the mind.

The buzzword in feminist circles these days is "backlash." And the question what to do about it. The '80s were not a good decade for the feminists. Just as "first-wave" feminists rebelled against the '50s June Cleaver image of the perfect wife, so many in the next generation rebelled against the feminists' tie-dyed shirts and political activism and preferred high heels and skimpy skirts. Others realized that the traditional family, which the feminists had been so busy tearing down, cannot be so easily dismissed if life is to have coherence and meaning. Feminists came to be seen as grumpy, unattractive hold-overs.

Feminism Gets Too Much Credit

Received wisdom has it that feminism is a victim of its own success. It is certainly true today that women have made great inroads in all spheres of the working world. They can be astronauts, soldiers, plumbers, surgeons, ambulance drivers, television news anchorpersons, even congresswomen and senators, though not yet combat pilots, much to the chagrin of Pat Schroeder. All this is commonly credited to the women's movement. Exactly how much it had to do with it is open to question, however. As noted by Oriana Papazoglou "Despising Our Mothers, Despising Ourselves," in *First Things*, the great ground shift began in the late '50s before the publication of Betty Friedan's call to arms in *The Feminine Mystique* in 1964, which launched radical feminism.

What's more, the polls that are often cited as proof that a double standard is at work in the new generation, which is supposed to have benefited from the feminist movement while at the same time rejecting the feminist label, can—like most polls—be read in many ways. "Has the women's movement improved your life?"

Time magazine asked women in its survey. Yes, say 39 percent. "Do women today have more freedom than their mothers did?" Yes, say 82 percent. "Do you consider yourself a feminist?" No, say 63 percent. Surely, this is evidence of a double standard, not to mention a certain amount of ingratitude. But what about those 54 percent in the survey who feel that feminism has had no discernible influence on their lives whatsoever?

Most Women Are Not Feminists

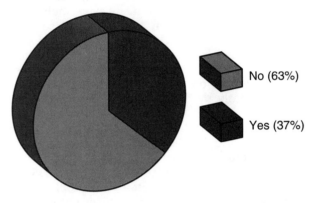

No (63%)

Yes (37%)

Response to the question: "Do you consider yourself a feminist?"

Source: *The Washington Times*, March 8, 1992; *Time*.

Whatever the reasons for women's progress in the work force—and economic necessity may have as much to do with it as ideology—the question remains: What do feminists have to offer in the 1990s? Has the rejection of radical politics in the 1980s taught the movement anything? Have the errors of the past been understood and absorbed? The denigration of women who preferred to be mothers and home-makers, for instance? Or attacks on women who like to look like, well, women, rather than short men or bundles of laundry?

On a superficial level, the rejection appears to have made an impression. Karen Lehrman in the *New Republic* notes that "second-wave" feminists led by Betty Friedan, Germaine Greer and Susan Brownmiller now argue that women should be free to choose whatever they want, raising kids or going out to work.

Some are trying to promote a sexier image. Naomi Wolf, also in the *New Republic*, rebuts Camille Paglia's contention that feminists are dour puritans. "The great feminists have been women of passionate impulses, sensuous beauty," writes Ms. Wolf, who as author of *The Beauty Myth*, is a leader in the feminist renaissance. "Orgasm is the body's natural call to feminist politics: if being a woman can be this good, women must be worth something." That ought to get somebody's attention.

Gloria Steinem, in her best-selling, *Revolution from Within*, finds that all her flamboyant radicalism of the past was rooted in an inferiority complex and goes searching for her "inner child," joining up with the self-esteem movement and the New Agers.

And yet, those who caught a glimpse of the 25th anniversary celebration of the National Organization for Women in Washington might doubt that the new feminism is a whole lot different from the old. The old radicalism, which put off so many of the American women that NOW claims to represent, was certainly still in evidence. There were the Socialist Women's International Caucus, the Lesbian Rights Caucus, etc. Workshops earnestly discussed the role of women in the environmental movement. And as noted recently by Elena Neuman in *Insight* magazine, as for NOW's claim to speak for all American women, the organization has basically ignored the battle for breast cancer research funding, as opposed to AIDS research—despite the fact that four times as many women (about 500,000) have died of breast cancer as have died from AIDS since 1981, when AIDS deaths began being recorded in the United States (133,000).

And the mindset of the new feminists turns out to be not so different from that of the old. "First-wave" feminists saw women as victims of a conspiracy by beastly men, society, the military-industrial complex, the ways of Judeo-Christian tradition and assorted other evils. Not much has changed here. Women, the new feminists assert, are still victims. This they will undoubtedly continue to assert, no matter how successful or how educated women become. Today women are victims of the famous backlash.

The Backlash

According to *Wall Street Journal* reporter Susan Faludi's *Backlash: The Undeclared War Against American Women*, it is a conspiracy concocted by the reactionaries and the media, seeking to drive women back into the safety of confining stereotypes through the use of "myths" such as the biological clock, the fast-receding marriage prospects for women over 30 or guilt inducing "toxic day-care" stories.

Ms. Wolf in *The Beauty Myth* blames the industrial-cosmetic complex, which has foisted on women eating disorders, breast implants, plastic surgery, plucked eyebrows and miniskirts. Fashion magazines, swimsuit issues of *Sports Illustrated*, beauty pageants, they all serve to beat successful career women into self-hating, pathetic submission.

That is a dreadful picture of course. What is wrong is that feminists are capable only of seeing women as victims, not as responsible individuals and human beings who have voices and opinions of their own. The primary fallacy of the women's movement is that its activists assume they somehow have been given a mandate to speak for an entire class of people, an entire gender in fact.

But most women are not victims. Certainly, there are some who are and who have the bruises of domestic abuse to prove it. But most women are more than capable of taking care of themselves. The enterprising and articulate Ms. Wolf and Ms. Faludi are no doubt good examples. And there is no reason to assume that all women share the same views. They have no need for a movement to speak on their behalf, any more than men need a bunch of bongo-banging weekend warriors to speak for them in the name of "the men's movement." The assumption that they do is insulting and condescending.

Periodical Bibliography

The following articles have been selected to supplement the diverse views presented in this chapter.

Johanna Brenner — "The Best of Times, the Worst of Times: U.S. Feminism Today," *New Left Review*, no. 200, July/August 1993.

Connexions — Entire issue on feminism, vol. 40, 1992. Available from 4228 Telegraph Ave., Oakland, CA 94609.

Midge Decter — "Farewell to the Woman Question," *First Things*, June/July 1991. Available from 156 Fifth Ave., Suite 400, New York, NY 10010.

Elizabeth Fox-Genovese and Nancy Hewitt — "Rethinking Feminism," *Tikkun*, June 1992.

Nancy Gibbs — "The War Against Feminism," *Time*, March 9, 1992.

Germaine Greer — "The Backlash Myth," *The New Republic*, October 5, 1992.

Wendy Kaminer — "Feminism's Identity Crisis," *The Atlantic Monthly*, October 1993.

Elissa Karg — "Symposium on Backlash: Is Feminism Out of Fashion?" *Against the Current*, March/April 1993.

Bonnie Pfister — "Communiqués from the Front," *On the Issues*, Summer 1993.

Phyllis Schlafly — "The Radical Goals of the Feminists," *The Phyllis Schlafly Report*, December 1991. Available from Box 618, Alton, IL 62002.

Social Policy — Entire issue on "The Women's Movement at a Crossroads: Where Do We Go from Here?" Summer 1993.

Barbara Taylor — "Old Passions, New Visions," *New Internationalist*, September 1993.

What Should the Goals of Feminism Be?

Feminism

Chapter Preface

Feminism is a broad movement that encompasses a vast number of people with varying goals and objectives. Liberal feminists, radical feminists, ecofeminists, and lesbian feminists, for example, may all support the broad goal of increasing equality for women, but they often disagree on the causes of women's inequality, the definition of equality, and how to improve women's status. These conflicts make setting goals for the feminist movement difficult.

For decades the primary goal of feminism was to gain for women the rights allotted men: the right to vote, the right to work in traditionally male jobs, the right to serve in the military. But as women have begun achieving these goals and making inroads into men's domains, some feminists are questioning whether seeking to be "just like men" is a worthwhile goal for women. As author Elizabeth Fox-Genovese explains in *Tikkun*:

> For some, feminism necessarily means the promotion of equality between women and men; for others, it just as necessarily means the celebration of the differences between women and men. . . . In practice, the debate between the two strands in feminism amounts to a disagreement over whether women simply need access to the same rights as men or whether women need protection on the basis of their irreducible differences from men.

Those feminists who favor deemphasizing the differences between men and women tend to fight for legal and social changes that gain women entry into corporate boardrooms, military jets, and other places women have not traditionally been welcomed. Most of these would argue that there are few meaningful differences between men and women and that there should be no difference in the opportunities given each.

Feminists who believe women and men are different in important ways also believe that women should not be denied opportunities. But they argue that by convincing women that they must become "like men" to gain equality, society demeans the unique nature of women. For example, these feminists might maintain that women are by nature more nurturing than men, and that men, women, and children would all benefit if nurturing occupations such as child care, nursing, and social work were more highly valued.

Whether feminists should strive for equality by deemphasizing the differences between men and women or by emphasizing women's unique nature is one issue explored in the following chapter. The authors in the chapter present differing feminist views and discuss how feminists can unite to establish goals.

"*Free markets are good for all women and men because they allow greater choice. This is what feminism is all about.*"

Feminism Should Promote Capitalism

Deborah Walker

Because capitalism provides prosperity and economic freedom to women, feminists should support capitalism and promote free enterprise, Deborah Walker maintains in the following viewpoint. Walker believes free markets allow businesses to operate efficiently, without government involvement. This strengthens the economy and provides both women and men with more freedom concerning their occupations. Walker is a Bradley Resident Scholar at the Heritage Foundation, a conservative think tank that promotes free enterprise and limited government.

As you read, consider the following questions:

1. What does Walker mean when she says she is not a "politically correct academic feminist"?
2. What did Ludwig von Mises state concerning feminism, as quoted by the author?
3. Who or what is to blame for the backlash against feminism, in Walker's opinion?

Abridged from Deborah Walker, "Feminism and Free Markets: Friends or Foes?" *The Heritage Lectures*, no. 443, November 19, 1992. Reprinted with permission.

The term feminism often conjures up images of angry women bashing men, criticizing capitalism, and turning to the state for answers. Indeed, as I researched the topic of feminism and free markets, I found that capitalism was often attacked not only by radical Marxist feminists, but also by the more mainstream feminists like Gloria Steinem, Susan Faludi, and Naomi Wolf, who have found themselves on best-seller lists. As an economist, my study of the market has led me to a deep appreciation of economic freedom. To me markets and prices are beautiful and wonderful. To understand how free markets work is to marvel at their ability to create wealth for a society that allows people like me to sit and think about such matters as feminism. So although my main interest in feminism is economic in nature, it does not stop there. I am not only an economist, I am a woman. There is a moral dimension to feminism that cannot be ignored.

In his recent book *Forbidden Grounds: The Case Against Employment Discrimination Laws*, Richard Epstein writes, "In my judgment, feminism is the single most powerful social movement of our time, one that addresses every aspect of human and social life." The feminist movement questions not only our economic order, but also the legal order upon which the economic order rests. And it also questions our moral order, upon which the legal order rests or should rest, in my opinion. In essence, feminism questions some of the basic cultural norms by which we live our lives. Is this questioning wrong? No, not necessarily. However, I disagree with how many people ask the questions. Moreover, I will argue that they give the wrong answers which, in turn, produce undesirable social and economic consequences.

Politically Correct? Not!

Let me begin by telling you what I am not. I am not a politically correct academic feminist. What does this mean? For those of you who are not in the academy, it means that I do not believe capitalism is bad for women. I do not believe men have deliberately designed every institution in history to enable men to dominate women. And I do not believe that there is only one research agenda for feminists. Most academic feminists today will not listen to alternative views of feminism. Ask, for example, Camille Paglia or Christina Sommers about feminist reactions to their alternative views.

Most academic feminists today are anti-capitalist statists. They are inconsistent, elitist, and, in my opinion, very anti-woman. They will say, for example, that men have deliberately designed institutions (capitalism for one) to dominate women. To quote one of the leading theorists in feminist legal theory, Catherine MacKinnon, "Here, on the first day that matters, dominance was achieved, probably by force. By the second day, division along

164

the same lines had to be relatively firmly in place. On the third day, if not sooner, differences were demarcated, together with social systems to exaggerate them in perception and in fact, *because* the systematically differential delivery of benefits and deprivations required making no mistake about who was who."

MacKinnon is saying that most of our institutions—private property rights, marriage, and exchange, for instance—were deliberately and consciously designed by men and that women throughout history have been passive agents. I believe this is insulting to women and gives undeserved credit to men. Genuine institutions are not deliberately designed by anyone; they evolve spontaneously out of the social interactions of men and women. To view free trade or market exchange, which is capitalism, as a deliberately designed method of domination is to be ignorant of why trade occurs and why private property rights emerge in civilization. . . .

Feminism and Freedom

There are natural differences between men and women and they manifest themselves in different ways. But I would argue that capitalism is responsible for technological advances which have changed the economic order from one in which physical strength and stamina are necessary for the production of goods to one in which they are no longer prerequisites for financial success. Women can now enter fields they could not enter earlier—remember, this is because capitalism has made possible technological progress. As a result, I am not afraid of how cultural norms may change in a free society as women make nonconventional choices. I am *as* opposed to social planning to preserve particular cultural norms as I am to economic planning. Both suffer from the same fallacy: the belief that there is a person or group able to know the subjective values and desires of others and the individual circumstances of their lives.

I think free markets and a free society are compatible with feminism. Let me define feminism and the principles to which I subscribe. I believe women have been treated as second class citizens, for lack of a better phrase, in one form or another throughout history. In the United States this has manifested itself in such laws as those which did not allow women to own property, to sue, to enter into contracts, to enter certain occupations, or to vote. Women have been governed—and in some cases still are governed—according to cultural norms which tell them that only certain types of behavior are appropriate. For example, speaking in a public place to a mixed audience of men and women was considered inappropriate 150 years ago. In essence, feminism as I understand it asks for equality under the law, but it also asks that women command the same respect as

165

complete human beings as men. Free markets not only support but promote this brand of feminism.

To make my position clearer I want to quote Ludwig von Mises. This is from his book *Socialism*: "So far as Feminism seeks to adjust the legal position of woman to that of man, so far as it seeks to offer her legal and economic freedom to develop and act in accordance with her inclinations, desires, and economic circumstances, so far it is nothing more than a branch of the great liberal movement which advocates peaceful and free evolution."

Peaceful and free evolution. I cannot say it any better than that. Professor Mises describes how man is dominant over woman in violent societies and in violent times. He explains that this domination breaks down in a free society, in the absence of violence, and that it is not in the interest of men to dominate women, even within the household. Societies that are based on the premises of socialism, on violence, on the premise that might makes right, or on the premise of *equality of outcome* will not be societies conducive to feminism.

Feminism and Statism

Unfortunately, what most feminists call for today are socialist, statist policies. These policies include affirmative action legislation, government-supported child care, mandated employment benefits such as family leave, and, worst of all, comparable pay for comparable worth. These policies undermine the workings of free markets.

But do these policies work? What are they designed to do? These policies are supposed to decrease discrimination in hiring and salary decisions by employers. They are supposed to increase the ease by which working mothers and fathers can enter the workforce by turning over the responsibility of raising children to the state, or by forcing employers to take on that responsibility and, in so doing, hasten cultural change. In short, the principles of a free society, or what Professor Friedrich Hayek terms its *general rules*, have been betrayed, and expediency has become the order of the day. These *specific commands*, the policies I have mentioned, undermine and contradict the general rules of a free society in several ways. They take day-to-day decision-making from individual hands and put it in the hands of legislators. They destroy freedom of contract and undermine private property rights. What are the consequences? Do these specific commands accomplish what is intended? Do they decrease discrimination? I argue that they do not. Actually, they do just the opposite. Let me explain.

There is a backlash against women in our society. But it was not created by the press as Faludi claims. The backlash stems from the fact that employers do not like to be told whom they can and cannot hire, and men do not like to be overlooked for jobs or promotions for which they are qualified simply because they are men. Unfortunately, this backlash (or increase in discrimination) is directed toward women. It should be directed instead toward the real cause of discrimination—the state.

Feminism Has Helped Women

Question: Since the women's movement got started in the 1960s, has it made things better for women, worse for women, or hasn't it made any difference?

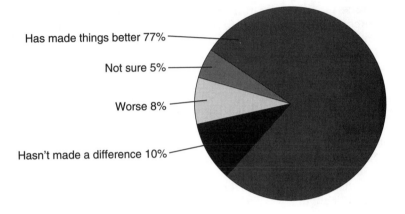

Source: Survey by Yankelovich Clancy Shulman for *Time* and CNN, October 23-25, 1989.

Discrimination increases when government mandates, e.g., child care or family leave policies, increase the costs of hiring women over men. True, there are individual women who have jobs they would not otherwise have because of these specific commands. But that does not mean discrimination has decreased or that we are better off as a society. On the contrary, many people are out of a job or are underemployed because of these specific commands.

Undermining the general rules of a free economy decreases the efficiency of the economy. Jobs are created when resources are put to productive or more productive uses. This can only come about if resources, including human resources, are moved in directions that entrepreneurs freely choose. Entrepreneurs have their pocketbooks on the line and are closest to the problems at hand. They do not always make the right decisions, but even their failures provide vital information to future entrepreneurs, and certainly no government agency can do a better job. My point is that specific commands hinder the entrepreneurial process. Resources are used less productively, and new jobs are *not created*. Unfortunately, no one can point to a *specific* unemployed person and say he or she is out of a job because of affirmative action legislation or family leave legislation. But any good economist can explain the relation of cause and effect.

Breaking the Rules

OK, you may say, but at least these specific commands have created social and cultural change. Oh, yes, change which has increased tension between the sexes and which, to some degree, is partly responsible for the breakdown of marriages. Domestic violence is with us in full force. These are the kinds of consequences that arise from favoring expediency over principle, from breaking down the *general rules* of a free society.

Women have made progress. However, that progress is the result of a cultural revolution that came about in spite of much government legislation. It began when the early feminists demanded equality under the law. Once women were on the same playing field as men, were allowed to play by the same rules, we began to make progress. It is those *general rules* and *free markets* that have created the kinds of cultural change favoring, in Professor Mises' words, *"peaceful and free evolution."*

So now we come to specifics. How do free markets break down discriminatory barriers for women and promote peaceful cultural change?

The Cost of Discrimination

First, discrimination against women in labor markets will decrease when it is in an entrepreneur's best interest. Discrimination on the basis of sex can be costly. Consider an instance of sexism in its purest form, i.e., as economist Thomas Sowell explains, "where people are treated differently because of group membership as such." If a firm decides that it will only hire men, for example, the firm must spend more time searching for qualified applicants who also must be men. The added search for men can be very costly, especially if there are very few qualified people in the relevant labor market. The discriminating firm can then face additional costs. In order to attract the few qualified persons to the firm who are men, it must pay them relatively higher wages. If other firms do not discriminate on the basis of sex, their labor pools are larger. They will not have to offer such high wages in order to attract qualified persons to their firms. Consequently, the discriminating employer faces higher costs in two ways: through longer and more extensive searches, the costs of which also include lost productivity, and through effectively decreasing the available (i.e., acceptable) labor supply, driving up the wages that the employer must pay.

Since firms only survive in markets if they make monetary profits, discriminating firms with higher costs will be at a competitive disadvantage and will have either to stop the discriminating behavior to remain competitive or lose profitability and perhaps even close their doors. In this way, competition in markets can, at times, decrease pure discrimination. However, the less competitive a market is, the more likely a discriminating employer will be able to bear the costs of discrimination. For instance, in industries where there are legal restrictions to entry or in government-operated firms and nonprofit organizations, discrimination is more likely to persist. Nonprofit or government-operated firms are not subject to competitive forces in the sense that they do not have to make a profit to survive. In essence, in many cases they can afford to discriminate when firms faced with more productive competitors cannot.

Third Party Discrimination

In some cases, third parties can be the real cause of employer discrimination. For example, customers or existing employees can insist that certain categories of potential employee be eliminated from consideration. In some cases, it can be economically desirable to discriminate. However, the market in some instances can also diminish third party discrimination. Customer discrimination, for example, can be reduced if customers do not have direct contact with all employees. Customers cannot push their preferences on an entire firm without assuming considerable costs. When one buys a loaf of bread, one does not usually ask the cashier if a woman or man baked it.

Discrimination Perceived as Cost Reducing

Turn now to a case where an employer may discriminate on the basis of a group characteristic. This is sometimes known as statistical discrimination. For example, women may be seen as less productive than men because, on average, they have higher turnover rates and are more likely to take leaves of absence than are men. Therefore, an employer may refuse to hire specific women because all women are perceived to be, on average, less productive.

Whether the characteristics are real or falsely perceived is important. As I have argued, if the perception regarding the group average is incorrect, competitive forces will tend to punish discriminating employers. However, if the perception is correct, women who fall in the upper range of the scale, i.e., those who are more productive than the average woman, will be punished because of their sex. Employers may decide to discriminate because the costs of screening individual women to discover if they fall in the upper range of the distribution will outweigh the estimated benefits of finding them.

On the other hand, most employers would rather screen individual employees and hire the most productive in any group. In essence, then, employers face a knowledge problem regarding which employees to hire. They must trade off the cost of screening individual employees against the cost of missing out on hiring very productive workers. This is why firms, indeed market forces, have come up with different ways to screen employees at lower costs. Employers use employment agencies, interviews, references, a variety of tests such as aptitude or skill level tests, and they look for brand names in the educational and vocational institutions which potential employees attended. All these devices decrease screening costs for employers and thereby increase the likelihood that potential employees will be hired on the basis of their individual attributes rather than on the basis of their group membership. . . .

Employment Contracts

Lastly, the employment contract itself is an important source of information for employers who are willing to hire from any group of employees, as long as they can in some way determine individual merit prior to employment. This can be especially important for women, who may be seen as less productive than men because of their biological ability to give birth. Through individual contract terms a woman can assure an employer that she will not leave the job within a specific period of time, will not ask for an extended leave if she does choose to have a child, and so on. In other words, she can legally promise the employer that she will take full responsibility for her personal choices and will not expect the employer's costs to increase because of those choices. In this way, women who have chosen to make their market career their top priority can signal that fact to employers and be judged on their individual merits. The freedom to make creative, individualized employment contracts can be a very important source of information to employers and it can thereby decrease discrimination.

When I once explained this theory to a reporter, her reply was, "But doesn't this put a lot of responsibility upon women?" And the answer is yes. If women want cultural change, they have to be the driving force behind it, they have to stop turning to the state, and they have to stop trying to force men to change. Freedom calls for individual responsibility. I am in complete agreement with Camille Paglia here. As she says, "This is my belief, that feminism begins at home. It begins with every single woman drawing the line."

I do want to note that there are other ways discrimination can be overcome in free markets. When wages are free to vary as the market sees fit, discriminatory practices can be broken down. If an employer is faced with hiring a highly skilled male employee or a less skilled female employee, an employer can be induced to hire the less skilled woman if the difference in the wage rates between the two workers justifies the difference in productivity. Two important points must follow. First, if the perception regarding the skill or productivity level is correct, then hiring the less skilled woman enables her to gain valuable experience and skills, increasing her market value and wage rate over time. Second, if the perception of productivity is incorrect, hiring a woman over an equally productive male at a relatively lower wage rate allows the woman to obtain the job and prove her productivity, thereby also allowing her to increase her wage over time—sometimes almost immediately upon discovery that the employer's perception was incorrect. . . .

Markets and Families

Besides decreasing undesirable discrimination over time, there is a second way free markets produce positive change. As I have argued, free markets lead to real job creation and a strong economy in general. And a strong economy translates into more choices, including the choice *not* to enter the workforce when support of the family requires only one working spouse. So, for those of you who think I have forgotten the women and men who do the most difficult work in the world—building a loving home and raising decent children—I have not. Free markets are good for all women and men because they allow greater choice. This is what feminism is all about. Feminism should not only address choices in the workforce, it should address choices about lifestyles. In this way, free markets are good for men and children too. I am convinced that if left alone, the creative forces of the market would generate a variety of positive responses enabling men and women to juggle careers and child-rearing.

And finally, free markets create positive cultural change, change which takes place slowly and from inside the social system. Markets create change through the free choices and mutual give-and-take occurring between men and women.

> *"It is time to retrieve our critique of capitalism and reassert the goal of economic justice as an explicit part of feminism."*

Feminism Should Promote Socialism

Ann Froines

Ann Froines teaches women's studies at the University of Massachusetts, Boston. In the following viewpoint, Froines describes socialist feminism and explains why feminists should once again work for a socialist society in the United States. Women are oppressed both economically and because of their gender, Froines contends. Because of this, feminists must combine socialism and feminism to fight class and gender oppression.

As you read, consider the following questions:

1. How did socialist feminists attempt to bridge the gap between white, middle-class feminists and poor women of color in the 1980s, according to the author?
2. What insights concerning women and work have socialist feminists formulated, according to Froines?
3. What aspects of Cuban society does the author admire?

Ann Froines, "Renewing Socialist Feminism," *Socialist Review* 92:4, pp. 125-31. Copyright Duke University Press, 1992. Reprinted with permission.

Recent socialist feminist analysis has tended to acknowledge social class difference primarily as one aspect of diversity, with an emphasis on understanding and appreciating class diversity, rather than analyzing the social and economic injustices of class difference. Yet what was distinctive about socialist feminist thought as it developed in the 1960s and 1970s was precisely the linking of social and economic class difference to a critique of capitalism as a whole, not as an abstraction, but as it exists today, in the world. This capitalism has created a world economic order that enriches the North (United States, Western Europe, and now Japan) at the expense of the South (Asia, Africa, and Latin America) and now perhaps Eastern Europe and the independent states of the former USSR. This capitalism relies increasingly on the global wage labor of women.

The decline or fall of socialist states worldwide and the inadequacy of socialist theory's analysis of gender inequality notwithstanding, I believe it is time to retrieve our critique of capitalism and reassert the goal of economic justice as an explicit part of feminism. Socialist feminism's critique of capitalism was based on an analysis of the relationship between women's work and women's liberation. The exploitation of women's labor power was a central concept. That analysis is still viable.

The History of Socialist Feminism

Attempts to establish socialist feminist women's organizations ended by 1980, and socialist feminist activism as such largely became socialist feminist theorizing in university Women's Studies programs. Yet socialist feminist activists remained in both left and feminist politics and, as several scholars have documented, have had a significant impact on the politics of women's issues in both settings.

Since the history of socialist feminism is a history of groups and tendencies rather than national organizations and agendas, a brief review of socialist feminism's place in women's activism over the last twenty years will help to demonstrate the importance of a new socialist feminist project. Many feminists who identify themselves as socialist feminists (myself among them) have been active in women's studies programs in academic institutions, labor organizing, antiwar and anti-intervention work, reproductive rights, and gay rights struggles. Moving beyond a heartfelt but naively one-dimensional view of sisterhood in the women's movement, in recent years we have explored, in a variety of forums, the reality of "difference" among women. We have struggled with the difficulties of creating a political activism that would transcend or better yet *utilize* difference. Socialist feminist thought is not an abstraction for us, but still guides decisions about, for example, how inclusive we need to be in creating a

173

syllabus, or in which women's groups we will participate. Some of us have been activists in trade unions and have represented women's concerns in that context. Women of color also identify with socialist traditions and theory as a solution to the quest for economic justice, but may identify primarily as African-American, or Latina, or Asian feminists, or community activists. I remember, however, that in the early years of the second wave of the women's movement in the United States—well before our current comprehensive discussions about inclusiveness—economic issues, as much as race and culture, separated white feminists from women of color and working-class women. Many of us in feminist organizations were middle-class, and articulated issues in a manner that made other women perceive feminism as a middle-class movement.

Helping the Poor

Socialist feminists responded to the perspectives of working-class women and women of color. We helped to broaden the goals of reproductive rights organizations to include the right to have children (by ending sterilization abuse) as well as the right to abortion. In the 1980s, national and local women's groups focused on women's and children's poverty in response to Reagan's attacks on the welfare state, and some feminist groups supported coalitions to restore lost welfare benefits for low-income families. The many obstacles to the participation of low-income women in women's organizations as presently constituted, however, meant that contact between low- and middle-income women was often transitory. And even though we are reminded every day, in a myriad of ways, that an economic system that cannot provide for basic needs certainly cannot foster the liberation of women, somehow issues concerning poverty, or the conflict between women's work in the family and in the labor force, did not keep pace, in our theoretical debates, with discussions of violence, reproductive autonomy, and the meaning of equality.

Socialist feminist insights about women's work remain dynamic concepts, inextricably linked to other issues of women's survival. These insights were precisely the underpinnings of early revelations which led to the formation of an autonomous women's movement: women wanted to move in the world of work, of public power, which was dominated by men, even as we envisioned transforming this male-dominated world we were entering. We rejected definitions of ourselves as primary sexual beings who, as adults, would inevitably fulfill our "main" purpose in life—motherhood. We did not, however, reject motherhood itself, and demanded that women's work in the home, though unpaid, be recognized as real work.

The theoretical formulations that followed from these insights include: (1) the vast majority of the women in the world must work in order to provide for themselves and their families; therefore, feminist theory must address fundamental economic issues of women and men in society; (2) there is a sexual division of labor both in production and consumption; (3) domestic labor—housework and childrearing—is socially useful work, and helps reproduce society (whether capitalist or socialist); (4) the patriarchal state has replaced many of the functions of the patriarchal family; (5) male supremacy exists in socialist as well as in capitalist societies.

Considering Diversity

Although classical socialist theory may not sufficiently recognize the place of race and gender in economic class relations, it doesn't follow from this that socialist feminist theory is inadequate to the task of theorizing about these issues. A socialist feminist perspective means paying consistent attention to women *in our capacity as workers,* and in all our variety. Zillah Eisenstein's *Socialist Review* article, "Specifying U.S. Feminisms in the Nineties: the Problem of Naming," is a good starting point for an exploration of socialist feminist thought in relation to the need for a new specificity in discussing women. Eisenstein develops the example of the "pregnant woman of color" as a more inclusive category of diversity. She argues that this "pregnant woman of color" lacks access to reproductive choice, so that even with the advance of reproductive rights she remains a "transcendent case of female need." The question then arises: how do we describe and analyze the relationship between the economic status of this woman and the economic organization of the society in which she lives?

Eisenstein's transcendent case of female need is incomplete unless we add "working" to "pregnant woman of color." As women have the capacity and right to reproduce, so do we have the capacity and the right to work, to have employment that sustains our physical, intellectual, and (dare we hope) spiritual needs. Work is required in this picture not only because women have to be able to feed ourselves and our children, but because we cannot imagine a society without work. To lose from our ethical vision of a just society the goal of a fair distribution of economic wealth, of employment for all, means a very narrow vision indeed, one which does not square with women's historical struggles or contemporary expectations.

The Basic Requirements of a Socialist Vision

The "working pregnant woman of color" requires access to an affordable quality health care center that offers counseling about birth control and pregnancy and provides both abortion services and good prenatal care. A socialist feminist agenda would include universal health care as a basic right available to all, thus addressing the problem of "access." Similarly, the "working pregnant woman of color" requires paid maternity leave, and the prospect of decent child care when she is ready to return to work. And of course, whether she is working in the labor force or receiving community-provided benefits for herself and her children, her level of existence should be a minimally comfortable standard of living, not one below a designated poverty line.

America's Classist Society Must Be Challenged

Women's oppression is integral to capitalism. This is why, despite the real reforms won by the last women's movement, so little has changed 20 years later. But, unfortunately, the last women's movement never aimed to transform society. The bulk of the women's movement was based upon the aspirations of middle-class women, which didn't attempt to challenge the class basis of society.

Sharon Smith, *Socialist Worker*, August 1992.

These have been the basic components of a socialist feminist vision for most of the twentieth century. The fact that socialist states failed to realize the vision of women's liberation—true equality and parity with men in the areas of employment and family life—does not render that vision invalid. In fact, there are things to be learned from some socialist societies where the state attempts to guarantee a minimal standard of living with extensive social welfare systems. We can learn from analyzing our responses to these experiences.

In the former German Democratic Republic, approximately 80 percent of pre-school-age children attended state-subsidized child care centers while their mothers worked full time. Socialist feminists in North America have been critical of the lack of state attention to the "double day" burden of women, sometimes even labeling child care services as a device to more fully exploit the labor of women. We are right to be critical, but we must address the underlying issues of the double day of women without undermining our support for publicly subsidized child care.

The Benefits of Cuban Socialism

Socialist Cuba has made a fundamental commitment to health care and education for all, and this strategy has benefited everyone. Cuba's health care system is regularly commended by international agencies as one of the best in the western hemisphere.

By the standard of health care for all, it is among the best in the world. The Cuban government also subsidizes child care for working families, though, as a poor country, not as extensively as the former GDR. Women are also entitled to paid maternity leave, and then subsequent leaves, though generally unpaid, if a child is sick. In Cuba today, there exists a net of social security that greatly reduces both the fears of parents about the future of their children, and the fear of growing old. Unfortunately, since 1989, economic dislocations in Cuba—due to events in Eastern Europe and the former USSR—have created unemployment and shortages of basic goods, which cannot help but undermine the population's sense of well-being, and threatens to force a reduction of funding for vital social services.

During a trip to Cuba in 1991, I discovered how Cuban work organizations must sometimes struggle to cope with the guaranteed maternity leaves and parental leaves to care for sick children. For example, professors at a pedagogical institute have to fill in for the female professor who has missed one month of classes due to her child's serious illness. Sometimes the father takes the leave if the mother is, for example, a doctor, or a high-level administrator. The assumption seems to be that the workplace has to adjust to fit family needs, not merely the other way around. Several professional women, however, pointed out to me that managers sometimes ask about a woman's family circumstances before they make hiring or promotion decisions, in part because they are inclined to believe that family responsibilities will affect a woman's work performance. This practice is illegal according to the Cuban constitution, but old attitudes take a long time to change. Some problems endure. But imagine how essential and reassuring these policies are for the many single working women and divorced mothers in Cuba: Their jobs will be there for them when they return from leave.

Women in Cuba acknowledge the need for entrenched ideas of male supremacy to change more rapidly, in accord with the dramatic improvements in the economic and legal status of women. I discuss these examples not because they are models for the United States necessarily, but because they demonstrate that policies emanating from a socialist vision can offer more equitable, rational, and democratic solutions to the pressing needs of women.

Class and Gender

Eisenstein argues, correctly, that socialist thinking has to "reinvent" the meaning of equality to include gender. Is it not equally appropriate to argue that feminist theory must reinvent the meaning of women's liberation to include access to a decent standard of living and meaningful work? This is not simply an

177

ideological requirement, but a human necessity, like living without fear of violence. We know that to debate which is more basic—class oppression or gender oppression—is a dead end. A socialist feminist analysis must keep them together.

Rather than abandon the socialist feminist project as an outmoded remnant of a passing historical era, I would like to see us find a way to reinvigorate our discussions of strategy *within* a socialist feminist framework. First, those of us who have become primarily scholars or teachers would have to find a way to reduce the distance between ourselves and women activists who share our perspectives. To talk about developing "strategy" implies making a commitment to activism of some kind. Some questions by which we might begin to renew our discussions include: (1) what are the possible points of solidarity among working women in the United States, and where do we (as professionals, service workers, or grass roots activists) "fit" in a working women's movement?; (2) could an organization of socialist feminists develop some direction which might help all progressive women's organizations unite around a national program of health care, housing, and welfare?; and (3) what will be the role of socialist feminists in the effort to develop a third party in the United States?

With these questions, I anticipate women activists sighing with exhaustion. How can we expect women's organizations, many of them continually struggling for their very existence, to embrace the universal demands of health care, employment rights, and a minimum standard of living? Organizations that focus on defending the right to abortion and reproductive autonomy may lack the resources to join the campaign for universal health care through a national health insurance program, for example. But any women's organization could start by endorsing this goal at every opportunity, and by attempting to work in coalition with senior citizens, trade unions, and other organizations which support a more socialist program for health care.

The socialist feminist vision is more successful than any other in addressing simultaneously and comprehensively social and economic injustice based on gender, class, and race. Though we may be uncertain about how to promote socialist feminism as an organizing agenda in these times, it is difficult to imagine getting up in the morning without the motivating power of its vision.

"The cultural agenda of feminism . . . has always been to encourage women to fulfill themselves as individuals."

Feminism Should Focus on the Rights of the Individual

Joan Kennedy Taylor

Individualism is the theory that the rights of the individual in society are paramount, and that only when these rights are secured and government involvement in people's lives is reduced are the rights of all people protected. In the following viewpoint, Joan Kennedy Taylor argues that early feminists believed in individualism. Unfortunately, she states, feminism has strayed from this belief and has embraced collectivism and government involvement as the answers to women's oppression. Taylor contends that feminism must reclaim its support of individual rights if all women are to prosper. Taylor, the national coordinator of the Association of Libertarian Feminists, is the author of the book *Reclaiming the Mainstream: Individualist Feminism Rediscovered*, from which this viewpoint is excerpted.

As you read, consider the following questions:

1. How does Taylor respond to the argument that individualism means "rampant egoism"?
2. How does individualism relate to cooperation and association, according to the author?
3. Why does Taylor oppose the idea of feminists creating special-interest groups?

From: Joan Kennedy Taylor, *Reclaiming the Mainstream: Individualist Feminism Rediscovered* (pp. 9-13, 233-35, 241-43). Copyright ©1992 by Joan Kennedy Taylor. Reprinted by permission of the publisher, Prometheus Books.

This is the age of feminism—or of post-feminism, depending on which issue of the *New York Times Magazine* you read. So obviously, since it has been so prominent, so important, so influential in our current society, we all know what it is. Or do we?

I am a believer in individualism and individual rights; in entrepreneurship and free enterprise; in civil liberties and minimal government. And I am a feminist. Does that surprise anyone? I am convinced that there are many people who would basically agree with me if they didn't have a soundbite image of what feminism entails.

What we now call "feminism" began early in the nineteenth century as an individualist movement, and it is this individualism that has been the defining characteristic of the mainstream of that movement ever since. This does not mean that individualism has always predominated. Since the early days of the movement, there have been two philosophical strands of thought within it: individualism and collectivism, and from time to time one or the other strand has become dominant. When the collectivists predominate, the individualists become less active and return to cultivating their gardens.

Individualism and Collectivism

We have all been brought up in an era of big, powerful government, in which being "law-abiding" doesn't just mean refraining from theft and murder but may require such positive actions as wearing seat belts, cutting one's hedge if it exceeds a certain height, or separating one's trash. And society is also exacting in nonlegal ways. Too much "individualism" is not necessarily seen as a good thing today. It may be viewed as antisocial, since it is sometimes taken to imply antagonism to the interests of others or even the sacrifice of others to the self.

Western culture assumes the importance of the individual even when societies endorse political programs that may downgrade or jeopardize individual rights (the "war on drugs" comes to mind as an example). It may therefore seem to be tautological to say that feminism is individualistic. But in recent years there have been attacks on that very aspect of feminism. For instance, Sylvia Ann Hewlett's 1986 book, *A Lesser Life*, criticized American feminism's emphasis on consciousness raising, reproductive rights, and equality before the law on precisely that ground. In 1991 Emory University professor Elizabeth Fox-Genovese called her book *Feminism Without Illusions: A Critique of Individualism*, and she describes her thesis thus:

> This book offers a critique of feminism's complicity in and acceptance of individualism. . . . Throughout, I am using "individualism" to mean the systematic theory of politics, society, economics, and epistemology that emerged following the

Renaissance, that was consolidated in the great English, American, French, and Haitian revolutions of the seventeenth and eighteenth centuries, and that has found its purest logical outcome in the laissez-faire doctrines of neoclassical economics and libertarian political theory. The political triumph of individualism has led to its hegemony as *the* theory of human nature and rights, according to which, rights, including political sovereignty, are grounded in the individual and can only be infringed upon by the state in extraordinary circumstances.

. . . Here I am arguing that individualism actually perverts the idea of the socially obligated and personally responsible freedom that constitutes the only freedom worthy of the name or indeed historically possible.

She goes on to suggest that individual rights should be seen as deriving from the community rather than as being "prior" to the claims of society. This she sees as a necessary underpinning for laws—her immediate example is laws against pornography—"that recognize liberties as interdependent and as inseparable from social responsibility." When you speak of community in this way, you are downgrading the importance of individual legal rights.

The Importance of the Individual

But community remains important. The seeming contradiction that the individualist-centered women's movement keeps foundering on is the tension between the concepts of the individual and of the group. If you believe in the importance of the individual, does that mean you deny any importance to groups to which the individual belongs? Or, on the other hand, is group identification more important than individuality? As Elizabeth Fox-Genovese asked, which is prior? Do you view each individual as empowering the group by entering it, or do you view the group as bestowing rights that it can then take back?

The consistent individualist holds that the individual is the basic unit. An individual joins with others in various ways to achieve goals. An individual does not receive identity by being a member of a group. Nor should an individual's political and legal rights be decided by being born into a group.

When the group being referred to is the state, there is a real tension between it and its individual members because the state can use the force of law to require the behavior it wants from its members. It can draft people, jail people, outlaw their livelihoods. Individuals can try to take over the power of the state for their own purposes, to force *other* people to behave in a certain way, but that always has unexpected consequences—the Prohibitionists didn't intend to foster the rise of mob gangsters or the social tolerance of public drunkenness, especially in women. Nongovernmental groups have less power than governments have, but they also can try to control by coercion.

181

When the group being referred to is a free association of people with a common goal uniting to achieve that goal, the group acts as an extension of its individual members and is no contradiction to individualism. A group formed by individual choices nourishes the individual—in fact, human nature is such that many life-serving goals can only be reached by people willing to act in concert. So the accusation that individualism means rampant and fragmented egoism is a misunderstanding of what individualism entails. Individuals need chosen groups of all sorts, and the existence of a multiplicity of such groups almost necessarily works to increase choices.

Individualism Helps Women Meet Their Goals

The individualist impulse brings women together. This is no paradox—once individuals set goals, they often find that supporting each other and taking joint action is necessary to achieve their goals.

Joan Kennedy Taylor, *Reclaiming the Mainstream*, 1992.

A number of women activists over the years have put their primary emphasis on the liberty of the individual and on the individual's freedom to make choices. Many of them have also felt that women could best be emancipated through various forms of communal action or communal living, which they sometimes thought of as utopian socialism, or "collectivism." That is not what I mean by collectivism. The real form of collectivism—of coercively subordinating and submerging the individual in the identity of the collective and looking at the individual only as a group member—has been present in some aspects of the women's movement, from the nineteenth-century days of social purity to contemporary Marxist feminism.

Classical Liberalism

It is, however, the individualist strand of feminism that has always reached a wider audience. My political view is the view called by some today "libertarian" or, more historically and formally, "classical liberal," but not many feminists since the actual classical liberal days in the eighteenth and nineteenth centuries share that view. So when I say that both the nineteenth-century Woman Movement (as it was called then) and the twentieth-century feminist movement are mainly individualist movements, I do not mean to imply that their members always, or even often, share my suspicion of the use of government power. I mean that they emphasize the importance of the individual woman's rights and happiness, even though they may think that this can be combined with some form of state power to enforce the policies they advocate.

Although I consider myself to be an adherent of classical liberalism, this [viewpoint] is not about classical liberalism or libertarianism. It is not about how libertarianism applies to women, or how all feminists should embrace the libertarian philosophy *in toto*. Rather, since I do not see feminism as a purely political philosophy or movement, my [view] has to do with the companion tradition of individualism in this country—understood to mean a tradition that holds it important to support the full flowering of the individual life. . . .

A Retreat from Feminism

Individualists are not speaking out in the name of feminism. In America today, uncounted numbers of women who would have been feminists like the abolitionist women or like the early twentieth-century feminists are not claiming to be feminists. On the contrary, they often look on many of the feminists they meet as bitter, as unhappy, as narrow. These women, like their predecessors, know they can do anything, try to do it, and want not to be hampered by state and society while they are trying. And there are men who would like to help such women.

One such man wrote a letter to the editor that was published in the *New York Times* in December of 1985. He claimed that the definition of a feminist as "a person who advocates the same rights for women as for men" is "exhaustive" and that he felt an article by a feminist the previous month excluded feminists who were conservative Republicans, or conservative Democrats, as well as all the women who had voted for Reagan, because the article "offers a platform only for women (and men) who embrace the philosophy of the liberal wing of the Democratic Party." But he insisted he is still a feminist. He concluded by saying, "The women's movement will start moving again only when it escapes the bondage of its liberal baggage and strives to unite both conservatives and liberals in the important but limited fight against a common enemy: the remaining barriers to true equality between women and men."

As for a nonfeminist who honors this individualist tradition of feminism, take Midge Decter, one of the most vocal critics of contemporary feminism. She wrote in a *Policy Review* article, "The Intelligent Woman's Guide to Feminism,"

Feminism properly understood is a view summed up in the simple proposition that women are the equals of men; that they are as intelligent, as competent, as brave, and above all, as morally responsible. It was this proposition, for example, that earlier in the century secured for women the right to vote, to educate themselves, to have and to spend their own money, and in general, to take upon themselves a share of the burden of civic responsibility. . . .

When I read "The Intelligent Woman's Guide to Feminism," . . . its positive vision of "feminism properly understood" was inspiring. It was my vision of what feminism has been in my life, and I wondered why anyone would settle for anything less. We feminists who believe in the inspiring history and classical liberal mainstream of American feminism should not give up our claim to the name *feminist*, any more than institutions supporting limited government should give up their claim to the name *liberal*. . . .

The Past as Vision of the Future

The political agenda of feminism has been to protest and try to change the respects in which the law has subjected women as a class to society and, at times, required the subjection of individual women to individual men. The cultural agenda of feminism has changed over the years, but it has always been to encourage women to fulfill themselves as individuals, whether this be through occupation, avocation, or relationship. The selective emphasis given each of these areas has, of course, shifted in different periods, depending on the climate of the time.

What I would like to see is a feminist movement that is more self-consciously individualistic, but also understands that individual action includes cooperation and association, which doesn't tie feminism to positive government programs but to taking action together to solve problems. If, like Suzanne LaFollette and Jean Bethke Elshtain, we don't feel it is helpful to consider government "Mr. Right" and if, like Betty Friedan, we think the only way to achieve the institutions we want is by a "passionate volunteerism," then we will have to rely on ourselves and on each other. Because we still need to expand our own options, to make our lives a little easier, to learn even more to help each other.

The classical liberal has moral objections to using government power to impose change on people by force. But there are also practical objections—no one knows what will work and what won't. Even the spontaneous changes that affected American women so profoundly since the 1960s brought problems that no one could have predicted. I've quoted Betty Friedan in 1963 saying that it would be no big deal for women to combine motherhood and work—and in 1981 saying that how to achieve such a combination happily was the problem of the second stage of feminism. Some people have felt that this was an indication that she was being revisionist or a turncoat, but the plain fact is, *she didn't know*, in 1963. Many women have complained that they weren't warned in advance of how complex their lives were going to become—but no one knew how hard it was going to be for women to change their lives. If women had then, in the late sixties, the unlimited political power to put into effect any government programs they wanted, no one would have known what government programs to design.

Gaining Power Is Not the Answer

There's another reason to stick to the original vision of feminism, instead of adopting one or another version of social feminism. Who is really inspired to join a movement to be a special interest? To seize the power of government and use it to create a spoils system to reward our own group? The only argument that can remotely justify such actions on moral grounds is the argument of past victimization, and that is not only a very specious argument, but a personally destructive one.

The ERA [Equal Rights Amendment] was lost when the women supporting it turned away from the vision of equal rights to a search for political dominance; to get a large enough voting bloc to wrest privileges from society. Do we really want to go from a subordinate to a dominant legal position? To get legislation to try to make the taxpayers in general make our domestic lives easier with child allowances and subsidized day care? Despite the blandishments of some government-enamored feminists, people in the welfare democracies of Europe are not happier than people here. They think they like their benefits, but they have to work very hard to pay for these supposedly "free" advantages. And now they are faced with changes and cuts, with no lessening of the work or the taxes, as these states, too, run out of money. This is a self-defeating and ultimately puny vision of democracy as a way of using the vote to get things from others. Our heritage is grander than that.

In her last public address, in 1892, "The Solitude of the Self," Elizabeth Cady Stanton said that the strongest reason for all the reforms to benefit woman that she had spent her life advocating—access to higher education; a voice in government, religion, and social life; the right to earn a living—was because of "her birthright of self-sovereignty; because, as an individual, she must rely on herself. . . . Seeing then, that life must ever be a march and a battle, that each soldier must be equipped for his own protection, it is the height of cruelty to rob the individual of a single natural right."

An internally contradictory view of liberty will not work. We have to choose between trying to build a special interest group, out for our own aggrandizement, and this view of the importance of rights. In a review of a collection of the correspondence, writings, and speeches of Elizabeth Cady Stanton and Susan B. Anthony, Vivian Gornick wrote, "The subject of Stanton's lifelong speculation was the nature and meaning of natural rights—women's rights was a euphemism—and her thinking took her

185

ever more inward, to the psychological heart of the matter."

It is that psychological heart of the matter that we are still discovering. We have to give up the idea that we can force others, either personally or by using the power of government, to treat us as we would wish. Instead, we have to live our lives as equal citizens of the world, establishing our networks of relationship, our ways to earn a living, our values, and our goals, by relying on ourselves and each other. There's a lot we don't know. We don't know how alike, or different, men and women really are. We don't know how to solve all the problems of living together and bringing up children. We don't know what institutions we really need to form or how to solve the problems of the inner cities, or the homeless, or the environment.

We do know that the idea of equal rights is a very powerful engine and that if enough individuals are inspired by it to transform their lives, they can make unforeseen changes together that will change a lot of their world. Feminists have done that, over the last thirty years. Some of the changes have been wonderful, and some have been hard. But we don't have to stop changing. Individuals inspired by a grand, idealistic tradition to link together in a community can do remarkable things.

"*Feminism has absorbed aspects of individualism,
which . . . it must resolutely oppose.* "

Feminism Should Not Focus on the Rights of the Individual

Elizabeth Fox-Genovese

In the past, feminism has focused on attaining specific individual
rights, such as the right to abortion and the right to job opportunities. In the following viewpoint, Elizabeth Fox-Genovese argues
that this focus has harmed women as a group and society as a
whole. Rather than trying to attain specific individual rights, she
says, feminism should work at creating a sense of community
among women and addressing social injustice. Fox-Genovese is
Eleonore Raoul Professor of the Humanities, professor of history,
and director of women's studies at Emory University in Atlanta.
She is the author of the book *Feminism Without Illusions: A
Critique of Individualism*, from which this viewpoint is excerpted.

As you read, consider the following questions:

1. What disagreements exist concerning the definition of
   "feminism," in the author's opinion?
2. What does Fox-Genovese mean by "individualism"? How has
   it harmed society, in her opinion?
3. What is the significance of the differences between different
   women and between women and men, according to the
   author?

Feminism enjoys a poor to middling press these days, among many women as well as men. One of my undergraduates at Emory University captured this unease in a paper she wrote for a Women's Studies course. When she had begun the course, feminism to her "meant the denial of femininity and womanhood. It suggested lesbianism. It led to 'bra burnings,' menhating, and an almost irritating aggressiveness." She has not been alone in her associations. To many women, feminism even betokens the destruction of family values and the defiance of divine and natural order. In the time-honored tradition of blaming the victims of injustice and those who protested against it for the consequences of injustice itself, some women and too many men find it easy to blame feminism for some of the most disturbing aspects of modern life: divorce, latch-key children, teenage alcoholism, domestic violence, the sexual abuse of children. From that indictment only a few short steps are required to arrive at an indictment of feminism for the collapse of academic standards and the decline of Western civilization. Many young women simply consider feminism outmoded—a relic of former times that no longer constructively affects their lives.

Feminists reply that only our vigilance protects and improves women's hard-won and still-precarious place in work and politics. Yet even those who call themselves feminists frequently disagree about the meaning and implications of feminism. For some, feminism articulates women's rights as individuals and as women, women's needs as parents, and women's opportunities as workers. Others insist upon the radical implications of women's experience for society as a whole, arguing that women speak "in a different voice" than men; have different "ways of knowing" than men; would, if given power, order the world more humanely than men. Some hold that justice can obliterate, or radically minimize, the differences between women and men. Others hold that those differences are fundamental and that our ideals of justice should be rewritten to take account of women's experience. Still others dismiss the very idea of difference as the product of invidious and hierarchical dichotomies that should be replaced by an appreciation of diversity.

A Reflection of Changes in Society

The differences over the meaning of feminism reflect the larger confusion of our times. Less the cause of the unsettling changes in our world than their symptom, feminism embodies a variety of dissatisfactions with things-as-they-are and a variety of visions about how they could be improved. Above all, feminism represents different attempts to come to terms with women's changing position in American society, particularly the economy. . . .

The question remains: What do we want for our daughters,

our students, the young women for whom we feel responsible? As the director of a Women's Studies program, I live with that question. As one who sees herself as temperamentally and culturally conservative, I harbor no consuming desire to turn the world upside down and by no means subscribe to all that is advanced in the name of feminism. But I am convinced that (1) the changes of which feminism is a symptom will not be reversed; (2) feminism is having a broad and profound impact on our society and our ways of thinking; (3) young women must be trained to support themselves, preferably by work that draws upon their talents and enhances their self-respect. . . .

The Supreme Court's recent *Webster* decision, which limited women's access to abortion and raised the possibility that *Roe* v. *Wade* might yet be reversed, is engaging the imagination of young women, who fear the implications for themselves, although that engagement does not guarantee their adherence to a broader feminist program, much less their concern with the problems of women of other classes and races. The fight for women's "right" to choice in the matter of abortion is being misguidedly waged in the name of women's absolute right to their own bodies and, ironically, on the grounds of reproduction as a private matter. It qualifies as ironical since so much feminist energy has been devoted to an insistence that familial relations are not private matters, that "the personal is political," and that women cannot, in justice, be excluded from the public business of society. But the fight over abortion is being waged more in the name of women's sexuality than in the name of their reproductive capacities. That confusion alone indicates the extent to which feminism has absorbed aspects of individualism, which, to be coherent, it must resolutely oppose.

The Dominance of Individualism

This [viewpoint] offers a critique of feminism's complicity in and acceptance of individualism—or rather of its contemporary atomized version that replaces the early and glorious recognition of the claims of the individual against the state with the celebration of egotism and the denial or indefensible reduction of the just claims of the community. Throughout, I am using "individualism" to mean the systematic theory of politics, society, economics, and epistemology that emerged following the Renaissance, that was consolidated in the great English, American, French, and Haitian revolutions of the seventeenth and eighteenth centuries, and that has found its purest logical outcome in the laissez-faire doctrines of neoclassical economics and libertarian political theory. The political triumph of individualism has led to its hegemony as *the* theory of human nature and rights, according to which, rights, including political sovereignty, are grounded in the individual and can only be infringed upon by the state in extraordinary circumstances.

That hegemony has proved so powerful that most of us intuitively associate individualism with the defense of individual freedom, our highest value. Here I am arguing that individualism actually perverts the idea of the socially obligated and personally responsible freedom that constitutes the only freedom worthy of the name or indeed historically possible. Theoretically, individualism does not contain the possibility of establishing necessary limits on the will of the individual, on what Nietzsche called the "will to power." The problem lies at the heart of every modern discussion of democracy since Rousseau: What can be the relation between the will of the individual and the will of the majority? Theorists of individualism have not, in fact, arrived at a better definition of the social good than the individualistic notion that what more people want must be accepted as better. In practice, modern individualistic societies have significantly curtailed individual right in the name of the public good, but they have done so apologetically, defensively, not on the grounds of the prior rights of the collectivity. (To be sure, socialist societies have proclaimed the priority of society in a way that has stifled the just claims of the individual, but that deeply disquieting problem lies well beyond the scope of this [viewpoint] and is today being recast by events with unpredictable consequences.) Western societies, in any case, have, as some conservative and feminist critics are beginning to argue, failed to develop a notion of individual right as the product of collective life rather than its justification.

The Failures of Individualism

The defense of individual freedom has properly prompted the most generous aspects of our national tradition, which includes the abolition of slavery and the growing recognition of women's rights. But we have had difficulty in separating the defense of individual freedom from the basic premise of individualism, namely that rights derive from the individual's innate being. The origins of the confusion lie in the theory of the social contract, dear to seventeenth- and eighteenth-century political theorists, according to which individual right derives from nature and, accordingly, precedes any form of social organization. The political institutions built on this theory did not, initially, expose the radicalism of the concept, if only because they did not acknowledge all people as individuals. Excluding propertyless men, slaves, and women from political participation, they perpetuated the illusion that individualism and collective life could coexist. But, as the dispossessed increasingly insisted that collective life depended upon the denial of their individuality, the last bastions began to fall and to expose individualism's growing inability to curtail any exercise of the individual will. No wonder, then, that free marketeers, who today call themselves conservatives as the result of a massive misunderstanding, probably choke when confronted with what they have wrought.

In our own time individualism, fueled by the capitalist market, threatens to swing the balance between the individual and society—the balance between personal freedom and social order—wholly to the side of the individual. In this process feminism has played an ambiguous and sometimes destructive role. The implementation of women's rights has whittled away at the remaining bastions of corporatism and community—notably the family—even as women, released to the dubious mercies of the public sphere, require new forms of protection from the state. The issues defy easy solutions but do suggest that we have reached a period in our history at which we can no longer deceive ourselves that individualism suffices to define our collective purposes as a people and a nation. . . .

Jeff Stahler/*The Cincinnati Post*. Reprinted with permission.

Individualism, like the Western tradition from which it emerged and which enthusiasts celebrate as its supreme realization, has firmly cast women as other, even as it has afforded men models of subjecthood and authority that women have tried to adapt to their own ends. Yet women have always had to wrestle with the knowledge that individualism's prestigious models of authoritative subjectivity have refused female identification. Feminism, as an ideology, took shape in the context of the great bourgeois and democratic revolutionary tradition. It thus owes much to the male-formulated ideology of individualism, as it does to the special experiences of women who have been excluded from the benefits of individualism.

During the twentieth century, American women have steadily increased their independent participation in the labor force, society, and the polity. Increasingly cut loose from the "protection" of husbands, families, and communities, they are behaving more and more like "individuals." But their growing personal freedom and independence from male authority have not automatically resulted in the hoped-for full equality with men. "Difference" persists and colors every assessment of women's real needs and wishes. The tension between difference and equality, which has informed feminism from the start, has steadily escalated until it now dominates feminist theory and policy. As successive gains for women reveal the inadequacy of earlier optimistic assumptions, feminists are being forced ever more directly to confront the intractability of difference and the elusiveness of equality. . . .

Feminism has followed the path of individualism in viewing "man" and "woman" as absolutes, in building the ideal of the individual (or, in the case of woman, nonindividual) directly from biology. Man and woman, respectively, embody nature. Feminism's temptation to follow individualism in this abstraction flows naturally from individualism's commitment to reducing women to female sexuality and to justifying men's superiority as a consequence of male sexuality. This strategy is sometimes compelling in the measure that feminism engages our culture's dominant models of being as encoded in its most prestigious texts and traditions.

Women Have Varying Experiences

Unfortunately the strategy too frequently leads to the assumption that a single, "orthodox" feminism can embody the aspirations of all women and thus mocks the multiplicity of female experiences, the range of female consciousness, and the varying strategies for coping with what remains overwhelmingly a man's world. The attempt to define and impose a feminist orthodoxy implies a totalitarianism that negates the very point of the feminist revolt—that substitutes the experience of privileged individuals for the discrete claims of countless others.

Feminism does embody the claims of women on the basis of what they share as women—what we might view as the claims of the female individual. In this spirit, feminism is frequently viewed, in Mary Wollstonecraft's words, as the proclamation of the "rights of woman." But contemporary experience also reveals feminism to be something more and something less. The goal of "the rights of woman" has revealed itself as deceptive. Rights have not granted women equality with men, much less obliterated centuries of discrimination against women. Rights, above all, have not transformed men's—or women's—consciousness in the sense dreamed of by those who yearn for the "liberated woman" of radical utopian thought. The failure of the campaign for woman's rights to deliver "new worlds" has, in part, resulted from our inability to eradicate the fundamental sexual difference between women and men, whatever the scope of that difference may be. It has also resulted from the inherent limitations of individualism in ideology and in practice. Individualism, in jumping from personal identity to political right, has itself abstracted from difference of condition among men. Feminism can ill afford to accept that sleight of hand. To prevail, it will have to assimilate a recognition of difference among women to the core of its meaning and program. . . .

The Harms of Radical Individualism

The individualism from which modern feminism was born has much to answer for but much in which to take pride. Individualism has decisively repudiated previous notions of hierarchy and particularism to declare the possibility of freedom for all. In so doing, it transformed slavery from one unfree condition among many into freedom's antithesis—thereby insisting that the subordination of one person to any other is morally and politically unacceptable. But the gradual extension of individualism and the gradual abolition of the remaining forms of social and political bondage have come trailing after two dangerous notions: that individual freedom could—indeed must—be absolute, and that social role and personal identity must be coterminous.

Following the principles of individualism, modern Western societies have determined that the persistence of slavery in any form violates the fundamental principle of a just society. But in grounding the justification in absolute individual right, they have unleashed the specter of a radical individualism that overrides the claims of society itself. To the extent that feminism, like antislavery, has espoused those individualistic principles, it has condemned itself to the dead ends toward which individualism is now plunging. Feminism, as the daughter of individualism, carries the potential of bringing individualism back to its social moorings by insisting that the rights of individuals derive from society rather than from their innate nature. Feminism, as the daughter of women's exclusion, understands that social opportunity must lie in access to the various roles that society offers. Above all, women, with the privileged knowledge of sexual asymmetry, which derives from their history of subordination, understand that justice must derive from a collectivity that grounds its deepest principles of individual right in the collectivity's commitment to honor and protected difference. . . .

Breaking the Legacy of Individualism

Today, the feminist critique of individualism is becoming ever more widespread. If my argument differs from those of others, it is primarily in my conviction that feminism, in all its guises, is itself the daughter of that (male) individualism which so many feminists are attacking. The attack on individualism has, in general, led to arguments that practices and values, from the organization of work to the law, should be refashioned and rethought to take account of women's distinct experience—perhaps even women's distinct nature. But our very conception of women's experience and nature has been filtered through the premises of individualism. For this reason, it seems to me that the metaphors of sisterhood and community that still enjoy much currency with many feminists should be recognized as, in some sense, hostage to the very institutions they are mobilized to oppose. Similarly, feminist politics have had difficulty in breaking with the legacy of individualism.

From my perspective, the central problem in the feminist critique of individualism lies in the difficulty of reimagining the collectivity—society as a whole—in such a way as to take account of women's legitimate needs. There can be no doubt that many, if not most, of our laws and institutions, including our vision of justice, have been constructed on the basis of men's experience. But it is a big step from an attack upon the biases inherent in those laws and institutions to a repudiation of the possibility of any "objective" standards. I am, accordingly, arguing that the dream of objectivity constitutes one of the great contributions of our civilization, however much it has been constructed by men for their own advantage.

This conviction that feminists have come perilously close to "throwing out the baby with the bath" also informs my discussion of the claims of a common culture. Feminism and postmodernism have both irrefutably demonstrated that, more often than not, the defense of a common culture has constituted the defense of the prerogatives and perspective of some over those of others. They have also taught us that culture is infinitely and richly diverse—that each of us has her or his own story. But to accept the overriding claims of those diverse stories is to accept a potentially dangerous and impoverishing fragmentation. It is also to risk the loss of our own history, which was, like it or not, fashioned in interaction with a dominant culture. In many academic circles, the Western tradition, not to mention the idea of an American national culture, enjoys scant popularity today. Yet neither feminism nor postmodernism is conceivable or comprehensible without them. To jettison them now means to forego the possibility of coming to terms with our history and perhaps the possibility of shaping our future as well.

The Consequences of Difference

American women are, as they always have been, members of American society and heirs to Western and American culture. The issue that confronts us is the terms of their membership in the present and future. That issue has led many feminists up against the dilemma posed by the juxtaposition of equality and difference. How can women, if they are different, ever hope to be equal? How can women, if they aspire to be equal, continue to insist that they are fundamentally different? I have become more convinced than I had previously been of the importance of difference. Even after discounting all of the ways in which our specific culture has constructed and represented difference, a biological difference remains. But the recognition of difference does not dictate the social consequences of difference. The consequences are a matter for the collective determination of society as a whole. We live in a world in which women must be able to support themselves and in which the survival of our species depends upon their bearing children. It is, accordingly, of the most pressing social concern that our laws and institutions permit them to do both.

In the end this is not so much an argument for a chimerical equality, but for equity—and an argument that equity requires a broader and more generous social vision than individualism alone can provide. It is, in sum, an argument that the realization of equity for women requires a view of individual right as derivative from collective social life.

"The overall picture is one of stagnation in women's economic status."

Feminism Should Work for Economic Equality

Teresa Amott

While many women have benefited tremendously from gains in women's economic status, feminism still has far to go to guarantee all women equal access to jobs and economic prosperity, Teresa Amott states in the following viewpoint. Amott describes how many women still suffer from discrimination in the workplace and in the economy in general. Feminists must work to end this inequality and to ensure that women have the same economic opportunities as men, she concludes. Amott is an economics professor at Bucknell University in Lewisburg, Pennsylvania, and editorial associate with *Dollars & Sense* magazine, and a welfare rights activist.

As you read, consider the following questions:

1. Amott describes the experiences of four women. What do these stories illustrate, in her opinion?
2. Why has the gap between men and women's salaries decreased in recent decades, according to Amott?
3. What are feminists doing to improve women's economic status, according to the author?

Teresa Amott, "How Far Have Women Come?" Reprinted with permission from the Winter 1993 issue of *Equal Means: Women Organizing Economic Solutions*, a triannual journal published by the Ms. Foundation for Women. Subscriptions available from *Equal Means*, 2512 Ninth St., #3, Berkeley, CA 94710, (510) 549-9931; four issues, $24.

In 1972, many of us thought that we were on the verge of a revolution in women's economic status. The combined energy of the sixties movements of women, African Americans, Latinos/as and American Indians gave us hope that structures of exclusion and oppression were crumbling. The next few years confirmed our hopes: the minimum wage was extended to cover domestic workers, labor union women came together to form their own organization (the Coalition of Labor Union Women), the federal government required businesses receiving federal contracts to develop affirmative action plans, the Equal Credit Opportunity Act barred gender discrimination in lending, welfare mothers in the National Welfare Rights Organization became a national force and women office workers organized around the country. These were just a few of the promising signs. The momentum seemed unstoppable.

Now, twenty years later, some women have realized their dreams. They fly in space or drive BMWs, sit on the Supreme Court or in the corporate board room, plan highways or develop new treatments for AIDS. But for most women, the dream of economic security and equality is further away than ever. Why? What happened to women's economic progress? How far have we really come?

Caught in the Crisis

Ina Mae Best's experiences, as reported by Barbara Barnett in *In These Times*, typify how women workers were caught in the economic crisis of the 1980s. Best was fired from her textile factory job at age 51 for supporting a union organizing drive. Best had come to work at Goldtex, Inc. in eastern North Carolina, 18 years ago after her youngest son started school, in order to supplement her husband's salary. But when union organizers came around, Best began to wonder about her working conditions: why had her salary increased only $2 during her 18 years of work? Why did the supervisors treat workers as though they were less than human? Why did the company lie to workers, claiming that profits were too slim to permit adequate wages? When Best began raising these questions, her job was doomed, and she was dismissed six months after the union organizers had begun their drive. Textile mill organizing has never been easy, but the risk of losing your job for union activity escalated during the 1980s, as the government agency charged with enforcing collective bargaining rules took a decided tilt towards management.

In Marshalltown, Iowa, Glenda Schmidt was also caught in the crisis, writes Peter T. Kilborn in the *New York Times*. A 39-year-old mother of five, Schmidt works part time as a nurse's aide, earning less than $6 an hour. Her employer calls her in when she is needed, so Schmidt can never count on a steady income from week to week. Until October 1991, she had received welfare benefits and Medicaid, the government-sponsored health care plan that provided free care to her family. Schmidt needs treatment for hypertension, migraine headaches and stomach problems, and her youngest child requires $180 worth of medication for kidney problems every month. The family now faces a Catch-22 situation: Schmidt's new job does not provide any health benefits, but her earnings are too high in most months for the family to qualify for continued Medicaid coverage. Prior to 1981, Schmidt would have been able to keep her coverage, but new regulations in the Reagan years tightened eligibility and stripped away health benefits from hundreds of thousands of families.

" YOU'RE RIGHT. YOU AND FRED DO THE SAME WORK AND SHOULD GET THE SAME PAY. I'LL LOWER HIS SALARY TO MATCH YOURS IMMEDIATELY!"

Stayskal. Reprinted by permission: Tribune Media Services.

In *The Progressive*, Louise Palmer describes how Felipa Perez, a sewing machine operator in an El Paso, Texas, factory found herself in jail in 1991 as a result of the economic crisis. Her employer shut down, owing Perez and other workers weeks of back pay, but soon started up operations again under another name. To dramatize her situation, Perez and five other women chained themselves to sewing machines in the new factory, and were carted off to jail by the police. A mother of four, Perez had never imagined that she would be in jail, facing angry disapproval from her family. During the 1980s, over 5,000 garment industry jobs were lost in El Paso, as factories relocated across the border. The Department of Labor, which was supposed to regulate the industry to ensure that workers received fair treatment when their plants shut down, had ignored Perez's plight.

But as Stephanie Strom points out in the *New York Times*, not all women suffered during the crisis. Linda J. Wachner is the only female CEO of a Fortune 500 company. Starting as department store buyer in 1974, Wachner rose to become the richest working woman in the U.S., catapulting into the stratosphere of executive pay in 1986 when she led a hostile takeover of Warnaco, Inc., a maker of lingerie and men's sportswear. In 1990, she earned $2.5 million in salary and bonuses, even though the company posted losses of over $28 million. Wachner was deeply enmeshed in the high-rolling world of takeover finance during the 1980s, using junk bonds to raise the funds to purchase Warnaco, and then selling off profitable divisions, such as the Speedo swimwear line, to help pay off the debt. Stock market analysts point out that although Wachner was part of the investment group that purchased Speedo and had a serious conflict of interest in the sale, the sale itself was legal. Today, they estimate Wachner's net worth at $100 million.

As these stories illustrate, the effects of economic crisis on women are not simple, or undifferentiated, because women are neither. Not all women are affected the same way, because not all women are the same. Class, race-ethnicity and sexual preference, along with age and family status, all play crucial roles in shaping the choices and structuring the opportunities for women.

Up the Down Escalator

Stepping back, it is apparent that women's progress got hampered by an economy that went haywire. Little did we know in 1972 that the long postwar boom that had put the U.S. on top of the global economic hierarchy was dying. As our capacity to dominate world markets eroded, inflation soared out of control, our paychecks lost their purchasing power and the younger generation of workers faced a labor market full of lousy jobs.

The past two decades, referred to by some economists as a "silent depression," have seen the U.S. economy slip from dominance into crisis. Businesses that had enjoyed high profit margins in the 1950s and '60s suddenly had to scramble to keep their shareholders happy. So, starting in the 1980s, a new set of business and government policies was put into effect by a newly powerful conservative coalition. Companies moved to lower-cost regions in the United States and abroad ["capital flight"]. They replaced full-time, permanent employees with part-timers and contingent workers. They attacked labor unions with sophisticated antilabor strategies. Government policies deregulated the economy, loosening enforcement of consumer, job safety and environmental regulations. Tax policies at the state and federal level shifted the burden of taxation from corporations and wealthy households to poor and middle-income households. Budget cutters shredded the government safety net.

All these policies were part of a plan to restore the profitability of U.S. companies and put the U.S. back on top. They were certainly not aimed at carrying out a women's economic agenda. In fact, they polarized economic opportunity, blocking mobility for millions of women while offering new opportunities to a select group. As a result, the pay gap between men and women workers narrowed. Ironically, the 1970s and 1980s brought women workers some equality with men, but not the way we wanted it. Men's wages have fallen and inequality among women has grown.

Women became an integral part of the corporate strategy to restore profitability since we represented a cheaper pool of labor, and were less organized by unions and more "flexible" in terms of hours and benefits. So, in a variety of industries and occupations, here and abroad, businesses substituted women for men. Businesses moved abroad in search of lower costs—a process known as capital flight—and the global assembly line, staffed predominantly by women, was born. Here, millions of women entered the labor force. Most of us took traditionally female jobs, since that is where most job growth took place. In fact, job growth in the services was rapid because women were available to work at relatively low wages and for few benefits. Lacking options for better jobs, most women had no other choice. Over the years, male-dominated manufacturing jobs disappeared in the United States, replaced by female-dominated service work (and female-dominated manufacturing abroad), most of it for very low pay.

The "Trickle Down" Job Market

Still, some women did make inroads into traditionally male, highly paid jobs, particularly those requiring advanced degrees. In 1989, for instance, women earned 40 percent of all U.S. law degrees (compared to 23 percent in 1977). However, white women were the major beneficiaries of the new opportunities for high-paid prestigious jobs. In 1990, one in six doctors were white women, but only one in a hundred were either African American or Latina. There was a "trickle down" job market, with growing numbers of white women gaining entrance into jobs formerly dominated by white men. Women of color, particularly African American women, took the white women's places. Census Bureau data suggest that African American women's gains in professional jobs came mainly by moving into the female-dominated jobs, such as social work and teaching, that were vacated by white women. (We will have to wait several more years before the government publishes data from the 1990 Census on Asian American and American Indian occupational status—for now, in 1993, all we have are data on whites, African Americans and Latinas.)

Resistance to Women Working

Blue-collar women didn't fare as well. The movement of women into highly skilled jobs was sharply limited by capital flight and by weakening enforcement of affirmative action. Resistance to women in the trades stiffened during the 1980s, when layoffs were common and union jobs were under attack. Moreover, all three major racial-ethnic groups of women lost ground in manufacturing jobs such as operators and laborers. Latinas saw the least improvements in occupational status—a greater share of Latinas were in service jobs at the end of the 1980s than at the beginning. (Employment discrimination against Latinos/as increased in the latter half of the 1980s because of changes in immigration laws. New immigrants, unable to find work in occupations for which they had trained in their native countries, faced limited job opportunities.)

In addition to capital flight, another key component of the corporate plan to boost profits involved the replacement of permanent workers by contingent workers. Here again, women's quest for economic security has been stymied. Temp jobs are by definition insecure. There are few fringe benefits, and wages are lower than those in permanent jobs, even when the work itself is the same.

Employers have also turned to home work to cut costs, sending us back to the cottage industry of the 19th century. Industrial home work had been illegal in the U.S. since 1949, but the Reagan administration dismantled the prohibition, legalizing industrial work in the home. As a result, clerical and industrial home work are growing in importance in the U.S. economy. Homeworkers must pay their own overhead, work at long hours for low piece rates and rarely receive any benefits.

While some jobs moved offshore and others were transformed into contingent work, still other jobs were moved underground. The sweatshop economy boomed in major cities, relying on the work of undocumented women and other new immigrants to assemble electronic components and sew garments. Since these jobs are off the books, workers lack the most basic protections, receive no Social Security credits, can be paid below minimum wage—when they are paid at all—and are forced to work overtime without receiving overtime pay.

Despite the growth of low-wage work, the gap between men and women's earnings narrowed for whites, African Americans and Latinas. During the 1970s and '80s, men of most racial-ethnic groups had to accept lower wages as unions declined in membership and as business and government policies took their toll on the manufacturing sector. About two-thirds of the increase in women's wages relative to men's resulted from the drop in men's earnings. If we compare median weekly earnings for full-time workers, all three groups of women improved their standing relative to men of the same racial-ethnic group.

Inequality Among Women

But if we compare all three groups of women to white men, we can see that white women had the greatest improvement: in 1990, white women earned 71 percent as much as white men (compared to 63 percent in 1980), while African American women only improved from 58 percent to 62 percent and Latinas from 50 percent to 54 percent. The ratio of African American women's wages to white women's actually fell, as did the ratio of Latinas' to whites'. Opportunities in the labor market, in other words, were not expanding as fast for women of color as for whites.

Together, these wage and job trends spelled increasing inequality among women workers (and among men workers). One Labor Department study found that the increase in inequality generally resulted from an increase in the share of earnings received by the top fifth of workers, while workers in the bottom three-fifths received a relatively lower share. During the 1960s, inequality among workers had declined. By contrast, during the 1980s, women workers who were able to establish and maintain positions in the top sectors of the labor market—the marketing executives, the accountants, the chemical engineers—did very well. Others, trapped in secondary and informal sector jobs—the typing pool, the chicken processing line, the cafeteria kitchen—earned less and less compared to those at the top.

Of course, these labor market changes don't reveal the whole story on women's economic status. Women get income from government and from family members, too, but the 1970s and 1980s have been even harder on these sources of income than they were on women in their roles as paid workers. Government checks such as welfare or unemployment compensation are smaller today than they were two decades ago. More and more women are the sole support of their households, and have little or no financial support from men. Added together with the job market, the overall picture is one of stagnation in women's economic status.

But the picture is not all bleak. We've learned a valuable lesson. In 1972, many of us thought that the economy would grow on its own and that all we needed to do was ensure that we got our share of the growing pie. Our strategies for economic equity assumed that the economy would continue to generate enough jobs at living wages for us to claim our share. Now, we know that we must challenge the structure of the economy itself. We don't want a larger share of this pie; we want a new recipe.

A Grassroots Movement

Today, at the grassroots level, there are hundreds of thousands of groups working for progressive change in the U.S., seeking to restructure the economy, the household and the state for democratic and participatory ends.

What do all these efforts have in common? They create collective possibilities for analyzing the causes of the crisis and overturning the existing relationships of exploitation and domination. They bring people together across lines of race, ethnicity, gender and sexual orientation in ways that reject the politics of division and scapegoating. They are democratic to their core, involving people at the grass roots in the decisions that affect their lives.

In each of these areas, women have taken the lead. Among women, creative strategies have been developed by women of color, poor women, lesbians and women with disabilities. Perhaps it is because these groups are so severely affected by the crisis, forced to assume new burdens of work and responsibility but deprived of safety nets and supports. Perhaps, caught in the crisis, these women have been able to see it more clearly than those whose privileges have insulated them from its worst effects. And finally, perhaps it is the very diversity of women's experiences that has given them a vision of alternative possibilities that is richer, more pluralistic and more democratic. At this moment of crisis, when the old framework is dead, women are giving birth to the new.

"Just as generations of men have succumbed to the lure of the American dream, so too have millions of women scrambled after an illusion."

Feminism Should Work for a More Caring Society

Suzanne Gordon

For too long feminists have focused on helping women make inroads into male-dominated fields, Suzanne Gordon writes in the following viewpoint. Along the way, she charges, feminists have forgotten their original goal of transforming society into a more caring, less competitive world. Rather than trying to become economic equals with men, Gordon believes feminists should work to create a world that is more nurturing and less focused on economic success and gain. Gordon, a frequent contributor to the *Boston Globe*, is the author of the books *Lonely in America*, *Off Balance: The Real World of Ballet*, and *Prisoners of Men's Dreams: Striking Out for a New Feminine Future*, from which this viewpoint is excerpted.

As you read, consider the following questions:

1. What does Gordon mean when she states that "women are in danger of becoming prisoners of men's dreams"?
2. Some feminists believed that when women entered male-dominated fields, society would be transformed. What was wrong with this assumption, in the author's opinion?
3. What must women do to transform society, according to Gordon?

From *Prisoners of Men's Dreams* (pp. 3-9, 15-16) by Suzanne Gordon. Copyright ©1991 by Suzanne Gordon. By permission of Little, Brown and Company.

Women and their vision of a more humane world are at risk. Only a few short years ago, women's liberation promised to change our world. Our emphasis on the value of relationships, interdependence, and collaboration sought to balance work with love, hierarchy with healing, individualism with community. Through our profound commitment to caring, we hoped finally to teach American society that care was neither a reward for hard work nor an indulgence meted out to the infirm and vulnerable, but rather a fundamental human need. Many women who participated in our movement demanded that equality make a difference—not only for our sisters and ourselves, but for men and for generations to come.

Now, two decades after the great social upheavals of the 1960s, women are in danger of becoming prisoners of men's dreams.

It has required centuries of excruciating struggle, but we have finally arrived on the shores of the masculine world. And yet, as we have moved inland, slowly, almost imperceptibly, too many of us seem to have been wooed away from our original animating goal of changing this landscape.

Women Are Now Part of the System

We have not attained as much power and influence as we'd hoped. Although millions of us live in poverty that has been increasingly feminized, we have nonetheless been assimilated into the American marketplace. Millions of us now participate in an economic, social, and political system that is highly competitive, aggressive, and individualistic; a system that values workplace success and the accumulation of wealth, power, and privilege above all else.

Many of us are now doctors and lawyers, bankers and stockbrokers, scientists and engineers, legislators and congressional representatives, mayors and even governors. We are telephone workers and underground miners, carpenters and house painters, auto mechanics, mailpersons, and cab drivers. A few of us sit on the boards of the nation's major corporations. We have started our own magazines and secured positions of influence in the media—editing newspapers, producing network news shows, writing and directing for television, running major motion picture studios, and determining the content of at least some of the films they make.

Some of us supervise not only other women but men. We boss secretaries, give orders to nurses, hire nannies, and are served by flight attendants as we fly the nation's skies. Not all of us, but some of us, participate in making the decisions that govern other women's lives.

We are lobbyists, political consultants, and politicians. We advise women—and sometimes men—how to run campaigns and shepherd bills through state legislatures and Congress. We may not have all the votes, and we certainly do not have the final veto—but to our constituents we interpret reality, define the possible, and help create the probable.

We have entered the male kingdom—and yet, we have been forced to play by the king's rules.

That is not what an important segment of the feminist movement promised.

A Transformative Vision

Feminism was, and remains, one of the most powerful social movements of the twentieth century. When women marched and protested and united to recast the contours of our world, many of us carried a very different transformative vision in our hearts and minds. Twenty years ago, a significant group of feminists believed in women, in the potential of femininity and the transformative power of feminism. It was clear, these transformative feminists argued, that our masculine socialization—our ingrained insecurity about our competence and talents outside of the domestic sphere—was a wound. But our feminine socialization, so many sensed, was a source of strength to be mobilized not only for the private but for the public good.

Socialized in the home, the community, and the helping professions, women devoted themselves to nurturing, empowering, and caring for others. In a society little dedicated to sustaining relationships, encouraging cooperation and community, recognizing the value of collaboration, or rewarding altruism rather than greed, women have historically defined, defended, and sustained a set of insights, values, and activities which, if never dominant, at least provided a counterweight and an alternative ideal to the anomie, disconnectedness, fragmentation, and commercialization of our culture.

Many of us saw women's experiences and concerns as the source of a sorely needed transformative vision. And our dream of liberation was fueled by the hope that we could carry this vision with us into the marketplace and encourage a new ethic of caring even as we demonstrated our own competence. Our vision of a more humane society was based on a profound commitment to caring—to the emotional and physical activities, attitudes, and ethical comportment that help people grow and develop, that nurture and empower them, affirming their strengths and helping them cope with their weaknesses, vulnerabilities, and life crises.

Thus we hoped to create a less hierarchal workplace, one in which people could help others grow and develop; in which knowledge, experience, power, and wealth could be shared more equitably. We wanted both the private and public sector to allow and even help us fulfill our caring responsibilities by implementing the kinds of social policies that are essential to any real integration of work and personal relationships. And we wanted to infuse our society with a greater respect for the caring work that women have so long performed and refined both inside and outside the home. Most importantly, we wanted men to value and share that caring with us in the home and the workplace.

THEY'RE ADVANCING MUCH FASTER THAN MEN. IN SHORT, IT LOOKS LIKE WOMEN WILL SOON BE RUNNING THE DAY-TO-DAY BUSINESS OF AMERICA.

MEN WIN AGAIN!

"RALL" by Ted Rall. Reprinted by permission of Chronicle Features, San Francisco, CA.

American society has made it enormously difficult for women—or men—to hold to such an alternative ideal. Many men have sabotaged women's struggle for equality and difference from its inception, and they continue to resist our every effort to improve our lives. When America's masculine-dominated, marketplace culture has not openly thwarted women's hopes and dreams, it has often tried to co-opt women's liberation. Thus while many women have remained faithful to this transformative vision and still struggle valiantly to make it a reality, it has been difficult for millions of others to resist a barrage of messages from corporate America and the media that define mastery and liberation in competitive, marketplace terms. Corporate America and the media have declared that feminism triumphs when women gain the opportunity to compete in what Abraham Lincoln once called the great "race of life." Following a classic pattern in which the victims of aggression identify with their aggressors, many prominent advocates of women's liberation within the highly competitive capitalist marketplace have themselves embraced this masculinized corruption of feminist ideals.

Placing competition above caring, work above love, power above empowerment, and personal wealth above human worth, corporate America has created a late-twentieth-century hybrid—a refashioned feminism that takes traditional American ideas about success and repackages them for the new female contestants in the masculine marketplace. This hybrid is equal-opportunity feminism—an ideology that abandons transformation to adaptation, promoting male-female equality without questioning the values that define the very identity it seeks.

Betty Friedan, whose important work launched the liberal branch of the feminist movement, was one of the first to give voice to this ideology, in 1963 in *The Feminine Mystique*. For her, feminism and competition seemed to be synonymous. "When women take their education and abilities seriously and put them to use, ultimately they have to compete with men," she wrote. "It is better for a woman to compete impersonally in society, as men do, than to compete for dominance in her own home with her husband, compete with her neighbors for empty status, and so smother her son that he cannot compete at all."

A Fear of Caring

From the equal-opportunity feminism first envisaged in *The Feminine Mystique* to that promoted today by *Working Woman* and *Savvy* magazines, and the dozens of primers that promote the dress-for-success philosophy that often pretends to speak for all of feminism, progress and liberation have been defined in male, market terms. While some equal-opportunity feminists pay lip service to the work of their more care-oriented sisters, claiming that they would support a broad agenda that addresses our caring needs, the overarching mission of many is to help women adapt to the realities of the masculine marketplace. This brand of feminism often appeals to women's understandable fears that to discuss human beings' mutual need to care for one another is to argue that only women—not men—shoulder the duty to care. Rather than reaffirming our caring commitments so that we can all—male and female alike—share them, equal-opportunity feminism often seems to define caring as a masculine attempt to imprison women in the home and caring professions.

In this environment, the goal of liberation is to be treated as a man's equal *in a man's world*, competing for oneself against a very particular kind of man—the artists, scientists, politicians, and professionals that Friedan speaks of throughout her book. Or, as a recent *New York Times* series about the progress of women and feminism stated, "The basic goal of the women's movement was to eliminate the barriers that kept women from achieving as much as men and which did not allow them to *compete* with men on an equal basis" (my italics).

For equal-opportunity feminism, then, the ultimate goal is traditional American success—making money; relentlessly accumulating possessions; capturing and hoarding power, knowledge, access, and information; grasping and clinging to fame, status, and privilege; proving that you are good enough, smart enough, driven enough to get to the top, and tough enough to stay there. In America—particularly the America of the Reagan and post-Reagan years—this is, after all, the meaning of "having it all."

In a world where allegiance to family, community, and politics has eroded, the American marketplace, with its glittering prize of success, has co-opted many of us, undermining our hopes and expectations. Others among us had a different vision. We had hoped that by going into the marketplace and taking our posts there as individuals, we would somehow subvert it. Many believed that our femininity would protect us, that the force of our feminism would make us invulnerable to the seductive logic of either patriarchy or capitalism.

Is the Fault with Men or the Market?

In fact, we were remarkably naive about this foreign land into which we had journeyed. Yes, we were quick to admit that American society is too ruthless, too violent, too aggressive and uncaring. But many of us believed that the market's ills were a direct result of the sex of those who ruled and served it—men. As Betty Friedan, among so many others, has said over and over again, "Society was created by and for men."

It seemed logical, therefore, to argue that the aggressive, elitist, hierarchal attitudes, values, and behaviors that kept women oppressed served the needs of and benefited all men, and that the natural solution was simply to change the sex of the players. It seemed natural to believe that putting women in power—without radically changing the system of power—would improve things for *all*. After all, like so many oppressed groups who believe oppression is a shield against the temptations of tyranny, women, who had been oppressed and subordinate for so long themselves, would never turn around and oppress and dominate others.

What we had not counted on was the strength of the marketplace, its ability to seduce and beguile the best and brightest, and its capacity to entrap us in its rules and entangle us in its imperatives. A few women have won great wealth and privilege. But, not unlike men in similar positions, many of them are unwilling to jeopardize what they've acquired in order to work for change. Some are so caught up in their own personal sagas of success that they have forgotten the women who have been left behind.

It is, of course, true that a great many professional women are deeply concerned about the fate of personal, political, and social life in modern America. They express great disenchantment but nonetheless seem caught in gilded cages—unhappy with their lot but too fearful of losing what they've gained for the promise of a richer life or the fulfillment of a common morality.

Just as generations of men have succumbed to the lure of the American dream, so too have millions of women scrambled after an illusion.

Just as transformative feminism insisted that following this fantasy did not make men winners but rather victims, so too it has made us victims of a different oppressor—the market. Instead of attaining mastery and liberation on our own terms, we have become clones of what economist Adam Smith called "economic man." Now standing beside him, we have economic woman—a group of women who have grown so competitive and individualistic that they can think of little but themselves and advancing in their careers. Committed to the bottom line of short-term profit, these women have become oblivious to the needs and ambitions of those who work with them or under them; some actually try to thwart other women's efforts to improve their own lives. . . .

What Do Women Want?

For the past decade, too many of us have lived out the fantasy that we could, individually and collectively, find happiness and completion in the marketplace, often as clones of economic man. Many believed that if an elite group of women benefited from the many victories of feminism, then millions of others would slowly follow in their footsteps. Well, now we have seen reality: women do not change the world by becoming more like men; many women who do not want to be like men feel they have no alternative but to leave the marketplace; even more women who are trying only to stay in place find that the bottom is falling out from under them and that the victories of their more fortunate sisters may be of little help.

Transformative feminists have been struggling to fulfill their vision of feminism in spite of the tyranny of the market. As more women realize that the dream of success in the male marketplace imprisons us as tightly as it has always imprisoned men, more of us can join in that struggle for real change. We can once again begin to dream our own dreams, to ask new questions and revise our goals. The question can no longer be, can we compete and succeed in traditional terms?

The question needs to be, what do we want to do, be, and become? The issue can no longer be only body counting—calculating how many women have attained positions of power and where—it must be quality counting. What kind of women are we putting in power? What do we want them to *really* stand for? What do they believe? Do they practice what they preach? To whom are they accountable? Will we make them accountable to the majority of women, not just an elite?

The task is no longer to find role models, it's to determine which kind of role models we want to promote. Are women who have succeeded in male terms and in male-dominated arenas the only women we want to emulate? Or are many of us looking for our role models only in the corporate headquarters of Exxon and American Express, rather than also in the caring professions, where some of the most interesting experiments in transformative feminism are taking place? Are we looking so intently at the model that we no longer ask what role that model actually performs in the world—what actions she takes, whom she serves?

The goal is no longer to work only for ourselves, but to regroup so that we can determine how best to work for others.

A Renewal Is Necessary

Many women have been working together for years to achieve equality with a difference. I believe those the market has disempowered can also relearn how to work with one another for real change. Indeed, we cannot afford not to. Individual inaction poses a far greater risk for most of us than does collective action. We must all become creators of and participants in a mass transformative feminist renewal. If we do not, then we risk losing whatever we have gained. If men and women do not work together to tame the market—and to forge a new definition of freedom and self-worth—then it will defeat us all in the end.

Recent debates about women and men, women and work, women and family, women and relationships have concentrated on the wisdom or folly of creating new tracks for women in the workplace. But the real issue is not what track women are on, or who will arrive first at the glittering station of individual success. What should concern us instead is the context in which we find ourselves today—a competitive, goal-oriented consumer culture that bears little resemblance to the balanced, more compassionate society envisaged by so many of us thirty years ago. I believe our most daunting problems represent, in fact, a great and exciting challenge: we must demystify the mistaken models of liberation that have been constructed for us of late and, using the vision of a more transformative feminism, together craft new alternatives based neither on a nineteenth-century sentimentalization of women's caring roles nor on a celebration of late-twentieth-century economic man.

"The fight for reproductive freedom is the foundation of all the others."

Feminists Should Protect the Right to Abortion

Ellen Willis

Ellen Willis is associate professor of journalism at New York University and former senior editor at the *Village Voice* newspaper. She is the author of the books *Beginning to See the Light: Sex, Hope, and Rock-and-Roll* and *No More Nice Girls: Counterculture Essays*, from the latter of which this viewpoint is excerpted. Willis asserts that the right to abortion is perhaps the most important feminist issue. Those who oppose abortion focus on the question of whether a fetus is a human being. This question is irrelevant, Willis argues. The crucial issue is that women are free human beings who must have the right to control their bodies, including their reproduction.

As you read, consider the following questions:

1. Antiabortion liberals argue that their prolife position concerning abortion is part of a "seamless garment" of respect for human life. How does Willis refute this claim?
2. How did the author's personal experience concerning pregnancy affect her attitudes about abortion?
3. How does the availability of abortion help women, in the author's opinion?

Reprinted from *No More Nice Girls: Counterculture Essays* (pp. 75-78, 80-81, 83) by Ellen Willis. Copyright ©1992 by Ellen Willis, Wesleyan University Press. By permission of University Press of New England.

I often feel isolated when I insist that abortion is, above all, a *feminist issue*. Once people took for granted that abortion was an issue of sexual politics and morality. Now, abortion is most often discussed as a question of "life" in the abstract. Public concern over abortion centers almost exclusively on fetuses; women and their bodies are merely the stage on which the drama of fetal life and death takes place. Debate about abortion—if not its reality—has become sexlessly scholastic. And the people most responsible for this turn of events are on the left.

The left wing of the right-to-life movement is a small, seemingly eccentric minority in both "progressive" and antiabortion camps. Yet it has played a critical role in the movement: by arguing that opposition to abortion can be separated from the right's antifeminist program, it has given antiabortion sentiment legitimacy in left-symp and (putatively) profeminist circles. While left antiabortionists are hardly alone in emphasizing fetal life, their innovation has been to claim that a consistent "prolife" stand involves opposing capital punishment, supporting disarmament, demanding government programs to end poverty, and so on. This is of course a leap the right is neither able nor willing to make. It's been liberals—from Garry Wills to the Catholic bishops—who have supplied the mass media with the idea that prohibiting abortion is part of a "seamless garment" of respect for human life.

What Is the Key Question?

Having invented this counter-context for the abortion controversy, left antiabortionists are trying to impose it as the only legitimate context for debate. Those of us who won't accept their terms and persist in seeing opposition to abortion, antifeminism, sexual repression, and religious sectarianism as the real seamless garment have been accused of obscuring the issue with demagoguery. *Commonweal*—perhaps the most important current forum for left antiabortion opinion—ran an editorial demanding that we shape up: "Those who hold that abortion is immoral believe that the biological dividing lines of birth or viability should no more determine whether a developing member of the species is denied or accorded essential rights than should the biological dividing lines of sex or race or disability or old age. This argument is open to challenge. Perhaps the dividing lines are sufficiently different. Pro-choice advocates should state their reasons for believing so. They should meet the argument on its own grounds. . . ."

In other words, the only question we're allowed to debate—or the only one *Commonweal* is willing to entertain—is "Are fetuses the moral equivalent of born human beings?" And I can't meet the argument on its own grounds because I don't agree that this

213

is the key question, whose answer determines whether one supports abortion or opposes it. I don't doubt that fetuses are alive, or that they're biologically human—what else would they be? I do consider the life of a fertilized egg less precious than the well-being of a woman with feelings, self-consciousness, a history, social ties; and I think fetuses get closer to being human in a moral sense as they come closer to birth. But to me these propositions are intuitively self-evident. I wouldn't know how to justify them to a "nonbeliever," nor do I see the point of trying.

A Deeper Understanding of Abortion

Feminist ethics will see a different and more complex human meaning in the act of abortion. Rather than judging universally in fixed categories of "right and wrong" it will be inclined to make graded evaluations of choices. . . . It will attempt to help women to orchestrate the various elements that come into play in the situation, including the needs of the woman as a person, the rights of women as an oppressed class, . . . the negative aspects of her situation in a society which rewards the production of unwanted children with shame and poverty.

Mary Daly, *Beyond God the Father*, 1973.

I believe the debate has to start in a different place—with the recognition that fertilized eggs develop into infants inside the bodies of women. Pregnancy and birth are active processes in which a woman's body shelters, nourishes, and expels a new life; for nine months she is immersed in the most intimate possible relationship with another being. The growing fetus makes considerable demands on her physical and emotional resources, culminating in the cataclysmic experience of birth. And childbearing has unpredictable consequences; it always entails some risk of injury or death.

Having a Baby

For me all this has a new concreteness: I had a baby last year. My much-desired and relatively easy pregnancy was full of what antiabortionists like to call "inconveniences." I was always tired, short of breath; my digestion was never right; for three months I endured a state of hormonal siege; later I had pains in my fingers, swelling feet, numb spots on my legs, the dread hemorrhoids. I had to think about everything I ate. I developed borderline glucose intolerance. I gained 50 pounds and am still overweight; my shape has changed in other ways that may well be permanent. Psychologically, my pregnancy consumed me—

214

though I'd happily bought the seat on the roller coaster, I was still terrified to be so out of control of my normally tractable body. It was all bearable, even interesting—even, at times, transcendent—because I wanted a baby. Birth was painful, exhausting, and wonderful. If I hadn't wanted a baby it would only have been painful and exhausting—or worse. I can hardly imagine what it's like to have your body and mind taken over in this way when you not only don't look forward to the result, but positively dread it. The thought appalls me. So as I see it, the key question is "Can it be moral, under any circumstances, to make a woman bear a child against her will?"

From this vantage point, *Commonweal*'s argument is irrelevant, for in a society that respects the individual, no "member of the species" in *any* stage of development has an "essential right" to make use of someone else's body, let alone in such all-encompassing fashion, without that person's consent. You can't make a case against abortion by applying a general principle about everybody's human rights; you have to show exactly the opposite—that the relationship between fetus and pregnant woman is an exception, one that justifies depriving women of their right to bodily integrity. And in fact all antiabortion ideology rests on the premise—acknowledged or simply assumed—that women's unique capacity to bring life into the world carries with it a unique obligation; that women cannot be allowed to "play God" and launch only the lives they welcome.

Yet the alternative to allowing women this power is to make them impotent. Criminalizing abortion doesn't just harm individual women with unwanted pregnancies, it affects all women's sense of themselves. Without control of our fertility we can never envision ourselves as free, for our biology makes us constantly vulnerable. Simply because we are female our physical integrity can be violated, our lives disrupted and transformed, at any time. Our ability to act in the world is hopelessly compromised by our sexual being. . . .

A Sexual Double Standard

Opposing abortion means accepting that women must suffer sexual disempowerment and a radical loss of autonomy relative to men: if fetal life is sacred, the self-denial basic to women's oppression is also basic to the moral order. Opposing abortion means embracing a conservative sexual morality, one that subordinates pleasure to reproduction: if fetal life is sacred, there is no room for the view that sexual passion—or even sexual love—for its own sake is a human need and a human right. Opposing abortion means tolerating the inevitable double standard, by which men may accept or reject sexual restrictions in accordance with their beliefs, while women must bow to them out of fear—or defy them at great risk. . . .

Certainly many women have had abortions they didn't want or wouldn't have wanted if they had any plausible means of caring for a child; and countless others wouldn't have gotten pregnant in the first place were it not for inadequate contraception, sexual confusion and guilt, male pressure, and other stigmata of female powerlessness. Forcing a woman to bear a child she doesn't want can only add injury to insult, while refusing to go through with such a pregnancy can be a woman's first step toward taking hold of her life. And many women who have abortions are "victims" only of ordinary human miscalculation, technological failure, or the vagaries of passion, all bound to exist in any society, however utopian. There will always be women who, at any given moment, want sex but don't want a child; some of these women will get pregnant; some of them will have abortions. . . .

The fight for reproductive freedom is the foundation of all the others, which is why antifeminists resist it so fiercely. . . . It's the antiabortion left that refuses to face the contradiction in its own position: you can't be wholeheartedly for "life"—or for such progressive aspirations as freedom, democracy, equality— and condone the subjugation of women. The seamless garment is full of holes.

"Historically, feminism has vigorously opposed abortion."

Feminists Should Oppose Abortion

Frederica Mathewes-Green and Haven Bradford Gow

In Part I of the following viewpoint, Frederica Mathewes-Green contends that abortion exploits women who feel pressured by family and society to abort children they cannot afford to raise. She suggests that feminists should help women who face unplanned pregnancies rather than encouraging them to resort to abortion. Mathewes-Green, vice-president for communications of Feminists for Life of America, has written for *World Policy Review* and other publications. In Part II, Haven Bradford Gow maintains that if feminists want to help the weak and powerless, they should oppose abortion, which kills the weakest and least powerful: unborn children. Gow is a contributing editor for the Catholic League for Religious and Civil Rights.

As you read, consider the following questions:

1. What does Mathewes-Green mean when she states that abortion cannot be just because it is "social engineering built on death"?
2. In what specific ways can feminists help women facing unplanned pregnancies, according to Mathewes-Green?
3. How does Gow respond to the feminist argument that "women must have control over their own bodies"?

Frederica Mathewes-Green, "Why I'm Feminist and Pro-Life," *Christianity Today*, October 25, 1993. Reprinted with permission of the author. Haven Bradford Gow, "True Feminism Is Anti-Abortion," *The Wanderer*, April 11, 1991. Reprinted by permission of *The Wanderer*.

I

The scene was an emotionally charged prolife rally, the kick-off of a petition drive to overturn a new proabortion law.

I was the last speaker of the evening. The crowd's excitement was at its peak. But as I rose to the podium, when the name of my organization was announced, part of that excitement turned to dismay. I am a vice-president of Feminists for Life.

Most People Are Feminists

Many people react negatively to the term *feminism*. To them, it means angry women who hate men and mock the family. But this is as unfair as believing that all prolifers bomb abortion clinics. In fact, if we adopt Gloria Steinem's definition of a feminist—"Anyone who recognizes the equality and full humanity of women and men"—most of us are probably feminists, too. This was a radical innovation two thousand years ago, when the first Christians proclaimed the equal value of all people.

I became a feminist over 20 years ago, in response to a culture that treated women as frivolous, gossipy creatures, endearingly silly, whose chief delight was the buying of hats. Today most of us believe women to be as intelligent and capable as men and see women's careers as appropriate, especially before and after their child-rearing years.

But if prolifers balk at "feminism," establishment feminists have an even harder time with "prolife." Yet, historically, feminism has vigorously opposed abortion.

Susan B. Anthony, Elizabeth Cady Stanton, and other early feminists saw abortion as proof of women's powerlessness and inequality. Anthony's newspaper stated, "When a man steals to satisfy hunger, we may safely conclude that there is something wrong in society—so when a woman destroys the life of her un-born child, it is an evidence that . . . she has been greatly wronged."

A century later, prolife feminists still charge that abortion is a convenience for sexually exploitative men, who find it easier to pay for an abortion than to be responsible for the life they helped to begin. In fact, abortion makes it easier for everyone—the woman's boss, her school, her landlord, her family, her church—to ignore her plight and the impositions it might cause them.

Even worse, abortion means death. And social engineering built on death can never be just. If it is "a woman's right to control her body," this right must first mean that she is protected from all forms of violence. This right must be hers no matter where she lives—even in her mother's womb.

But true feminism has something to say to the prolife movement as well. Sometimes prolifers hate abortion so much they begin to hate the woman who is tempted by it. But she deserves our help and love as much as her unborn child does.

History's most famous pregnancy was a difficult one: a peasant girl, pregnant out of wedlock, finding shelter in a stable in a friendless town. In our cities today there are many women like her, women for whom pregnancy is a frightening burden, prey to the wheedling, sympathetic voice of the sellers of annihilation. In this lonely place, will we be like Caesar's tax collectors, concerned only that there be one more name for the census? Or will we be wise innkeepers, searching our resources, offering whatever we have to share?

How to Help

Ultimately, we are not called to save her unborn child; the mother is the one appointed to be the child's protector. Our job is to find ways to be her servant so that she can love her child to life. Far from dreamy theory, this involves concrete and unglamorous action. It may mean volunteering at your local pregnancy center, offering hope to women in need, or even opening your own home to a pregnant woman. It may call you to political action, seeking not just limits on abortion, but also strengthened child-support laws, compassionate maternity-leave policies, and adequate, accessible medical care.

Prolifers need not fear feminism; feminists need not fear the cause of life. Prolife feminism is the natural flower of both movements: over a century of saving babies by serving their mothers, and helping them to choose life.

II

According to the Pro-Life Office of the National Conference of Catholic Bishops, true feminism affirms and defends "virtues such as nonviolence, the sharing of power, and equal rights which could transform and even save lives. True feminism recognizes the equal rights of all living beings. But pro-abortion feminists such as [the National Organization for Women] distort these values by insisting that women can only achieve equality if a 'right' to abortion is legitimized. They justify their position by claiming that poverty, abuse, and career derailment are worse than the violent killing of abortion."

When feminists who support abortion on demand argue that they simply are defending the rights of the weak and powerless, antiabortionists must respond: "Your definition of feminism means 'my rights are more important than anyone else's rights.' You say feminism respects the rights of the weak and powerless, the voiceless members of society. Aren't unborn babies weak, powerless, and voiceless? Where is the respect for their right to life?"

When pro-abortion feminists say women must have reproductive freedom to control their destinies, pro-life people must reply: "The tragedy is that pro-abortion women think they must abort their babies to obtain equality with men. They don't mean freedom to reproduce, to bring beautiful and innocent new life into this world, but freedom to resort to the violence of abortion."

Abortion Is Violence

Abortion is violence: a deep, desperate violence inflicted by a woman upon, first of all, herself.

Adrienne Rich, *Of Woman Born*, 1976.

When pro-abortion women argue that antiabortionists want to push women back 100 years in their fight for social equality, antiabortion people must say "Feminism holds that each individual can make an equally important contribution to society and the world, that there are no second-class people. Therefore, it is ironic and tragic that pro-abortion feminists complain about women being oppressed and victimized by men when these women are doing the very same thing to their innocent unborn babies."

When pro-abortion feminists tell us that "no woman should be forced to give birth to a baby that is unwanted. Women should have control over their own bodies," pro-life people must respond: "What you are saying is that an unborn child is your property. Feminists were appalled when women were once seen as a husband's property, and today it is completely unacceptable to view any life—including the life of the unborn child—as mere property."

Indeed, it is a significant fact that the founders of the feminist movement in the United States were principled and courageous foes of abortion; they rightly insisted that abortion is the killing of innocent unborn babies and that it scorns the sacredness of sex, marriage, family, and human life.

Susan B. Anthony, for example, described abortion as "child murder," while Elizabeth Cady Stanton referred to abortion as "infanticide." Alice Paul, author of the original Equal Rights Amendment, said "abortion is the ultimate exploitation of women," while Victoria Woodhull, the first woman to run for President of the United States, observed that "the rights of children as individuals begin while yet they remain the fetus."

Matilda Gage, a writer and leader of the women's suffrage movement, discerned that abortion is a great male convenience because it allows men to evade responsibility for their self-centered, hedonistic sexual activities.

Since 50% of the unborn babies butchered in their mothers' wombs are little baby girls, it seems fair to say that proponents of abortion on demand are the real foes of women; and pro-abortionists likewise are the true enemies of freedom of choice because abortion denies the unborn child her choice to live.

Periodical Bibliography

The following articles have been selected to supplement the diverse views presented in this chapter.

Jean L. Cohen and Cynthia Fuchs Epstein	"Women and Rights," *Dissent*, special section, Summer 1991.
Barbara Ehrenreich	"Beyond Gender Equality: Toward the New Feminism," *Democratic Left*, July/August 1993.
Susan Faludi	"Looking Beyond the Slogans," *Newsweek*, December 28, 1992.
Suzanne Gordon	"Feminism and Caregiving," *The American Prospect*, Summer 1992.
Issues in Reproductive and Genetic Engineering	"Feminist Framework on Reproductive Technology Declaration," vol. 4, no. 1, 1991. Available from Pergamon Press, 660 White Plains Rd., Tarrytown, NY 10591-5153.
Nannerl O. Keohane	"Educating Women for Leadership," *Vital Speeches of the Day*, July 15, 1991.
Katherine Kersten	"What Do Women Want?" *Policy Review*, Spring 1991.
Karen Lebacqz	"Feminism and Bioethics: An Overview," *Second Opinion*, October 1991. Available from Park Ridge Center, 676 N. St. Clair, Suite 450, Chicago, IL 60611.
Ursula K. Le Guin	"Pornography plus Responsibility," *Civil Liberties*, Fall 1993.
John Leland	"Our Bodies, Our Sales," *Newsweek*, January 31, 1994.
The Minority Trendsletter	Special issue on "women's organizing," Winter 1992/93. Available from Center for Third World Organizing, 1218 E. 21st St., Oakland, CA 94606.
Jocelynne A. Scutt	"Infertility, Sexuality, and Health: Toward a New World for Women," *Issues in Reproductive and Genetic Engineering*, vol. 4, no. 1, 1991.
Camille S. Williams	"Thoughts of a Pro-Life Feminist," *The World & I*, October 1991. Available from 3600 New York Ave. NE, Washington, DC 20002.

For Further Discussion

Chapter 1

1. In the early 1900s many Americans considered suffragists to be "radicals" and antisuffragists to be women with common sense. Today, however, the controversy over women's suffrage has been resolved, and voting is recognized as the constitutional right of women and all other adult citizens. After reading the two viewpoints in this chapter concerning women's suffrage, what is your opinion of the authors? Think of the controversial issues of today. In eighty years, which of these issues do you think will be resolved? How will they be resolved?

2. Margaret Sanger and Vance Thompson present opposing arguments concerning the morality of birth control. One of today's controversies concerning reproduction is abortion. What similarities and what differences exist between the debate concerning birth control and the debate concerning abortion?

3. John Martin and John Stuart Mill disagree concerning women's abilities and strengths. How are men and women compared to each other today? If possible, discuss with other class members their views concerning the ways in which men and women are similar and different. Do their answers surprise you? Explain your response.

Chapter 2

1. Marianne Wesson and Nadine Strossen are both feminists. Yet Wesson believes that feminists must censor pornography, while Strossen believes that censoring pornography harms women. Explain how they come to opposite conclusions. Who makes the most persuasive case, and why?

2. What do Diane Crothers and Kenneth Lasson argue is feminism's effect on family law? How do their arguments differ? After reading their viewpoints, what conclusions can you draw concerning the law's effect on the family and feminism's effect on the family?

3. Explain how surrogacy helps and harms women, according to Barbara Katz Rothman and Katherine B. Lieber. After reading their viewpoints, what is your view of surrogacy? Does it seem to be a form of reproductive enslavement or a reproductive opportunity? Defend your answer. Do you think your gender affects your opinion concerning surrogacy? If so, how?

Chapter 3

1. How would feminist teachings improve education, according to Dale Spender? What criticisms does Karen Lehrman make of feminist courses? After reading their viewpoints, do you think you would consider taking a course on women's issues? Explain your answer. If you already have taken such a course, explain how it affected your attitudes concerning women and feminist teachings, if at all.

2. Ivone Gebara and Kay Ebeling define "ecofeminism" in different ways. Explain how each defines the term. How might their definitions affect the reader's attitude concerning ecofeminism? Which view is most similar to your own? Why?

3. How do Tibor R. Machan's and R.W. Connell's views concerning men and feminism differ? If you are male, explain how feminism has affected your life, if at all. If you are female, explain the attitudes concerning feminism held by those males closest to you—father, brother, husband, son, friend.

Chapter 4

1. Sally Quinn and the editors of the *Washington Times* believe feminism is a dead movement with nothing to offer today's women. Consider your own life. Does feminism play any role in your life? Why or why not? How, if at all, have the viewpoints in this book changed your views concerning feminism?

2. Why do Paula Kamen and Flora Davis believe feminism is still a powerful force in society? What do they believe feminism offers today's women? Do you agree with their analyses? Explain your answer.

3. Consider the position of women in society today. Do you think women still need a mass movement to address their needs? Explain your answer. Which of the four authors in this chapter do you believe has the best perspective concerning feminism's future? Why?

Chapter 5

1. What do Deborah Walker and Ann Froines each believe concerning feminism and economic systems? How do capitalism and socialism affect women, in their opinions? State which system you believe would most benefit women and why.

2. What is individualism? What do Joan Kennedy Taylor and Elizabeth Fox-Genovese each think about the role individualism plays in feminism?

3. Many feminists aim to make women equal with men. What does Suzanne Gordon believe about this goal? Explain her view of feminism's most important goals.

Organizations to Contact

The editors have compiled the following list of organizations concerned with the issues debated in this book. The descriptions are derived from materials provided by the organizations. All have publications or information available for interested readers. The list was compiled on the date of publication of the present volume; names, addresses, and phone numbers may change. Be aware that many organizations take several weeks or longer to respond to inquiries, so allow as much time as possible.

American Civil Liberties Union (ACLU)
132 W. 43rd St.
New York, NY 10036
(212) 944-9800

The ACLU champions the human rights set forth in the U.S. Constitution. It works to protect the rights of all Americans and to promote equality for women, minorities, and the poor. The organization publishes a variety of handbooks, pamphlets, reports, and newsletters, including the quarterly *Civil Liberties* and the monthly *Civil Liberties Alert*.

Catalyst
250 Park Ave. S.
New York, NY 10003
(212) 777-8900

Catalyst is a national research and advisory organization that helps corporations foster the careers and leadership capabilities of women. Its information center provides statistics, print media, and research materials on women in business. It publishes a wide variety of reference materials, pamphlets, career guidance books, and research reports, including *Beyond the Transition: The Two-Gender Work Force and Corporate Policy* and *New Roles for Men and Women*. It also publishes a Career Series for women searching for their first jobs and a monthly newsletter, *Perspective on Current Corporate Issues*.

Center for the American Woman and Politics (CAWP)
Eagleton Institute of Politics
Rutgers University
90 Clifton Ave.
New Brunswick, NJ 08901
(908) 828-2210
fax: (908) 932-6778

CAWP is a research and public service organization for women in politics and government that encourages women's involvement in public life. It disseminates information about the backgrounds, status, and impact of women legislators; holds conferences and seminars about women in American politics; underwrites grants for specific, related projects; and takes surveys on women's issues. In addition to its newsletter *CAWP*

News and Notes, the organization publishes books, monographs, and reports, including *Women as Candidates in American Politics, In the Running: The New Woman Candidate, Women Make a Difference,* and *Women's Routes to Elective Office: A Comparison with Men's.*

Center for Women Policy Studies (CWPS)
2000 P St. NW, Suite 508
Washington, DC 20036
(202) 872-1770
fax: (202) 296-8962

CWPS is an independent feminist policy research and advocacy institution established in 1972. The center's programs combine advocacy, research, policy development, and public education to advance the agenda for women's equality and empowerment. CWPS programs address educational equity, family and workplace equality, violence against women, girls and violence, women's health, reproductive rights, and women and AIDS. The center publishes reports, articles, papers, bibliographies, and books such as *The SAT Gender Gap, Violence Against Women as a Bias-Motivated Hate Crime,* and *Guide to Resources on Women and AIDS.*

Eagle Forum
PO Box 618
Alton, IL 62002
(618) 462-5415

The Eagle Forum is dedicated to preserving traditional family values. It believes mothers should stay at home with their children, and it favors policies that support the traditional family and reduce government intervention in family issues. The forum opposes feminism, believing the movement has harmed women and families. The organization publishes the monthly *Phyllis Schlafly Report.*

Family Research Council
700 13th St., Suite 500
Washington, DC 20005
(202) 393-2100
fax: (202) 393-2134

The council is a conservative social policy research, lobbying, and educational organization. It promotes the traditional two-parent family in which the husband is the breadwinner and the wife stays home with the children. The council supports government policies that protect and promote the traditional family. It publishes the monthly newsletter *Washington Watch,* the bimonthly *Family Policy,* and reports such as *The American Family Under Siege.*

Feminists for Life
811 E. 47th St.
Kansas City, MO 64110
(816) 753-2130
fax: (816) 753-7741

Feminists for Life is a group of individuals united to secure the right to life, from conception to natural death, of all human beings. It seeks legal and social equality for all people and views respect for life and equality for all as necessary, compatible goals. Feminists for Life publishes the quarterly *Sisterlife* as well as position papers, booklets, and books such as *Prolife Feminism: Different Voices*.

Fund for the Feminist Majority

1600 Wilson Blvd., Suite 801
Arlington, VA 22209
(703) 522-2214
fax: (703) 522-2219

The organization seeks to encourage women to fill leadership positions in business, education, media, law, medicine, and government. It sponsors projects and a speakers bureau and compiles statistics on women in leadership roles. The fund publishes the quarterly *Feminist Majority Report* as well as a newsletter, fact sheets, books, and videos.

The Heritage Foundation

214 Massachusetts Ave. NE
Washington, DC 20002
(202) 546-4400
fax: (202) 544-2260

The Heritage Foundation is a public policy research institute that advocates limited government and the free market system. It opposes affirmative action for women and minorities and believes the private sector, not government, should be relied upon to ease social problems and improve the status of women. The foundation publishes the quarterly journal *Policy Review* as well as hundreds of monographs, books, and papers on public policy issues.

Male Liberation Foundation (MLF)

701 NE 67th St.
Miami, FL 33138
(305) 756-6249
fax: (305) 756-7962

MLF is a men's organization dedicated to counteracting feminist influence. It attempts to stop the rising divorce rate, to inform men that women now hold more power and money than men do, to motivate young men to achieve the career success that young women have, and to encourage women to be housewives. MLF believes men and women have distinct biological and psychological differences. It believes feminism has harmed men and male/female relationships and opposes all affirmative action legislation. The foundation publishes the monthly newsletter *Male Liberation Foundation* and a book titled *The First Book on Male Liberation and Sex Equality*.

National Coalition Against Censorship
275 Seventh Ave., 20th Fl.
New York, NY 10001
(212) 807-6222
fax: (212) 807-6245

The coalition comprises more than forty national nonprofit organizations united to preserve and advance freedom of thought, inquiry, and expression. It opposes censorship, including censorship of pornography, as "a dangerous opening to religious, political, artistic, and intellectual repression." The coalition educates the public concerning the dangers of censorship. Its publications include the quarterly *Censorship News*, a newsletter, and reports.

National Coalition of Free Men
PO Box 129
Manhasset, NY 11030
(516) 482-6378

The coalition's members include men seeking a "fair and balanced perspective on gender issues." The organization promotes the legal rights of men in issues of abortion, divorce, child custody, the draft, false accusation of rape, sexual harassment, and sexual abuse. It conducts research, sponsors educational programs, maintains a database on men's issues, and publishes the bimonthly *Transitions*.

National Council for Research on Women
530 Broadway, 10th Fl.
New York, NY 10012
(212) 274-0730
fax: (212) 274-0821

The council is a network of organizations representing the academic community, government, media, business, public policy and nonprofit institutions, and others interested in women's issues. It conducts research and education programs and acts as a clearinghouse. The council publishes an annual report, directories, and reports such as *Sexual Harassment: Research and Resources*, *To Reclaim a Legacy of Diversity: Analyzing the Political Correctness Debates in Higher Education*, and *Women in Academe: Progress and Prospects*. Its quarterly newsletter is titled *Women's Research Network News*.

National Organization for Women (NOW)
1000 16th St. NW, Suite 700
Washington, DC 20036
(202) 331-0066
fax: (202) 785-8576

NOW is one of the largest and most influential feminist organizations in the United States. It seeks to end prejudice and discrimination against women in all areas of life. NOW lobbies legislatures to make laws more equitable and works to educate and inform the public on women's issues. It publishes the bimonthly *NOW Times*, a newspaper, policy statements, and articles.

NOW Legal Defense and Education Fund
99 Hudson St., 12th Fl.
New York, NY 10013
(212) 925-6635
fax: (212) 226-1066

The NOW Legal Defense and Education Fund is an independent national nonprofit women's advocacy organization. The fund is separate from the National Organization for Women (NOW), although the organizations are affiliated. The fund works to promote equality for women by educating the public concerning women's issues and by providing legal assistance to women. It conducts research and compiles information on women's issues. The fund publishes reports such as the *State by State Guide to Women's Legal Rights*, legal resource kits, surveys, brochures, and pamphlets such as *Facts on Reproductive Rights*.

Women Against Pornography (WAP)
PO Box 845, Times Square Station
New York, NY 10036-0845
(212) 307-5055

WAP is a feminist organization that seeks to change public opinion about pornography so that Americans no longer view it as socially acceptable or sexually liberating. It offers tours of New York's Times Square intended to show firsthand that "the essence of pornography is about the degradation, objectification, and brutalization of women." WAP offers slide shows, lectures, and a referral service to victims of sexual abuse and sexual exploitation. Its publications include *Women Against Pornography—Newsreport*.

Women's Action Alliance
370 Lexington Ave., Suite 603
New York, NY 10017
(212) 532-8330
fax: (212) 779-2846

The alliance, established in 1971, is a national nonprofit organization dedicated to helping women achieve equality in education, work, and health care, and to help them combat sexual harassment and domestic violence. The alliance's programs at community centers, women's centers, and schools provide information and assistance to women and girls to help them succeed in life and fight oppression. The organization has a library and information service and publishes reports and pamphlets such as *Alcohol and Drugs Are Women's Issues*.

Bibliography of Books

Carol J. Adams, ed.   *Ecofeminism and the Sacred*. New York: Continuum Publishing, 1994.

Kathryn P. Addelson   *Impure Thoughts: Essays on Philosophy, Feminism and Ethics*. Philadelphia: Temple University Press, 1991.

Jules Archer   *Breaking Barriers: The Feminist Revolution from Susan B. Anthony to Margaret Sanger to Betty Friedan*. New York: Viking, 1991.

Himani Bannerji et al.   *Unsettling Relations: The University as a Site of Feminist Struggles*. Boston: South End Press, 1992.

Janet Biehl   *Finding Our Way: Rethinking Eco-Feminist Politics*. Boston: South End Press, 1991.

Claudia Card   *Feminist Ethics*. Lawrence: University Press of Kansas, 1991.

James L. Cooper and Sheila M. Cooper, eds.   *The Roots of American Feminist Thought*. Boston: Allyn and Bacon, Inc., 1973.

Drucilla Cornell   *Beyond Accommodation: Ethical Feminism, Deconstruction, and the Law*. London: Routledge, 1991.

Nancy F. Cott   *The Grounding of Modern Feminism*. New Haven, CT: Yale University Press, 1989.

Nancy F. Cott   *Root of Bitterness: Documents of the Social History of American Women*. New York: Dutton, 1972.

Nicholas Davidson   *The Failure of Feminism*. Buffalo, NY: Prometheus Books, 1988.

Flora Davis   *Moving the Mountain: The Women's Movement in America Since 1960*. New York: Simon & Schuster, 1991.

Susan E. Davis, ed.   *Women Under Attack: Victories, Backlash, and the Fight for Reproductive Freedom*. Boston: South End Press, 1988.

Alice Echols   *Daring to Be Bad: Radical Feminism in America, 1967-1975*. Minneapolis: University of Minnesota Press, 1989.

Barbara Ehrenreich   *Fear of Falling: The Inner Life of the Middle Class*. New York: HarperCollins, 1990.

Zillah R. Eisenstein   *The Female Body and the Law*. Berkeley: University of California Press, 1988.

Susan Faludi

Backlash: The Undeclared War Against American Women. New York: Crown, 1991.

Warren Farrell

The Myth of Male Power. New York: Simon & Schuster, 1993.

Martha Albertson Fineman and Nancy Sweet Thomadsen, eds.

At the Boundaries of Law: Feminism and Legal Theory. London: Routledge, 1991.

Elizabeth Fox-Genovese

Feminism Without Illusions: A Critique of Individualism. Chapel Hill: University of North Carolina Press, 1991.

Marlene Gerber Fried

From Abortion to Reproductive Freedom: Transforming a Movement. Boston: South End Press, 1990.

Greta Gaard

Eco-Feminism: Women, Animals, and Nature. Philadelphia: Temple University Press, 1993.

Joyce Gelb

Feminism and Politics: A Comparative Perspective. Berkeley: University of California Press, 1989.

Rose Glickman

Daughters of Feminists. New York: St. Martin's Press, 1993.

Suzanne Gordon

Prisoners of Men's Dreams: Striking Out for a New Feminine Future. Boston: Little, Brown, 1991.

Sandra Harding

Whose Science? Whose Knowledge? Thinking from Women's Lives. Ithaca, NY: Cornell University Press, 1991.

Marianne Hirsch and Evelyn F. Keller, eds.

Conflicts in Feminism. London: Routledge, 1990.

bell hooks

Talking Back: Thinking Feminist, Thinking Black. Boston: South End Press, 1989.

Carolyn Johnston

Sexual Power: Feminism and the Family in America. Tuscaloosa: University of Alabama Press, 1992.

Gloria Joseph and Jill Lewis

Common Differences: Conflicts in Black and White Feminist Perspectives. Boston: South End Press, 1981.

Paula Kamen

Feminist Fatale: Voices from the "Twentysomething" Generation Explore the Future of the "Women's Movement." New York: Donald I. Fine, 1991.

Wendy Kaminer

A Fearful Freedom: Women's Flight from Equality. Reading, MA: Addison-Wesley, 1990.

Alvin F. Kimel Jr., ed.

Speaking the Christian God: The Holy Trinity and the Challenge of Feminism. Grand Rapids, MI: W.B. Eerdmans, 1992.

Michael S. Kimmel and Thomas E. Mosmiller, eds.	*Against the Tide: Pro-Feminist Men in the United States, 1776-1990: A Documentary History*. Boston: Beacon Press, 1992.
Rita Kramer	*Ed School Follies: The Miseducation of America's Teachers*. New York: Free Press, 1991.
Morchen Leidholdt and Janice G. Raymond, eds.	*The Sexual Liberals and the Attack on Feminism*. Tarrytown, NY: Pergamon Press, 1990.
Michael Levin	*Feminism and Freedom*. New York: City University of New York, 1987.
Catharine A. MacKinnon	*Feminism Unmodified: Discourses on Life and Law*. Cambridge, MA: Harvard University Press, 1988.
Catharine A. MacKinnon	*Toward a Feminist Theory of the State*. Cambridge, MA: Harvard University Press, 1989.
Rita C. Manning	*Speaking from the Heart: A Feminist Perspective on Ethics*. Lanham, MD: Rowman & Littlefield, 1992.
Pam McAllister	*This River of Courage: Generations of Women's Resistance and Action*. Philadelphia: New Society Publishers, 1991.
Wendy McElroy	*Freedom, Feminism, and the State*. Washington, DC: Cato Institute, Laissez Faire, 1991.
Henry L. Mencken	*In Defense of Women*. New York: Knopf, 1926.
Juliet Mitchell and Ann Oakley	*What Is Feminism? A Re-examination*. New York: Pantheon Books, 1986.
Robyn Muncy	*Creating a Female Dominion in American Reform, 1890-1935*. New York: Oxford University Press, 1994.
William L. O'Neill	*Feminism in America: A History*. 2nd ed. New Brunswick, NJ: Transaction, 1989.
Camille Paglia	*Sexual Personae: Art and Decadence from Nefertiti to Emily Dickinson*. New Haven, CT: Yale University Press, 1990.
Judith Plant, ed.	*Healing the Wounds: The Promise of Ecofeminism*. Philadelphia: New Society Publishers, 1989.
Margaret Randall	*Gathering Rage: The Failure of Twentieth-Century Revolutions to Develop a Feminist Agenda*. New York: Monthly Review Press, 1992.
Laurel Richardson and Verta Taylor	*Feminist Frontiers II: Rethinking Sex, Gender, and Society*. New York: Random House, 1989.

Katie Roiphe	*The Morning After: Sex, Fear and Feminism on Campus*. Boston: Little, Brown, 1993.
Sheila Rowbotham	*Hidden from History: Rediscovering Women in History from the Seventeenth Century to the Present*. New York: Pantheon Books, 1973.
Sheila Rowbotham	*The Past Is Before Us: Feminism in Action Since the 1960s*. Boston: Beacon Press, 1991.
Rosemary Radford Ruether	*Gaia and God: An Ecofeminist Theology of Earth Healing*. New York: HarperCollins, 1992.
Ruth Sidel	*On Her Own: Growing Up in the Shadow of the American Dream*. New York: Viking Penguin, 1991.
Elizabeth Cady Stanton	*Eighty Years and More: Reminiscences, 1815-1897*. Boston: Northeastern University Press, 1993.
Donna Steichen	*Ungodly Rage: The Hidden Face of Catholic Feminism*. San Francisco: Ignatius Press, 1992.
Gloria Steinem	*Revolution from Within: A Book of Self-Esteem*. Boston: Little, Brown, 1992.
Carol Tavris	*The Mismeasure of Woman: Why Women Are Not the Better Sex, the Inferior Sex, or the Opposite Sex*. New York: Simon & Schuster, 1992.
Joan Kennedy Taylor	*Reclaiming the Mainstream: Individualist Feminism Rediscovered*. Buffalo, NY: Prometheus Books, 1992.
Joan Kennedy Taylor	*Women's Issues: Feminism, Classical Liberalism, and the Future*. Stanford, CA: Hoover Institution, 1993.
David Thomas	*Not Guilty: The Case in Defense of Men*. New York: William Morrow, 1993.
Ellen Willis	*No More Nice Girls: Counterculture Essays*. Hanover, NH: University Press of New England, 1992.
Linda Witt, Karen M. Paget, and Glenna Matthews	*Running as a Woman: Gender and Power in American Politics*. New York: Free Press, 1993.
Naomi Wolf	*The Beauty Myth: How Images of Beauty Are Used Against Women*. New York: Doubleday, 1992.
Naomi Wolf	*Fire with Fire: The New Female Power and How It Will Change the Twenty-First Century*. New York: Random House, 1993.

Index

236